COLLEGE OF SAN MATEO LIBRARY
3 9367 03053750 8
D0872321

many
futures
many
worlds

many futures many worlds

theme and form in science fiction

edited by Thomas D. Clareson

The Kent State University Press

Library of Congress Cataloging in Publication Data
Main entry under title:

Many futures, many worlds.

Includes bibliographical references and index.
1. Science fiction—History and criticism—Addresses, essays, lectures. I. Clareson, Thomas D.
PN 3448.S45M3 823'.0876 76-42448
ISBN 0-87338-199-8
ISBN 0-87338-200-5 pbk.

Library of Congress Catalog Card Number 76-42448
ISBN: 0-87338-199-8 cloth
0-87338-200-5 paper
Manufactured in the United States of America
Designed by Harold M. Stevens

Contents

Introduction

On several occasions, as I have done briefly in "Lost Lands, Lost Races: A Pagan Princess of Their Very Own," I have suggested that science fiction belongs to a literary tradition traceable back to and beyond the medieval travel books. In passing, one may note that those early tales, like *The Travels of Sir John Mandeville*—together with the multitude of imaginary voyages of the eighteenth century enumerated by such men as Philip Babcock Gove, as well as the "scientific romances" of Verne and Wells and their contemporaries—display the same sense of wonder at the marvels of the Earth that Asimov, Clarke, Heinlein, and James Gunn, for example, have more recently expressed in terms of the galactic universe. Another factor worth noting is that whatever the period, the writers have made use of those narrative structures and conventions available to them at the time of writing—the voyage or quest frame, the manuscript found almost anywhere—so long as the device contributed to the credibility of the ensuing tale. Or again: there is no essential difference between the settings of Wells's *The Island of Dr. Moreau* (1896) and Larry Niven's *Ringworld* (1970). Wells made use of a supposedly unexplored corner of the Earth; Niven, a corner of the galaxy. In terms of the interests of their period, both adapted the same device—a hitherto unknown locale, an unknown world—and, like the other writers cited, both wrote of those settings with awe and excitement.

One result of an awareness of this continuing tradition has been that during the past decade or so in courses dealing with fiction, I have not emphasized the concept of a single "mainstream" and the existence of a periphery—a backwater—of questionable subliterary stories; rather, I have tried to show that two equally important streams, or traditions, have developed in fiction, both having their "modern" origins in the intellectual climate of the eighteenth century. The first, of course, with which readers in general are more familiar, scrutinizes the everyday social-psychological world and has given increasing attention to character study. The second focuses upon scene and action, and it may well be the continuation of the heroic or epic mode of Homer, the Beowulf poet, and Malory. Andre Malraux has written of the need for the heroic to be far distant in time. To obtain its vision, perhaps it can also be far distant in space—and, perhaps, in the future as well as the past. In "Many Futures, Many Worlds," I have tried to trace something of the evolution of the tradition to which science fiction belongs. Indeed, one is tempted to suggest that both traditions have moved from the "realistic" to the absurd because of the intellectual temper of the various periods.

I mention these matters primarily because I deem unnecessary the attempts of some current critics to defend science fiction or define it rigidly—thereby often imposing restrictions which raise more questions than they answer. On the one hand, for example, they seem to overlook or simply disregard any historical perspective. They would make science fiction a creature solely of this century, or even more preposterous to my mind, a product solely of the specialist magazines from 1926 onward. To do this is to ignore what had occurred in the earlier magazines, both British and American, to say nothing of the Continent. While individuals will nod courteously to Wells and Verne and even to Mary

Shelley, perhaps, on the whole many dismiss the entire body of "scientific romance," for example, as some inferior, little-related precursor. One senses, too, that for some critics a work of science fiction must present a specified philosophical point of view in order to be counted among the troops. Nor should one forget that this issue of philosophical stance was at the core of the controversy involving the supposed "New Wave" in the 1960s.

On the other hand, one can encounter that type of academic jargon which may well have had an instrumental role in alienating many readers from the body of literature traditionally dealt with in the schools (this possibility may be what concerns those writers and "fans" who seem to bewail the increasing academic attention given to science fiction) or one comes upon the plea which asks that special criteria be created by which to judge the field, as though there were something so special or so inferior about science fiction that it cannot be evaluated in the same terms or manner as other fiction.

I have tried to keep these problems in mind while bringing together the essays which make up *Many Futures, Many Worlds: Theme and Form in Science Fiction.* I have wanted to emphasize some of the various ways in which one may examine the field, but at the same time to have the individual items complement one another so that one may see at least some of the same authors and works from different perspectives. When they are taken as a group, I hope that they will provide the reader with an appreciation of various of the critical methods by which science fiction may be explored, as well as with an insight into the manner in which themes both change and yet unify the field.

The College of Wooster
May 1976

Perception and Value in Science Fiction

Thomas L. Wymer

In the "Afterword" to his "Monitored Dreams and Strategic Cremations" in *Again, Dangerous Visions* (1972), Bernard Wolfe acknowledges that his two stories are "about matters which embrace certain scientific considerations," but denies that they are SF:

> whose premise is that science embraces all matters and that therefore any SF work, which is about nothing but science or the superficialities of science deftly skimmed off, is by definition about everything. SF is in the nature of things about things, sometimes disguised as people. A very different kind of fiction becomes necessary when you're interested in people not reduced to things. . . . you can't get any fiction of consequence out of science unless you gain enough elevation over the subject to see that science is not coterminous with the human condition, however much its increasingly demonic and mindless energies seem nowadays to be devoted to curing that condition through the process of elimination.[1]

A slightly different version of this article was published in *Extrapolation*, 16 (May 1975), 103-12.

In an essay published only a year earlier, Isaac Asimov argued that SF is "a literature of ideas . . . the *only* literature of relevant ideas, since it is the *only* literature that, at its best, is firmly based on scientific thought."[2]

The juxtaposition of these two passages reveals the remarkable fact that in spite of Wolfe and Asimov's obvious disagreement in their judgment of SF, they are in surprising agreement in their definition of the genre: science fiction is a literature of ideas, the relevance of which is based on its conviction that science is coterminous with the human condition. But in an essay which appeared in the same year as *Again, Dangerous Visions,* Gary K. Wolfe argued against such a definition and insisted that there is no limit to what SF can achieve as an art form except the limits created by the arbitrary imposition of culturally and aesthetically provincial standards such as Asimov's.[3]

Such passages could be multiplied endlessly, but there is a way, from the point of view of cultural history, to make sense out of such contradictions and, if not to define SF, at least to place it within a framework which makes its development and its internal controversies more clearly understandable, and that is to look at science fiction as a movement, a series of events in the history of ideas. This is an especially useful approach to SF since it is a genre which has come in recent years to sum up, in fact to recapitulate, some of the major developments of the last three hundred years or so of Western culture. For the sake of containing this discussion, I am basing my generalizations on a selection of primarily American works from the last four decades, the period during which SF began to take itself seriously as a movement in literature and ideas.

Because of its concern with science, SF has centered its attention on the problems of perception and knowledge, and it has derived its sense of value from these concerns. In one sense this puts SF in the mainstream of Western thought, which has, since the seventeenth century, placed its primary emphasis on the epistemological branch of philosophy, theory of knowledge. At the time, however, when SF began to take itself seriously, the theories of knowledge with which it dealt were characterized by a rather narrow empiricism which was, for all its claims for insight into the future, rather dated. John W. Campbell's "Twilight" (1934) can serve as an illustration of this point.

"Twilight" concerns a time traveller from the fourth millennium of our era who journeys several million years into the future and discovers a society of human beings being cared for by a complex network of perfect machines. We are presented with a problem, the fact that the human beings, though intellectually vastly superior to us and to the time traveller, are nevertheless in a state of decline which promises their eventual extinction. The key to their decline, we are told, is their loss of curiosity. After much nostalgic eulogizing about the glory that was man, our time traveller hits upon a solution: he programs the five biggest thinking machines to work on the problem of creating a curious machine—"It is only fitting it should be done. The machine can work on it, not for a thousand years, but for a million, if it must. . . . So I brought another machine to life, and set it to a task which, in time to come, it will perform."[4]

This is a story which is likely to strike the contemporary reader as exceedingly strange. If we catch the sense of satisfaction and fulfillment which Campbell evokes for his "solution," we might well suppose that the problem has been solved in more familiar terms, that mankind has been saved—but that is not so. Campbell makes it quite clear that mankind's decline to extinction has not been arrested; instead, curiosity has been saved, preserved to live another day in a set of machines. If, on the other hand, we recognize that mankind will soon expire, we might just as well suppose that the story is an attack on technology, a variation of Forster's "The Machine Stops" (1909). But this is not true either. The story is filled with unequivocal admiration for those perfect machines, and although it is ironic that there will be no one for the machines to serve, they are clearly identified as a lasting symbol of the greatness that was man, and the irony is directed against man's own failure to maintain his capacity for growth. The story is consistent with Campbell's characteristic attitude of defense for progress defined in terms of technological growth. Indeed, the most remarkable point in the story is precisely the fact that our regret over man's decline is supposed to be compensated for by our satisfaction and fulfillment over this solution, a point which reveals an unusual set of assumptions about knowledge and value.

The major function of man, for instance, the operation for which he is most prized, is his capacity to know and to engage constantly in the quest for and accumulation of knowledge. The chief value is placed not on man himself but upon this function, which is why it can continue as an operative value in the absence of man; we are to be satisfied that knowledge will continue to progress regardless of who—or what—is doing the knowing. Moreover, the time traveller's conviction that the curious machine will be created, even if it takes a million years, implies the belief that the universe is essentially knowable and that progress, the growth of knowledge, is its fundamental law. This is essentially an Enlightenment world view, modified somewhat by the nineteenth-century discoveries of geologic time, evolutionary theory, and astronomical distance so that the idea of progress is expanded to a grander scale, while satisfaction, almost religious awe, is achieved through the consciousness of partaking in the universal process.

Asimov's "Nightfall" (1941) may be a clearer example. Like the Enlightenment it argues for the critical examination of traditional assumptions, most of which are rejected as the products of prejudice and superstition, and it champions the quest for a body of truth which can be confirmed by direct observation and demonstration and tested by universal applicability. The hoped-for result is a break from the cyclic bonds of ignorance and the discovery of a new world of knowledge, power, and growth—in short, progress. The ideals are embodied in a group of scientists who are set against a group of fanatic religionists, a conflict which literally pits the forces of Enlightenment against those of darkness.

Asimov's links with the Enlightenment can be even more clearly illustrated by another bit of juxtaposition: take the following passage from his essay quoted earlier (keeping in mind that Asimov first hit the pulps in 1939 at the beginning of the era of Campbell's editorship of *Astounding Stories*):

> If we consider Literature (with a capital L) as a vehicle of ideas, we can only conclude that, by and large, the ideas with which it is concerned are the same ideas that Homer and Aeschylus struggled with. They are well worth discussing, I am sure; even fun. There is enough there to keep an infinite number of minds busy for an infinite amount of time, but they weren't settled and aren't settled.
>
> It is these "eternal verities" that are precisely what science fiction doesn't deal with. Science fiction deals with change. It deals with the possible advance in science and with the potential changes—even in those damned eternal verities—this may bring about in society.[5]

and place it beside the following passage from an essay on Lord Bacon which Thomas Babington Macauley wrote in 1827:

> The ancient philosophy was a treadmill, not a path. It was made up of revolving questions, of controversies which were always beginning again. It might indeed sharpen and invigorate the minds of those who devoted themselves to it; and so might the disputes of the orthodox Lilliputians and the heretical Blefuscudians about the ends of eggs. But such disputes could add nothing to the stock of knowledge.[6]

Macauley is a post-eighteenth-century Enlightenment thinker, prophet of progress and the scientific method, and Asimov is in a very similar position.

Science fiction, however, began to expand beyond its Enlightenment beginnings in the late 1940s and early 1950s. Again the history of ideas can help define the major direction of its growth, for its first major steps out of the Enlightenment were in the direction of romanticism; that is, in the direction of a radically enlarged and expanded empiricism which recognized the creative element in perception and explored the possibilities of new modes of consciousness and of knowing. This is a strain of thought which entered American SF primarily through the work of British writers, like Olaf Stapledon and Charles Harness, and particularly through the most popular British science-fiction writer in America, Arthur C. Clarke, whose *Childhood's End* (1953) is an especially good example of science fiction's early use of romantic epistemology.

Mark Hillegas comments on Clarke's novel in a way which illustrates the importance of recognizing its romantic element. He uses the novel as an example of what he calls "the Baconian faith that by the systematic investigation of nature man can master the secrets of this mysterious universe and in so doing improve the human condition."[7] In *Childhood's End,* he says,

> the Overlords, a manifest symbol of science, invade our Earth just in time to prevent men from turning their world into a radioactive wasteland and, by introducing reason and the scientific method into human activities, transform Earth into a technological Utopia where each individual can develop his potentialities to the fullest.
>
> —p. 273

Hillegas stops here with what is an accurate description of about the first half of the novel. But in *Childhood's End* the technological Utopia constitutes perfection of only a limited kind which, when achieved, sets the stage for the discovery of new modes of knowing and value. These new modes, associated with the Overmind, literally transcend the Overlord mind, limited as it is to passionless observation and collection of data, rationalistic analysis, and personal individualism. Set against this Enlightenment view is the romantic Overmind, with its emphasis on the intuitional, aesthetic, and creative, its transcendental vision and group mode of being. (The Overlords' lack of a capacity to understand or join the Overmind is linked to their having no art or music, while man's breakthrough into the Overmind begins in an artist colony among the most creative human minds, persons who have not found the technological Utopia satisfying.) The novel's first half sets up science fiction's standard conflict, as in Asimov's "Nightfall," between science/reason and religion/superstition, but the triumph of the former leads to its conflict with the aesthetic/creative: the romantic vision transcends that of the

Enlightenment and even ends by annihilating Earth, spirit destroying the material basis of Enlightenment epistemology.

Hillegas's error, however, is easy to make because, while Enlightenment and romantic views are different, certain manifestations of the romantic movement share assumptions with the Enlightenment. One of the first manifestations of romanticism was the breakdown of Enlightenment empiricism as it reached a dead end in Hume and led to Kantian transcendental epistemology. A similar crisis occurred in science in the early twentieth century when Einstein and Heisenberg overturned Newtonian physics (Heisenberg showed scientifically what Kant had shown philosophically, that one cannot assume an objective observer or the objective reality of what one observes.) In the nineteenth century the crisis was especially one of value, at least for the major literary figures of the movement, but the century as a whole managed to ignore or adapt the implications of the new epistemology so that it ended up reaffirming major Enlightenment values. We can see the effect in *Childhood's End* in the response its conclusion evokes, which is very like that evoked at the end of "Twilight": we feel that the author is setting us up to experience a sense of satisfaction over something that really isn't very satisfying. Jan Rodericks achieves a sense of fulfillment as he witnesses the transformed human children joining the Overmind, as though an early amphibian would feel fulfilled by the knowledge that his cousins would become dinosaurs. The basis for this feeling is a kind of racial pride in the knowledge that humans will go on knowing in a higher mode, which constitutes an affirmation of the same Enlightenment values as "Twilight."

Donald Wollheim helps further illustrate how science fiction's first major romantic symptoms were adaptations of the new epistemology to an Enlightenment value structure. In *The Universe Makers* (1971) he describes "the vision of a purely mechanistic universe" which flourished during the nineteenth century: "The laws of nature were fixed and permanent and merely awaited our discovery . . . the universe could be understood. Complex and wonderful it was, but essentially it was a vast clockwork mechanism which could be mapped and mastered."[8] He goes on to point out that this vision of a mechanistic universe "was dealt its death blow by the discoveries of Einstein" (pp. 24-25), which created a new and more complex vision reflected in SF. But later on Wollheim praises van Vogt as among the most popular of SF writers because "he believes in the invincibility of humanity, he refuses to accept the boundaries of time and space. The fact is that science fiction readers agree with him. They, too, cannot believe that humanity has limitations" (p. 48). Wollheim is enthralled by the fact that "modern SF writers are coming around to the idea that, given enough time (centuries, millennia, millions of years) and sufficient data (all that there is to know), our descendants can duplicate to their design anything at all" (p. 50). Without realizing what he has said, Wollheim implies that SF has finally caught up with the nineteenth century and that recent writers are finally coming around to an idea that Campbell propounded in his most famous story in 1934.

Wollheim, like many SF critics and writers—and many scientists—says he understands the implications of Einstein or Heisenberg, says he recognizes that we live in a world of probabilities, not laws, but then goes on to act out the Enlightenment assumptions he thinks he has transcended. In Heinlein's "The Roads Must Roll" (1940) the hero declares, "One man might be unpredictable, but in large numbers personnel were as dependable as machines, or figures. They could be measured, examined, classified,"[9] and this is a position which the story's outcome confirms. In effect, Enlightenment mechanism has been replaced with a romantic version of mechanism. But whether one's metaphor for man and the universe is based on Newtonian physics or quantum mechanics, the metaphor is still mechanical. Whether man is a cog in a clock or a subatomic particle, he is still an object, not a human being. Whether progress takes place by means of the slow grind of the clockwork mind or by the quantum leaps of evolution or theoretical breakthrough, progress is still the law of life, which sets the stage for the great drama of the conquest of life, which sets the stage for the great drama of the conquest of the universe. And that drama reveals the same value structures in both its Enlightenment and romantic versions: it places its emphasis on the stereotypically masculine virtues of mastery, control, power, and a personal superiority which is accompanied by imperialistic kinds of attitudes varying from contempt to paternalism toward the lower orders (the masses, women, and other alien beings.) Appropriately enough, robots are among the least alien of beings in this kind of SF; conceiving of the universe as a grand mechanism it admires systematic structures of all kinds—those of Asimov's *I, Robot* (1950) and Mike in Heinlein's *The Moon is a Harsh Mistress* (1966) are good examples, and the robot Jenkins is the most memorable character in Simak's *City* (1952). This preoccupation helps explain why so much SF is built around intellectual games and puzzles: a puzzle is by definition a problem that has an answer, and science fiction, as our twentieth-century Macauley conceives of it, is concerned only with questions that have definite answers; those other questions, the eternal problems (as Gary Wolfe points out, "verities" is a false and misleading term), are simply not worth asking. There is, of course, nothing intrinsically wrong with such puzzles; they are even fun. To turn Asimov against himself, "There is enough there to keep an infinite number of minds busy for an infinite amount of time." But too much SF has extended that habit into a conception of the human condition as merely a set of problems which some theoretical or technological breakthrough will "solve." Such is the nature of the Null-A philosophy of van Vogt's *World of Null-A* (1948), the Seldon equations of Asimov's *Foundation* series (1951), the various kinds of disciplines, from material to mental, which Heinlein's heroes master, even Juwain's discovery in Simak's *City* of "a new concept of philosophy . . . that will remake the solar system, that will put mankind ahead a hundred years in the space of two generations."[10] Both Wollheim and Asimov defend the lack of concern for character in this kind of SF as a proper symptom of its being a literature of ideas, but the fact is there is no room for character in so dehumanizing a vision, and van Vogt's kind of faith in the invincibility of a humanity without limitations, like Heinlein's preoccupation with transcendent heroes, is in reality an expression of contempt for an attempt to escape from some of our most human characteristics. It is little wonder that SF writers like Thomas Disch, Kurt Vonnegut, Jr., and Bernard Wolfe try to deny their association with the genre.

But SF did not stop growing. In order to understand its growth, however, it is necessary to recognize that it had developed something approaching a vision, a coherent and consistent way of perceiving man and the universe, a world view which identified it and set it off from other literary forms and which I have described as an Enlightenment value structure. Turning back to the critical comments with which this essay began, perhaps we can see now that Asimov's definition is an accurate description of the spirit which dominated SF in its Enlightenment stage. Bernard Wolfe's is probably a just judgment of the SF written in that spirit, but it is made without recognizing the fact that that spirit has ceased to dominate SF. Gary Wolfe is aware of the more positive directions that SF has explored in the last two decades, and he tries to establish a critical perspective in terms of which that growth can be appreciated and encouraged. This essay is an attempt to contribute to that effort by trying to define the nature of SF's growth.

Again, the models from cultural history can help, for, having established its vision, SF has since undergone a kind of spiritual crisis in which the Enlightenment faith of its fathers has been questioned and rejected, leading to SF's entrance into the mainstream of modern literature. This is much like the spiritual crisis in terms of which scholars currently describe romanticism and connect it with the modern tradition. Here, for instance, is how Robert Langbaum describes the crisis in a chapter called "Romanticism as a Modern Tradition":

> Whatever the difference between the literary movements of nineteenth and twentieth centuries, they are connected by their view of the

> world as meaningless, by their response to the same wilderness. That wilderness is the legacy of the Enlightenment which, in its desire to separate fact from the values of a crumbling tradition, separated fact from all values—bequeathing a world in which fact is measurable quantity while value is man made and illusory. Such a world offers no objective verification for just the perceptions by which men live, perceptions of beauty, goodness, and spirit. It was as literature began in the latter eighteenth century to realize the dangerous implications of the scientific world-view, that romanticism was born.[11]

Romanticism, Langbaum goes on to show, was not simply a rejection of the mechanistic values of the Enlightenment, but a quest for new values, a reconstructive process, the beginning of a new exploration of human consciousness in a spirit committed to doing justice to its organic complexity. This, I think, is what is happening currently to SF.

The transition, however, has not been sudden. The last forty years of SF can be characterized by the tension between the Enlightenment and romantic values, with the dominant spirit gradually shifting from the former to the latter, from the mechanical to the organic. Any full history of that shift would have to note the early manifestations of more humanistic values in writers as far back into the Campbell era as Sturgeon and would have to trace its development through writers like Bradbury, Bester, Pohl, Kornbluth, Blish, and Miller. But for the purposes of this essay, it is enough to illustrate the strength of the shift as it has been achieved. Disch and Vonnegut, for instance, are only the most notable examples of writers who have attacked the preoccupation not just of SF but of Western man with solutions, and both have shown how all ultimate solutions to the problem of being human are reducible to the same result, extermination, the ultimate case of murdering to dissect. In *Dune* (1965) a fundamental assumption Herbert begins with is that "the mystery of life isn't a problem to solve but a reality to experience,"[12] and the novel goes on to explore with extraordinary sophistication and honesty the paradoxical and limited ways in which human freedom manages to exercise itself in a largely deterministic universe. In Ursula LeGuin's *Left Hand of Darkness* (1969) technology is not attacked; it is simply revealed as of little relevance to the fundamental human problem which the novel exposes, the agony involved in human beings overcoming their alienation from each other and the drama of their finding the wisdom, courage, and compassion to communicate honestly with and love one another. The problem is not so much how to know or triumph but how to be and let be, an ontological, not an epistemological problem. In "Riders of the Purple Wage" (1967) Philip José Farmer presents a Joycean vision of our own world, warns of a possible future, and exposes the perennial problem of how the individual consciousness struggles to maintain its integrity in an insane world.

There will no doubt always be a market in SF for its more ephemeral manifestations, like adventures, escapes, puzzles, and scientific speculations, and certainly SF will remain in many ways a literature of ideas; indeed, it may even effectively extol the quest for knowledge as James Gunn does in *The Listeners* (1972). But instead of human beings existing to add drama to the exploration of science, technology, or the future, these latter elements have come to exist in a more sizable body of literature to heighten and expose a central concern with what it means to be a human being. What is especially delightful about this development is that in the process SF has grown from being a manifestation of the interests of a small coterie of specialized readers into a truly popular literature, and its growth in popularity has paralleled its growth in depth, sophistication, and understanding of the Western literary tradition. Science fiction reveals that popular literature need not be inferior, that it can function as the means by which a culture critically explores and creates its own values and consciousness.

NOTES

1. Bernard Wolfe, "Monitored Dreams and Strategic Cremations," in Harlan Ellison, ed., *Again, Dangerous Visions* (Garden City, N.Y.: Doubleday & Company, Inc., 1972), pp. 335-36.
2. Isaac Asimov, "When Aristotle Fails, Try Science Fiction," *Intellectual Digest,* 2 (December 1971), 75.

3. Gary K. Wolfe, "The Limits of Science Fiction," *Extrapolation* 14 (December 1972), 30-38.
4. John W. Campbell, "Twilight," in Robert Silverberg, ed., *The Science Fiction Hall of Fame* (Garden City, N.Y.: Doubleday & Company, Inc., 1970), pp. 40,41.
5. Asimov, p. 75.
6. Lady Trevelyan, ed., *The Works of Lord Macauley* (London: Longmans, Green, and Co., 1879), 6:207-08.
7. Mark R. Hillegas, "Science Fiction as a Cultural Phenomenon: A Revaluation," in Thomas D. Clareson, ed., *SF: The Other Side of Realism* (Bowling Green, Ohio: Bowling Green Popular Press, 1971), p. 272.
8. Donald A. Wollheim, *The Universe Makers* (New York: Harper & Row, 1971), p. 24.
9. Robert A. Heinlein, "The Roads Must Roll," in Robert Silverberg, ed., *The Science Fiction Hall of Fame,* p. 81.
10. Clifford D. Simak, *City* (New York: Ace Books, n.d.), p. 63.
11. Robert A. Langbaum, *The Poetry of Experience* (New York: Random House, 1957), pp. 11-12.
12. Frank Herbert, *Dune* (New York: Berkley, 1975), pp. 31, 508. Paul first states this as a quotation from the Bene Gesserit Reverend Mother, whose judgments are not always reliable, but in this case Paul agrees with her, recognizing the connection between her words and "the First Law of Mentat"; the same statement is repeated later in one of the appendices as a principle central to the religion of Dune.

Many Futures, Many Worlds

Thomas D. Clareson

In various articles I have speculated that the seeming isolation and neglect long imposed on science fiction by "serious" critics, teachers, and scholars arose in large part from the basically anti-scientific stance taken increasingly by the literary establishment, among others, since the turn of the century when both literary realism and naturalism and the "scientific romance" were daring innovations. These literary expressions remained largely incomprehensible to those critics who recoiled in horror from the vision of man in a meaningless universe. Not until the 1950s and 1960s when, quantitatively, the dystopian motif seemed to move SF closer to an anti-scientific position did the genre receive significant attention.

The result is intriguing, if one looks closely at literary naturalism as it occurs in John Steinbeck, James T. Farrell, and John Dos Passos, for example, and such contemporary SF works as John Brunner's *Stand on Zanzibar* (1968) and *The Sheep Look*

A different version of this article was prepared for the two-day, pre-convention conference held for teachers of SF at the annual NCTE meeting in New Orleans at Thanksgiving, 1974.

Up (1972), Robert Silverberg's *The World Inside* (1971), or Frank Herbert's *Hellstrom's Hive* (1973). These writers, whatever else they do, give attention to the description of an external world. Whether they write of the Salinas River Valley, Chicago, America in the near future, or a happy day in the year 2381, their works show a social awareness and are infused with a pessimism. If someone says that one of them portrays man as a helpless victim of social, economic, political, biological, or psychological forces over which he has little or no control and which derive from his own makeup, from the nature of the physical world and/or from the society created by the new technology, of which writer is he speaking? Only if one points out either the spice of pollution and overpopulation or a setting cast into the future do we call the work science fiction. The dehumanization, alienation, isolation, and estrangement which have become bywords of contemporary criticism apply equally well to literary naturalism and science fiction.

So pervasive has this emphasis upon the dystopian mood of current SF become among contemporary critics that in the issue of *Studies in the Literary Imagination* devoted to "Aspects of Utopian Fiction," the editor wondered "how accurately the pessimism implicit in a preoccupation with counter-utopia reflects the spirit of our age,"[1] while in a review of that issue, Patrick G. Hogan noted that "there is the chilling impression that some critics find little but what they want to find in a work under scrutiny" and that "perhaps the present collection would have been made more exciting had at least one essay been included which, deliberately and seriously, represented" an optimistic point of view.[2] The essays of Carolyn Rhodes and Patricia Warrick in this volume reflect something of the distrust long felt toward the potentials of technology developing in this century. Yet, however much the dystopian, cautionary warnings of countless science-fiction writers attract us and reflect our contemporary mood, the majority of science fiction—from before Wells until at least the last years of the 1940s—*was* optimistic. Rather than cringing before a meaningless universe from which the ancient verities had been ripped, SF writers celebrated the imminence of an "Earthly Paradise" which would see the perfection of man and his society and, then, his ascent to the stars themselves.

Several years ago Samuel R. Delany urged academic critics not to approach science fiction solely from the utopian-dystopian axis. He urged that instead they observe how certain myths basic to Western literature sit in concert in a given story. S. C. Fredericks has given implicit support to the idea that SF may be a continuation of the heroic tradition by showing how contemporary writers make use of ancient mythologies. J. Norman King speculates as to the influence of science fiction on traditional religious beliefs. In contrast, Robert Canary has suggested that we consider SF as fictive history and thereby, among other things, see what it tells us of the historical process. And Isaac Asimov declares that it is "a literature of ideas . . . the *only* literature of relevant ideas. . . ."

This leads to a perspective of the field which Asimov might not anticipate. Thomas Wymer has observed that such a remark as Asimov's provides a framework which makes the genre's development more understandable as a movement—a series of events —in the history of ideas.

From its beginnings to the so-called "hard-core" associated with the editing of John W. Campbell and the writing of Campbell, Asimov, Heinlein—and, more recently, such individuals as Larry Niven, James Gunn, and Jerry Pournelle—the basic stance of science fiction has been that of the Enlightenment. Partaking of a concern for epistemology, the central core of science fiction has accepted the concept that reason is the highest quality of mind and, as a result, both man and society are perfectable. This has important ramifications perhaps not immediately discernible. As Wymer points out, "the major function of man, the operation for which he is most prized" by Campbell and Asimov, for example, "is his capacity to know and to engage constantly in the quest for and accumulation of knowledge." To state it another way, with reason supreme (and thus the universe itself of a unified, rational nature), all knowledge can be attained.

Man must simply persist in his collection of data. Thus in these stories the study of characterization gives way to the exploration of idea. "What if" becomes the classic verbalization of the formula. The plot can thus assume the structure of a puzzle or a problem to be solved. This is the heart of science fiction—contemporary as well as that of the past.

During an episode of *Outer Limits,* for example, the announcer stated that the story to be presented dealt with the attempts of the inhabitants of Planet X to solve the problem of disposing of their criminals. The *Star Trek* episodes are all exercises in problem solving. In Murray Leinster's highly regarded "First Contact" (1944), when the ship from Earth encounters an alien ship near the Crab Nebula, the problem becomes how each will return to its own planet without giving away its position to an "alien" who may possibly seek to destroy it. Such an analysis helps to explain why Edgar Allan Poe contributed significantly to both the early detective story and science fiction—both are puzzles in his fiction. It explains why Isaac Asimov has successfully produced detective stories within science-fiction worlds, as in *The Caves of Steel* (1953) and *The Naked Sun* (1956).

Asimov stated that science fiction is "the *only* literature of relevant ideas, since it is the *only* literature that, at its best, is firmly based on scientific thought." If SF elevates reason, then it celebrates science and the scientific method with an almost mystic fervor. In Asimov's early story, "Trends" (1939), a new religious fanaticism brings scientific investigation to a standstill for various reasons; the "great vision [space travel] is hailed as 'defiance of God.'" Yet after the protagonist has secretly built a ship and returned from a flight to the moon, "Secret discontent, combined with a heroic tale of man against overwhelming odds—the sort of tale that had stirred man's soul since the beginning of time—" causes "the pendulum [to swing] back again."[3] The action is off-stage; the mere announcement of the accomplishment causes "the fickle world [to go] wild." The event leads to a new awakening of the human spirit. In *Prelude to Space* (1951), which concentrates upon the preparations for the first manned flight to the moon,

Arthur C. Clarke gives voice to the dream of a new Renaissance; he concludes an epilogue set in the moon colony twenty years after the success of that first flight, saying:

> . . . Once more the proud ships were sailing for unknown lands, bearing the seeds of new civilizations which in the ages to come would surpass the old. The rush to the new worlds would destroy the suffocating restraints which had poisoned almost half the [twentieth] century. The barriers had been broken, and men could turn their energies outwards to the stars instead of striving among themselves.
>
> Out of the fears and miseries of the Second Dark Age, drawing free—oh, might it be forever—from the shadows of Belsen and Hiroshima, the world was moving towards its most splendid sunrise. After five hundred years, the Renaissance had come again. The dawn that would burst above the Apennines at the end of the long, lunar night would be no more brilliant than the age that had now been born.[4]

In this passage Clarke enunciates the continuing, optimistic vision of the potential of rational man using science to loosen himself from old, dark bondages. This is the vision that lay at the heart of science fiction—perhaps at the heart of the American specialist magazines in particular—at least into the late 1940s.

Yet, if science fiction originated in the spirit of the Enlightenment, it did undergo a romantic sea-change. This is apparent at one level in its indebtedness to the Gothic. Nowhere in *Frankenstein,* for example, is there a problem to be solved as there is in the stories already cited. The scientist and his creature are locked in the chase across the Arctic ice, for Dr. Frankenstein has been overwhelmed by his sense of guilt at the outcome of his experiment (his solution to a puzzle)—that is, his creation of human life. As for the monster, he suffers as a result of what he regards as the injustice of a world he never made and lashes out after he has been ostracized by society (including his creator) and then refused a chance to live a full and meaningful life separate from European society. Similarly, although it lacks the Faustian dimension of Mary Shelley's novel, FitzJames O'Brien's "The Diamond Lens" (1858) perhaps even more vividly illustrates this indebtedness to the Gothic in its presentation of the first-person narrative of "Linley, the mad Microscopist," who tells of his dissatisfaction at not having a perfect lens and then of his fascination for the sylphlike girl whom he finds in the world within a drop of water. Both stories wear the cloak of madness, and that unbalance measures how terrible can be the world into which science may take an individual. This emphasis upon the irrational and terrible continues through the fantasies of A. Merritt and H. P. Lovecraft—as may be seen in the latter's Cthulhu Mythos, as well as such individual SF stories as "The Colour Out of Space" (1928)—and appears as late as Harlan Ellison's "I Have No Mouth, and I Must Scream" (1967), although Ellison's theme and tone differ from those of his predecessors.

The second level at which the Romantic influence may be discerned is in the mystic, transcendental themes of such writers as Olaf Stapledon, to whom so many writers, including Arthur C. Clarke, pay homage. Germane to all of Stapledon's fiction, although perhaps having most impact in his first book, *Last and First Men* (1930), in which he adopts a cosmic perspective tracing the development of eighteen species of man against a backdrop of several billions of years, he records the "huge fluctuations of joy and woe, the results of changes not only in man's environment but in his fluid nature." Although he disagrees with those romancers of the future who "too easily imagine a progress toward some kind of Utopia, in which beings like themselves live in unmitigated bliss among circumstances perfectly suited to a fixed human nature," his Last Men do achieve "spiritual maturity and the philosophic mind," thereby overcoming present human limitations.

This concern for transcendence stands behind a myriad of tales of mutants, robots, humanoids, supermen, and aliens ranging from Philip Wylie's *Gladiator* (1930) and Stapledon's *Odd John* (1937) through such examples from the pulp magazines as Ed Earl Repp's "The Gland Superman" (1938) and A. E. van Vogt's *Slan* (1940) to Arthur C. Clarke's *Childhood's End* (1953), John Wyndham's *Chocky* (1968), and Robert Silverberg's *Tower of*

Glass (1968). Significantly, this legion of mutants and humanoids and supermen provided science fiction with its first, basic method of exploring the possibilities (and consequences) of new modes of consciousness and knowing—what has recently been termed the "exploration of inner space"—a tradition which can be followed to such experimental novels as Robert Silverberg's *Son of Man* (1971) and Brian Aldiss's *Barefoot in the Head* (1969). One of the important expressions of this basic dream occurs in Clifford D. Simak's story, "Desertion" (1944)—included in *City* (1952)—in which "a new sharp clarity of thought" grips the protagonist who has been transformed into a Lopar, a creature of Jupiter: ". . . he had found something greater than Man had ever known. A swifter, surer body. A sense of exhilaration, a deeper sense of life. A sharper mind. A world of beauty that even the dreamers of Earth had not yet imagined."[5] In general, these mutations and transformations echo the certainty felt at the turn of the century that the next step in man's evolution must be "spiritual." Unless this theme is used in the occasional story—or, more often, in the SF film—to create a monster and evoke horror, the change produces something better. Man becomes *More Than Human* (1953), to cite Theodore Sturgeon's novel tracing the appearance and development of *homo gestalt* (the ending of the novel implies that this superior species has long been among us).

Nor should one forget that the heightened, romantic awareness of self characteristic of so many of these stories reflects that sense of estrangement, alienation, and isolation which has grown ever more abrasive in two centuries. Significantly, this feeling is shared by Frankenstein's creature, the Ancient Mariner, and David Selig, the protagonist of Robert Silverberg's *Dying Inside* (1972)—certainly one of the finest achievements of character study and metaphor within the genre.

The importance of setting to science fiction, however, leads one to what is perhaps the most salient feature of this romantic sea-change. One senses something of it in Coleridge, Wordsworth, Byron, Shelley, and the Romantic painters—in such works as John Martin's *Sadak in Search of the Waters of Oblivion* (1812) or *Manfred on the Jungfrau* (1837), John Constable's *Weymouth Bay* (undated), J. M. W. Turner's *The Shipwreck* (c. 1805), or Caspar David Friedrich's *Mountain Landscape with Rainbow* (c. 1809), in which one finds the human figure, often miniscule and alone, immersed in an expansive nature. Here certainly is one wellspring of two moods important to science fiction. First, the sense of wonder at the vastness, the beauty, and the terror of nature. (In Friedrich's *The Wreck of the 'Hope'* (1821), for example, one foresees something of what is best in the artistry of Chesley Bonestell.) Secondly, man's awareness of his aloneness. (This may cause him to reach out to science and the scientific method as he tries to impose an order upon a universe which may not be comprehensible; one thinks of Poe's dramatization of the epistemological paradox of the end of the eighteenth century, *The Narrative of A. Gordon Pym,* in which one can trust neither his senses nor the appearance of the world.) The latter mood causes Arthur C. Clarke to voice his loneliness as he waits for the first contact with an intelligence with whom he may share the awesome splendor of the galaxies; the advent of the Overlords in *Childhood's End* (1953) leads him to declare: ". . . the stars—the aloof, indifferent stars—had come to him. This was the moment when history held its breath, and the present sheared asunder from the past. . . . The human race was no longer alone."[6]

This concern for the relationship between man and nature led, in science fiction, as it did in the work of such nineteenth-century artists as Gaugin, to a neoprimitivism which included such figures as Rider Haggard, Conan Doyle, Edgar Rice Burroughs, Charles B. Stilson, as well as two of the earliest works of Edison Marshall, and Austin Tappan Wright's utopian *Islandia* (1942), among others. Frequently these stories gained their thematic teeth from a rejection of contemporary urban-industrial society.

This concern, however, has an even greater importance to the bulk of science fiction. Whether the narrative be concerned with the portrait of a utopia; with a journey into the depths of Asia, the polar regions, Africa, or the Americas—that is, into some unfamiliar corner of Earth; with a voyage to a far-distant planet or galaxy; or with travel into some alternate or future world, much of the fascination of author and reader alike arises from the encounter with the strange world. The reader accompanies the protagonist as he leaves the familiarity of his home, so to speak, to venture from the known into the unknown, the exotic, and often the terrible. The protagonist may go home again, as in countless space voyages such as A. E. van Vogt's "Far Centaurus" (1944), in which the problem of returning to Earth is solved by such pseudo-scientific gimmickry as "bachelor suns" and "adeledinander power"; its theme, of course, is the inevitability of progress. Or the protagonist may become an inhabitant of the new world, as does John Carter in Burroughs's Martian stories.

However tempting to our present mood, simply because the many worlds are different from the familiar one about us, one must not generalize that the creation of these imaginary settings provides a narrative strategy by which to dramatize man's alienation and estrangement. To say this is to ignore historical perspective; specifically, to ignore thematic content. For example, in Stephen Vincent Benet's "By the Waters of Babylon" (1937), the young initiate into the priesthood, seeking a medicine vision, enters the forbidden ruins of New York City. He learns that this "Dead Place" resulted from a "Great Burning"—from a bombing not unlike that at Guernica or Coventry or Dresden; he learns that its inhabitants were men, not gods; and he declares, "We must build again." Certainly this has an affirmative tone; the story is cautionary only in its warning that "Perhaps, in the old days, they ate knowledge too fast."[7] As science fiction, this story indicates how the Enlightenment and the romantic may fuse together. More recently, another exploration of an exotic setting occurred in Arthur C. Clarke's *Rendezvous with Rama* (1973), whose central fascination is with the nature of the automated spaceship which has intruded into the solar system; any political element in the plot remains essentially incidental to the main interest. Such forays lie, in large part at least, behind David Young's assertion that science fiction affords the most viable contemporary form of the pastoral.[8]

Benet portrays a post-catastrophic future. It is the so-called catastrophe motif—ranging from H. G. Wells's *The War of the Worlds* (1898), John Wyndham's *The Day of the Triffids* (1951), and Robert Merle's *Malevil* (1972, 1973) to the crop of current, often seemingly hurried best sellers and films—which provides the most vivid insights into the changes within science fiction. In the sense that a cataclysm threatens to destroy civilization, as in Garrett P. Serviss's *The Second Deluge* (1912), or confronts the protagonist with a destroyed or vanished civilization to rebuild, as in George Allan England's *Darkness and Dawn* trilogy (1914), it provides a problem to be solved. It often has had utopian overtones, as when Wells refers in "The Star" (1897) to a "new brotherhood [which] grew presently among men." In *The Day of the Triffids* Wyndham speaks of a crusade to destroy the triffids and reclaim the lands which they have usurped. Both Serviss and England enshrine science and technology and worship at the feet of the scientist and engineer as hero. And, of course, in that the protagonist is immersed into an often terrible world, the motif emphasizes the pastoral.

Yet as early as *The Time Machine* (1895) and "The Sea Raiders" (1896) Wells warned how precarious was man's position in the natural order. In "The Machine Stops" (1909) E. M. Forster foresaw the downfalls of a technological civilization which had burrowed into the Earth as it denied nature and direct experience. The "lost race" novelists, as noted, inveighed against the new urban industrialization. Zamiatin, Huxley, and Orwell damned those easy utopias to which Stapledon referred at the outset of *Last and First Men.* Clifford Simak's harsh judgement in *City* of man's surrender to technology marked a turning point in magazine science fiction. Kurt Vonnegut's *Player Piano* (1952) implies that man's imagination has been forever captured by the machine, while Walter Miller, Jr.'s *A Canticle for Leibowitz* (1959) re-enacts the cycle of history from medieval faith to atomic holocaust. Others might be cited: Anthony Burgess's *A Clockwork Orange* (1962) and *The Wanting Seed* (1962); John Christopher's *No Blade of Grass* (1957) or *Pendulum* (1968); Harlan

Ellison's "A Boy and His Dog" (1969). These writers no longer foresee the "Earthly Paradise" envisioned in early science fiction; they belong, instead, among *Hell's Cartographers.*[10]

The most recent mood of science fiction, however, goes deeper than a simple shift from a utopian to a dystopian perspective. Perhaps it was Mark Twain who first saw most clearly what was happening to the modern world. He gave expression to that insight in a short story written about 1898, "The Great Dark" (1962), in which his protagonist plunges through a microscope to voyage forever, without chance of landfall, aboard a ship on the endless sea of a drop of water beneath the indifferent lens—tortured by heat and cold, light and dark, microbe-monsters who swam beneath the surface. Bohr, the Curies, Roentgen, Einstein—these were among the ones to undercut "the laws of a mechanistic universe which were fixed and permanent and merely awaited discovery"—so Donald Wollheim described the natural order which stood behind *The Universe Makers* (1971).[11]

Twentieth-century science has replaced that order which is at the heart of the spirit of the Enlightenment—and therefore at the heart of early science fiction—with, at best, a world of probability, one which Loren Eiseley has called *The Unexpected Universe* (1969). Again one can name individual authors and individual works, among them, J. G. Ballard, Ursula LeGuin, George Alec Effinger, R. A. Lafferty, Joanna Russ, James Tiptree, Jr.; P. A. Zoline, "The Heat Death of the Universe" (1967); Philip José Farmer, "Riders of the Purple Wage" (1967) and "After Kong Fell" (1975); Gene Wolfe, "The Island of Dr. Death" (1970). These writers are some of those who, in perhaps the best of their work, ask the question which Frederic Brown once used as a title: *What Mad Universe?* Several years ago Alec Effinger suggested that instead of dystopian, the new mood of science fiction—which took form in the 1960s—should be called Absurdist. Such a judgement seems sound, for the basic shift has been one in philosophical stance— away from the idea of an ordered, rational universe toward the idea of a universe which is, ultimately, incomprehensible. And so once again the science-fiction writers reflect the intellectual climate of a period. These writers use SF materials to achieve the same ends that Ishmael Reed does in *Yellow Back Radio Broke-Down* (1969) or Robert Coover in such a story as "Babysitter" in *Pricksongs and Descants* (1969).

But one must remember that these three distinct moods exist side by side in the science fiction being written at present. Keith Laumer's *Retief of the CDT* (1971) still manages to keep "full control of the galaxy" in a manner befitting the most notorious of the space-opera formulas, as he solves all problems besetting the Corps Diplomatique Terrestrienne. In England they are still finding lost races, if not enchanting princesses, as in Ian Cameron's *The Lost Ones* (1968)—the basis of the recent Disney film—in which his protagonists find the Vikings, while in *The Mountains at the Bottom of the World* (1972), they find *Paranthropus,* a missing link, deep in an unexplored area of the Chilean Andes. Meanwhile, Samuel R. Delany experiments in *Dhalgren* (1975) and *Triton* (1976). It seems quite proper that all three exist simultaneously, for in so doing, they not only encapsulate and dramatize the intellectual history of the past several centuries, but they underscore the complexity of the human condition during a period when all of the supposed verities—the traditional systems—are being severely questioned.

NOTES

1. Jack Biles, "Editor's Comment," *Studies in the Literary Imagination,* 6 (Fall 1973), xi.
2. Patrick G. Hogan, Jr., "Reviews and Brief Mention: A Study of Utopia," *Extrapolation,* 16 (December 1974), 43.
3. Isaac Asimov, "Trends," in Thomas D. Clareson, ed., *A. Spectrum of Worlds* (New York: Doubleday & Company, 1972), pp. 125, 143.
4. Arthur C. Clarke, *Prelude to Space* (New York: Lancer Books, n.d.), pp. 172-73.
5. Clifford D. Simak, *City* (New York: Ace Books, n.d.), pp. 115-16.
6. Arthur C. Clarke, *Childhood's End* (New York: Ballantine Books, 1953), p. 11.
7. Stephen Vincent Benet, "By the Waters of Babylon," in *A Spectrum of Worlds,* pp. 119, 120.
8. David Young, *The Heart's Forest: A Study of Shakespeare's Pastoral Plays* (New Haven and London: Yale University Press, 1972), p. 199.
9. H. G. Wells, "The Star," in Robert Silverberg, ed., *The Mirror of Infinity* (New York: Harper & Row, 1970), p. 19.

10. Brian W. Aldiss and Harry Harrison, eds., *Hell's Cartographers: Some Personal Histories of Science Fiction Writers* (London: Weidenfeld and Nicholson, 1975). There will soon be an American edition of this collection of six essays in which Alfred Bester, Damon Knight, Frederik Pohl, Robert Silverberg, Aldiss, and Harrison reflect upon their ventures in the field of science fiction.
11. Donald A. Wollheim, *The Universe Makers: Science Fiction Today* (New York: Harper & Row, 1971), p. 24. Perhaps in no other single work devoted to the study of science fiction is the faith in man's immortality, as a race, and in his conquest of the galaxy so fervently stated.

The Science in Science Fiction

Stanley Schmidt

I suppose it's reasonably obvious from the name that science fiction has something to do with science. But the exact nature of the connection seems to be a perennial source of confusion, especially among people relatively unfamiliar with the field. On several occasions I have cringed slightly when someone asked me about my science-fiction "articles," at a time when I had (I hoped) published only *stories.* Perhaps the speaker in such cases has merely been using the word differently than I do, lumping all short printed works together as "articles," whether fiction or nonfiction, instead of making the sharp distinction that I do. But sometimes such questions raise the nagging suspicion that here is a person who thinks a science-fiction story is simply an essay about a scientific idea, thinly sugar-coated with fictional trappings.

No doubt some science-fiction stories have actually fit that description. I am told that in the early days of science fiction (somewhat prior to my own) a great many stories came quite close to it. Come to think of it, I have written some myself—but I soon learned that nobody wanted to buy them anymore, and I no longer (consciously) waste time writing or trying to sell such things. Times have changed; readers and editors have come to demand considerably subtler relationships between scientific speculation and storytelling. These relationships vary widely in the amount and kind of science and the way in which it is used in the story. But a pretty good formulation of a common denominator might be one attributed to Theodore Sturgeon: "A science fiction story is a story built around human beings, with a human problem, and a human solution, which would not have happened at all without its scientific content."[1]

Applied full-strength, this definition would tend to rule out a good deal of what has been passed off as science fiction, and to cast doubt upon a good deal more. I suspect it might even rule out some stories which I would persist in considering good science fiction—even with the added proviso that "human" in this context needs to be interpreted a lot more broadly than "*homo sapiens.*" No matter; this whole field is so big and varied that I have long since given up on finding a concise definition with no loopholes or exceptions. I don't think this one is perfect, but it's one of the best I've seen. If nothing else, it gives a good idea of what conscientious science-fiction writers are usually *trying* to do.

Sam Lundwall gives an example of a type of story which rather clearly fails to satisfy this criterion: the type which is effectively just a cowboys-and-Indians (or cops-and-robbers) story with the names changed. One of my favorite short examples of a story which *does* meet Sturgeon's test is Bob Shaw's "Light of Other Days."[2] This is first and foremost a psychological story, dealing with the emotional interaction of a married couple. But the way it works itself out is absolutely dependent on "slow glass," one of the more striking scientific speculations in recent science fiction.

Speculation is a key word; Damon Knight recommended inserting the word "speculative" before "scientific" in Sturgeon's statement. The late John W. Campbell, long-time editor of *Astounding* and *Analog,* once observed, "That group of writings which is usually referred to as 'mainstream literature' is, actually, a special subgroup of the field of science fiction—for science fiction deals with all places in the Universe, and all times in Eternity, so the literature of here-and-now is, truly, a subset of science fiction."[3] In ways, I think I like that definition best of all: the literature of all possible times and places. The trouble with it is that it includes too much. What we usually mean by science fiction is different from contemporary realism and historical fiction. What sets it apart is the inclusion of conditions (but *possible* conditions) outside the way we know things are or the way they have been in recorded history. In other words, speculation—usually about the future, sometimes (as in Lester del Rey's "The Day is Done")[4] about little-known parts of the past.

One way or another, that speculation usually involves scientific matters. In "The Day is Done," the underlying speculation is about what happened to Neanderthal man. In the more usual case of "future-based" science fiction, the speculations may concern, for example, future inventions, new scientific principles, future societies, or alien cultures that might be encountered in interplanetary or interstellar explorations.

There is one very important precaution that should be noted carefully before pursuing this matter further: "The mistake you must never make about science fiction is in thinking that, because it is about the future, it is necessarily about *the* future."[5] Even though science fiction has described many things which have since come to pass (and many more which haven't), it is rarely actually attempting to predict what *will* happen, and it should not be judged by its predictive accuracy. Rather, it examines various things which *might* happen and tries to imagine their consequences if they do. In effect, it tries out alternatives in imagination (where the bad ones do less damage than they would in reality)—which led Thomas N. Scortia to describe it, in an essay which elaborates on this idea, as "the imaginary experiment."[6]

I sometimes find it convenient to divide the scientific speculations in science fiction into two rough categories: *extrapolation* and *innovation.* (I say "rough" categories deliberately. Like all classifications which I may introduce in this article, these will be found to accommodate some examples easily, while others will more or less stubbornly resist being stuffed into pigeonholes.)

Let me try to illustrate each type of speculation with a straightforward example or two. "Extrapolation," as I use it here, means speculation based on extensions, developments, and applications of well-established scientific knowledge. No new principles are postulated, so it can be said with a fair degree of assurance that these speculations are things that we know are possible. Examples abound in the works of Robert A. Heinlein: future human societies worked out in minute detail, using technologies which we have never needed or got around to, but based entirely on sound engineering applications of thoroughly understood principles. Consider, for instance, *The Moon is a Harsh Mistress* (1966), which describes the breaking away from Earth of a lunar colony a century hence. To be capable of doing this—in fact, to be physically, economically, and politically feasible even as a colony—the lunar society had to solve a large array of engineering, economic, and social problems; and the solutions are worked out in enough detail to include numbers, which some readers may be expected to challenge if they're wrong. These include such things as air, water, and food recycling systems, as well as the ingenious catapults used for Moon-to-Earth shipping—which are based on sound physics and would in fact be much preferable to rockets for any serious shipping.

Extrapolation of another kind is particularly prominent in stories by Poul Anderson and Hal Clement: the development of whole alien worlds, ecologies, and cultures, internally consistent and believable but very different from the Earth we know, by the application to unfamiliar conditions of what is already known about astronomy, physics, chemistry, and biology. In *The People of the Wind* (1973), Anderson has humans mingling with Ythrians, a race of intelligent, flying ornithoids—something long casually assumed to be impossible. But he describes them in great detail, including not only the special adaptations which enable them to overcome the usual objections, but the evolutionary history which led to those adaptations. Clement, in *Mission of*

Gravity (1953) and *Starlight* (1971), has beings adapted to living and working on extremely massive gas-giant planets, with strong gravities and dense reducing atmospheres—environments which are utterly different from anything we have experienced directly, but which we know can exist and might well lead to life something like that imagined by Clement.

Conveniently, both Anderson and Clement have written essays giving rather detailed examples of the kind of reasoning that goes into world-making; these are printed back to back in Reginald Bretnor's symposium, *Science Fiction, Today and Tomorrow.*[7]

"Innovation" I distinguish from extrapolation by the fact that it does depend on the assumption of new—i.e., now unknown—principles. Classic examples include faster-than-light travel, anti-gravity, and time travel. Sometimes, as in the case of the "quasi-materials" in my own *Newton and the Quasi-Apple* (1974) such innovations were inspired by *analogies* with something already known, which may be mentioned somewhere in the story by way of "explanation." But they are innovations nonetheless, and the explanations are correspondingly nonrigorous, if they cannot actually be derived from known principles.

How do innovative speculations fit in with my definition some pages back of science fiction as the literature of all *possible* times and places? By definition, an innovative speculation cannot be proved possible. If it could, it would no longer be innovative, but would have been assimilated into the body of "established [accepted might be a better word] scientific knowledge." And yet such ideas are an important part of science fiction. What is reasonable to expect, I think, is that nobody should be able to prove it's *impossible* at the time of its writing. This requirement is what I call the "negative impossibility" test. It means that new principles must be introduced in such a way that they don't contradict any accepted principles *in any region of experience where the accepted ideas have been experimentally verified.*

It's no coincidence that this is almost exactly the main criterion which must be met by new theories in actual scientific research: the new, generalized theory must give the same answers as the old in the regions where the old one worked. A hundred years ago mechanics was described entirely by Newtonian equations. As long as nobody had ever seen anything moving very fast, they worked fine—meaning that, if you independently measured the quantities on both sides of one of those equations, they came out equal, within experimental uncertainties. For things moving at appreciable fractions of the speed of light, this turned out not to be true, and new equations were needed. Those developed by Albert Einstein under the heading of special relativity are known to work nicely at all speeds up to some value very near the speed of light—including the low speeds where the Newtonian equations worked. It's just that the two sets of equations give answers which are experimentally indistinguishable at those low velocities, and only gradually diverge as the velocity is increased. In much the same way, if I'm going to use faster-than-light travel in a story and try to explain anything about how it's supposed to work, I have to make sure the theory I'm using gives the same results as relativity in the range of speeds where relativity has been tested. (It just so happens that I've done this to some extent in a couple of groups of stories. A partial explanation of one of them appears incidentally in an article in *Analog*.)[8]

The easier and safer way out, of course, is to give as little explanation as possible.[9] By judicious and artfully glib vagueness, it is often possible to avoid the kind of close scrutiny which may lead to embarrassment, and perhaps this is just as well with many innovations. If A. E. van Vogt "explains" the operation of the Distorter in *the World of Null-A* (1945) in terms of a "twenty-decimal similarity" principle, who can argue with him? (*The World of Null-A,* by the way, is a book for which I have the highest admiration, lest anybody misconstrue this reference.) The question arises: how much explanation is an author obligated to give (or how little can he get away with)?

If he doesn't care whether the story is considered science fiction or fantasy, there would seem to be no need for explanation at all. But if he is interested in satisfying science-fiction readers who look closely for plausibility and internal consistency, he had better make at least a passing attempt at explaining any new principles he's using. Otherwise they just look like "magic."

Except . . .

Sometimes the available viewpoints make it impossible to give as much explanation as some readers (or even the author) might like. In Anne McCaffrey's *Dragonflight* (1968), for example, there are background questions which can never be fully and explicitly answered because none of the characters is in a position to know the answers, even if the author does.

Also, most people interested in science fiction very long have read a lot of it. There are some things which were once innovative, have not even remotely become part of accepted scientific knowledge, and yet are now readily accepted by readers without explanation. These are things like the aforementioned faster-than-light travel, anti-gravity, and time travel. Several authors *have* offered explanations, of sorts, for each of these things. That having been done, and these devices being so useful for generating stories, they have gone into a body of science-fictional *conventions* which are widely accepted as "potentially explainable" and are freely drawn upon by writers who may never bother to explain them. But once in a while an author will still venture a more detailed description of a new variation on one of these ancient themes, and the result may well be a story of surprising freshness. See, for example, the new twist on anti-gravity in Isaac Asimov's "The Billiard Ball" (1967) or on the time machines in his "The Dead Past" (1956).

Really new ideas, in fact, are rather rare these days. Even when an author has one, he needs to build a lot more around it before he can call it a story. Bob Shaw's slow glass (in "Light of Other Days") is one of the more commonly cited recent examples of a really innovative idea—a kind of glass through which light travels very, very slowly. Yet something strikingly similar to even this (with an angle which Shaw didn't emphasize) was mentioned casually in L. Sprague de Camp's "The Exalted" (1940) some twenty-six years earlier. This fact doesn't seem to have been widely noticed, but it wouldn't really matter in any case. Shaw's approach is still different enough to be fresh, and the novelty of the idea, though intriguing, is by no means the whole (or even the main) value of "Light of Other Days."

A couple of final comments before I leave this subject of kinds of speculation. I have talked about criteria for plausibility of innovations. Curiously, it is probably easier to be convincing with a wildly innovative idea than with a purely, tightly extrapolative one. Or perhaps it's not so curious after all. Consider this: if the speculative elements of your story deal with space travel within the solar system, using only classical mechanics and electrodynamics, those are understood in such detail that it's quite possible to work out things like trajectories and travel times and fuel requirements very specifically—and a lot of people know how to do it. If you don't bother, some reader is likely to—and let the world know. There's considerably less danger of that happening with a time machine for which you haven't given any equations. (But it still pays to take some pains to avoid implicit or explicit logical inconsistencies.) For just this reason, many writers tend to shy away from attempting the closely reasoned, meticulously worked out technical backgrounds characteristic of so-called "hard" science fiction. And those who do this sort of thing well—such as Asimov, Heinlein, Anderson, Clement, Larry Niven, and Frank Herbert—earn a special added bit of respect from those readers in a position to appreciate what they've done.

I conclude this section by remarking once more that the classification of speculation as extrapolative or innovative is not nearly as clear-cut as it might sound. For one thing, some ideas are themselves not entirely clear as to their status. How about "psi," the whole area of parapsychological phenomena such as telepathy and telekinesis? There appears, to some, to be a considerable amount of evidence scattered through history, folklore, and police files that some things of this sort do sometimes happen. But that evidence is so sketchy, uncontrolled, and seemingly nonreproducible that many scientists claim there's no real evidence at all, much less an explanation. So are stories about psi phenomena postulating totally new phenomena, or extrapolating from real but at least poorly understood ones? The question may well be more academic than useful. And still less can whole stories often be categorized in this way. In *The People of the Wind,* for example, the very carefully developed Ythrians participate in a plot which is completely dependent on the routine, taken-for-granted use of faster-than-light travel.

So much for the nature of science-fictional speculation. A question perhaps still more important is that of how it is *used* to help make a *story.* Many approaches to this question are conceivable, but a more or less historical one will perhaps prove useful here.

Asimov has suggested that most science fiction stories fall into one of three categories, according to how they use their speculative material: "gadget" stories, "adventure" stories, and "sociological" stories. Naturally, these classifications are not rigidly partitioned or universally applicable—a story may, for example, have elements of two of them—but they are useful for purposes of discussion. And they do have a fairly clear connection with the historical development of science fiction.

To illustrate what is meant by these classifications, consider the various kinds of stories that might result from different approaches to a single speculative idea. To use an example where we have the benefit of enough hindsight to have a pretty full idea of the possibilities, imagine that a science-fiction writer three centuries ago had conceived of the automobile and wanted to write a story about it.

A "gadget" story might describe the trials and tribulations of the car's inventor as he developed it and finally made it work. The idea that such a contraption was possible would be the *raison d'être* of the story, which might therefore tend to contain sizable expanses of explanation aimed at convincing the reader.

An "adventure" story might take the automobile as given, but unusual, and have an early driver using it to carry out a journey-with-adventurous-episodes which might not have been possible without it—as in the movie, *The Great Race.*

A "sociological" story would likely jump considerably farther into the future and envision a society (such as ours) in which automobiles had become commonplace and vital. It might deal, for example, with the problems of a family whose home is about to be seized to clear the way for an expressway, or with an automotive engineer in conflict with his company management on a question of pollution control. A really farsighted author might go still farther and imagine a society which has become dependent on cars in a myriad of interrelated ways and is in danger of collapse because of an impending cutoff of its oil supplies. The main point implied by the word "sociological" here is that the main emphasis is not on the car *per se* but rather on its impact—quite likely through quite indirect and unobvious consequences—on the lives of people. The actual possibilities cover a huge range.

This kind of retroactive hunting for examples of science-fictional thinking may seem peculiar, but I think it can provide helpful insights. Sociological science fiction might be thought of as "history in reverse." Where the historian looks backward for past causes of present conditions, the science-fiction writer postulates a significant change ("cause") and looks ahead for its future consequences. Historians, in my limited experience, have rarely seen fit to turn things around and look at them from this science-fictional point of view, but I remember one striking example where one has done exactly that. Read Alistair Cooke's "A Firebell in the Night,"[10] a nice example of the kind of thinking that a very good sociological science-fiction writer might have done in the late eighteenth century about the social changes that might result from a couple of simple inventions (the cotton gin and interchangeable parts). And then read Stephen Vincent Benet's epic *John Brown's Body* as an example of the kind of story that might result from that thinking—a story with the technological gadgets lurking far off backstage, but ultimately underlying all that's happening to the dozens of human lives woven into this story of the Civil War.

There weren't any sociological science-fiction writers in those days. If there had been, they might have been able to make some useful suggestions (though whether anybody would have listened is another question). Science fiction itself is, with a few scattered exceptions, quite a recent development. And as I hinted earlier, it has tended to develop through the categories I've named, though not neatly or monotonically—in particular, both gadget and adventure stories were common in the 1930s. But neither of them is common any more, while sociological stories have blossomed into a great variety of forms.

My personal familiarity with the early days of the magazines is somewhat limited. I was born too late to experience them directly, and relatively few of the stories from those magazines found their way into anthologies which came my way. But Isaac Asimov has recently compiled a big historical anthology of science fiction of the 1930s, containing over two dozen stories and liberal autobiographical comment.[11] These stories and Asimov's commentary together provide, I think, a good introduction to what kinds of things were being written and what kinds of changes were taking place then.

In general, and again with exceptions, those stories tended to be rather crude by present-day standards, both literary and (more important for the restricted purposes of this article) scientific. Asimov cites examples of stories containing scientific errors easily identifiable even at the time of writing, such as radium producing "repulsion rays" in Neil R. Jones's "The Jameson Satellite" (1931). In all fairness, such things still happen occasionally. Science is far too big for anybody to know all of it; some writers (probably more at the moment than just a few years ago, in fact) have relatively little scientific background; and some editors don't have enough to catch everything an author might slip by them. But it happens less often now than at some times in the past, if only because some standards of accuracy did rise to such a level that writers would tend either to know what they were talking about or to steer clear of statements that they couldn't support and which somebody else might be able to check.

The qualifying phrase "at the time of writing" seems to be essential in judging the accuracy of scientific content of stories. Research is constantly turning up new facts and even overturning old ones which were long taken for granted. This, if allowances are not made, may change the apparent validity of stories. For example, Stanley G. Weinbaum, who wrote briefly in this period and was in many respects far ahead of his time, did a couple of stories set on Venus ("Parasite Planet" [1935] and "The Lotus Eaters" [1935]) which were direct causes of my own present addiction to science fiction. Asimov has praised them highly: "The super-jungle of the dayside of Venus as pictured in 'Parasite Planet' is, in my opinion, the most perfect example of an alien ecology ever constructed."[12] In the light of recently acquired knowledge about Venus, however, this ecology couldn't possibly exist there, and the notion of a permanent dayside is no longer tenable. Does all this mean that the story is obsolete and no longer worth reading? I can't believe that. The world Weinbaum described could exist *somewhere.* Nitpicking over a name seems hardly fair either to Weinbaum—possibly the most amazing science-fiction writer who ever lived—or to readers who might still find his stories both entertaining and thought-provoking.

Another common fault which Asimov mentions, particularly in the early "gadget" stories, lies on the borderline of scientific and literary values. The scientific explanations tended to go on at great length, in large chunks of pedantic lecturing at the beginning of the story or here and there in the course of it. Either way, lectures obstruct the flow of the story and may anesthetize some readers. More recent writers have learned to give only such background information as is needed for the story (though they usually know more than they tell), and to work that smoothly into the story in a continuing series of small doses, rather than bringing the action grinding to a halt to explain everything at once. (They have learned to do this largely because readers and editors have learned to insist on it.) Lectures still occur in some modern stories, but they have become uncommon, and it takes considerable skill to use this technique without alienating readers. Poul Anderson gets away with it oftener and more successfully than most, and even he has occasionally been criticized for it.

Sometimes the line between a gadget story and an adventure story appears a bit nebulous. How about "Submicroscopic" (1931) by Capt. S. P. Meek, wherein the hero uses an "Electronic Vibration Adjuster" to shrink himself to explore a submicroscopic world? It starts out looking very much like a gadget story, complete with lecture and description of invention. But that's only the beginning. Most of the story is clearly and primarily a tale of adventure encountered in that world; the gadget functions (literarily) merely as a means of getting the hero there.

The simple "gadget-adventure-sociological" classification is perhaps best suited to stories based on single ideas, and a great many stories pretty well fit that description. In general, it is advisable for a writer to avoid making too many new assumptions in the same story. Often, even if there is more than one, one is central and the others are incidental. But the adventure and sociological categories can easily grow into things where a multitude of speculative ideas are prominent. I am thinking in particular of the super-adventure stories which E. E. "Doc" Smith and John W. Campbell were doing in the late 1920s and early 1930s. These have been variously described as "super-science epics" or "space operas," depending on whether the person doing the describing admired them or looked down on them. They featured action on an unprecedented scale, carried out with huge starships and dazzling arrays of "super-scientific" weapons and other inventions. They have been criticized on both literary and scientific grounds, but it is hard to deny their popularity at the time—or their mind-opening importance in first dealing with such ideas as human activity extending beyond the solar system and beyond the light-speed barrier.

In view of his prominence in connection with "space opera," it might seem somewhat surprising that Campbell played the role he did in the rise of "sociological" science fiction. There had been sociological science fiction earlier—Laurence Manning's "The Man Who Awoke," for example, might well be considered such. (Asimov likes to point this story out as an example of miscalled "escape" literature—it deals with a future society forced into hard times by its ancestors' waste of fossil fuels.) But it was rare. When Campbell took over *Astounding* in 1937 (or 1938, depending on how you figure), there began a transformation which rapidly made sociological science fiction the overwhelmingly dominant kind. In 1938 began the so-called "Golden Age" of *Astounding*; writers from the years before came to be known as "pre-Campbell" writers. Throughout the "Golden Age," *Astounding* clearly dominated the field. Even after other magazines of comparable stature appeared in the 1950s, and *Astounding* changed its name to *Analog* around 1960, a certain broad type of science fiction—usually quite sociological, but characteristically with a very solid scientific and technical foundation—continued to be referred to in such terms as "the Campbell/*Analog* tradition."

How did an editor have such far-reaching influence? Actually, it began even before he became an editor. Already in the middle and late 1930s, he had begun to envision a new kind of story—a kind in which the science was there, but mood and character took on dominant importance—and to write such examples as "Twilight" (1934) and "Who Goes There?" (1938) under the pseudonym Don A. Stuart. The Stuart stories were something new and they were popular, but, beyond inspiring a few imitators, they did not put Campbell in a position to revolutionize the field.

But as editor of *Astounding,* he could and did. The reasons, in retrospect, seem fairly simple. He had a clear idea of what he wanted, he was a magnificent teacher (and very willing to work with new writers), and he paid the highest rates in the business. These factors conspired to enable him to fill his magazine with writers doing the new kind of story he had conceived. And word quickly got around that this new kind of story was so much better than anything else on the market that readers and writers alike gravitated toward *Astounding*. The extent of its influence may be gauged by examining the credit lines for the stories in the *Science Fiction Hall of Fame,* an entirely disproportionate number of which originally appeared in *Astounding,* or by looking into the publishing history of such writers as Anderson, Asimov, Heinlein, Simak, Sturgeon, and van Vogt.

I don't think it's quite as easy to verbalize what makes a Campbell/*Astounding* story as some people have made it out to be. However, having read a lot of them and written a few, I think I can point out a few more or less common denominators. Campbell himself explained some of what he was looking for in some of his writings, e.g., his introductions to *The Astounding Science Fiction Anthology*[13] and some of the *Analog* anthologies. Essentially, he was looking for stories in which equal stress was placed on each of the two definitive words, *science* and *fiction.*[14] *Fiction* might be considered primary in the special sense that readers would judge the stories first as *stories,* and that the science should be incorporated not so much for its own sake as for its effects on people and societies.

But the science was in no way subservient in terms of the attention the writer was expected to give it—*neither* scientific nor literary considerations were to be slighted in favor of the other. Campbell himself had a strong scientific background. He had a degree in physics, and right up to his death in 1971 he kept up with research in many fields, both through reading and through personal contacts with active workers at places like MIT and Bell Labs. He could usually spot sloppy science or lazy thinking; I don't think I've ever met another man whose mind seemed to work quite as fast and incisively. He insisted on accuracy and thoroughness in thinking about both scientific background *and* its human consequences. In both areas, through conversations and letters, he was constantly prodding authors to pursue ideas and their consequences further than they might have without that goal. And in that, I think, lies a good deal of what sets the Campbell tradition apart—that, and the fact that he was also demanding more attention to believable plots and characters than had usually been demanded before. (One other characteristic which might be cited has little to do with science directly, but a great deal to do with people's attitudes toward it. That is the generally "upbeat" philosophical slant of *Astounding/Analog* stories—the idea that most [not all] problems have solutions, and if story characters fail to find those solutions, it should be because the problems are too big, not because the characters are too small.)

Since 1950 or so, *Astounding/Analog* has not dominated the field so completely. It is still there, and still going strong—now under the editorship of Ben Bova, who has in significant ways continued the tradition, but without hesitating to add the characteristic imprint of his own personality. But now there are other major publishers and editors as well, with their own distinctive tastes and goals, providing outlets for a wider spectrum of science fiction. There are other magazines such as *Galaxy* and *The Magazine of Fantasy and Science Fiction*; there are more original books than there used to be; there are the periodic original anthologies such as *Orbit* and *Universe.* How do these outlets differ from the one we have been considering, with particular regard to their scientific content?

I think it is fair to say that, of the magazines and original anthologies (which function somewhat like the magazines), *Analog* is still the most consistently and deeply concerned with careful scientific and technological speculation as such—with "hard" science fiction. Not *all* of its stories have this emphasis, but a substantially higher percentage than those in the other magazines do. *Galaxy,* for example, has often been associated with social satires (including some very good ones) which concentrate on examining possible *sociological* developments, without incorporating any new technological underpinnings beyond well-established science-fiction conventions. As for books, they run the whole gamut of possibilities.

That gamut, in both books and magazines, has come to include quite an extensive spectrum. Even in the realm of "hard" science fiction, the role of the so-called hard sciences varies enormously. There is a misconception in some circles that hard science fiction and sociological science fiction are mutually exclusive—that, for example, *Analog* is habitually preoccupied with machines rather than people (a claim which I or probably just about any other *Analog* writer would dispute vigorously). Hard science fiction can be very sociological—many of the stories of Anderson and Heinlein, for example, including the ones already specifically mentioned, are both very "hard" and very sociological.

On the other hand, it doesn't *have* to be. There is still science fiction in which the science *is* of primary thematic concern. In this connection, an Anderson story such as *The People of the Wind* or *Fire Time* (1974) and a Clement story such as *Mission of Gravity* or *Starlight* make an interesting contrast. Both as classic examples of the kind of science fiction in which the physical setting is worked out rigorously and in painstaking detail; I would find it hard to name other writers who excel or even approach either Anderson or Clement in the arts of world-building and alien-building. But what they *do* with their alien worlds is very different (and I humbly submit that there is plenty of room for both approaches). In the Clement story, a scientific or technical problem is central and forms the whole backbone of the plot; characterization and social issues are clearly secondary. An Anderson story, on the other hand, is very much a story of people and sentient aliens, with an abundance of highly developed individual characters, strong emotions and sensory impressions, and richly multifaceted cultures in conflict. The combination of this with the solidly crafted background—a relationship so intimate that the very nature of the alien civilizations in *The People of the Wind* and *Fire Time* grows inevitably out of their astronomical and planetary backgrounds—leads to what I personally consider the most fully realized alien worlds in the business.

There are other cases, not requiring (or lending themselves to) quite as much of that kind of detail work, in which science contributes directly to the theme, rather than just the background, of a story. The themes may, for example, be directly related to central concepts of scientific philosophy, as in Tom

Godwin's "The Cold Equations."[15] Here is a painful moral dilemma with no "right" answer—because the universe follows fixed laws and does not make exceptions, even for nice people.

Or a story may deal with questions of how science develops (and civilization develops with it) as in the strange cyclic civilization of Asimov's "Nightfall," or the gently perturbed quasi-medieval theocracy of my *Newton and the Quasi-Apple*. Or it may deal with the related (and far from simple) questions of social responsibility of scientists and government control of research; as examples of this, I could recommend Asimov's "The Dead Past" and Harry Harrison's *The Daleth Effect* (1970)—particularly to anybody with *either* a simplistic anti-technology or a simplistic pro-technology bias.

And then there is the large expanse of "not-so-hard" science fiction, in which the scientific speculation is present only as the key to something else, or as part of the background for purely social speculation or satire. A good example of the former is Daniel Keyes's *Flowers for Algernon* (1966), a most remarkable piece of writing detailing the rise and fall of a mentally-retarded man whose intelligence is surgically raised to a very high level—temporarily. The possibility of the operation is not the central point of the story; Keyes makes no attempt to describe it in detail, and I'm not at all sure that a surgical approach could actually do what was done in the story. But *maybe* it could, and the assumption opens the way to an unforgettable inside look at the central character's mind—and the world he has to live in because of it.

The "mere background" handling of science pervades a good deal of that nebulous phenomenon of, approximately, the late 1960s sometimes known as the "New Wave"—too much of which, in the eyes of some of us, overemphasized literary experimentation at the expense of solid ideation, and thus too often came across as blindly anti-technological or anti-scientific on emotional rather than rational grounds. But it also applies, to a considerable extent, to some very tightly reasoned, solidly-crafted speculation about man's future, such as many of Gordon R. Dickson's stories—for example, "Call Him Lord."[16]

In these last paragraphs I have been talking about books and magazines; perhaps I should say a few words about the visual media. Here, unfortunately, I have seen little that really qualifies as science fiction, by any of the partial definitions I have cited. A great deal has come out of movie and television studios which has been *called* science fiction, but most of that has been a pretty feeble imitation of either science or fiction. (Ironically, one of the few actual examples of good science fiction I have seen come out of Hollywood never mentioned science fiction in any of its advertising, and probably half the students in my science-fiction class have seemed surprised that I considered it such. That was *Charly,* a quite creditable filming of *Flowers for Algernon.*)

Probably the best-known sorts of visual "science fiction" are the innumerable low-budget "monster-from-outer-space" films and their television counterparts such as *The Outer Limits.* Unfortunately, giant spiders trampling through New York City—and most of their ilk—represent appallingly elementary violations of sound speculation. To cite just one reason, scaling an object of that shape up by such a factor would increase its weight so much more than its strength that it would have no hope of being able to stand up if constructed of any known material.

There have been occasional respectable attempts at science fiction in movies and television, though. I have already mentioned *Charly*; a few other movies which qualify in my opinion and/or those of people I respect are *Destination Moon, The Andromeda Strain,* and *2001: A Space Odyssey.* (Though *2001,* in my judgment, was presented far too obscurely to be intelligible to a viewer who didn't already know what was going on, and that ruined it as communication.) The one solid series I know of on television was *Star Trek*; I personally saw only a few episodes, and those struck me as competent but not outstanding. But even "competent" is a giant step upward for television science fiction, and I'm told by sources I tend to trust that there were some outstanding episodes. Not surprisingly, a major secret of *Star Trek's* success is one well known to any successful science-fiction writer: the stories were set against a large, self-consistent background that was worked out carefully and in considerable detail before the actual storytelling began.[17]

In conclusion, just how important is science—and which sciences—to a science-fiction writer, or to a reader who wants to understand and evaluate what a writer has done in terms of its speculative as well as its literary content?

The answers, as might be gathered from the preceding paragraphs, depend very much on the kind of story. Keyes, writing in a contemporary setting about an operation whose sole importance to the story lay in its consequences, needed very little detailed scientific background to produce *Flowers for Algernon*—and a reader needs very little to get a lot out of the story. *Mission of Gravity,* at the other extreme, could not possibly have been written by anybody without a very extensive and solid grounding in the physical sciences, and it can probably be only dimly appreciated by a reader who doesn't have at least a fair grounding in them. A typical Asimov or Anderson or Heinlein story lies somewhere in between. It is possible for a reader with little scientific knowledge to get quite a bit of enjoyment from one of these (though possibly marred by just an occasional brief spell of unintelligibility). But he will also be missing quite a bit; the reader who does know a fair amount of science gets a significant "something extra," and the more he knows, the more he gets.

Sometimes the author has considerable choice in how prominent to make the science in the background. For example, Ursula K. LeGuin's recent novel, *The Dispossessed* (1974), is first and foremost a story about human beings and human values; she herself describes it on the title page as "an ambiguous utopia." Even though it is about a scientist and is set on two planets of Tau Ceti, science really plays a surprisingly small role in both the background and the thematic material. It could very conceivably have played more—I find myself in the minority position of wishing, for example, that she had shown me a little more about the astronomical and planetological background of Urras and Anarres. What she did with the human issues involved was commendable, enough to enable her to easily win a Nebula for *The Dispossessed,* but I can't help thinking it could have been still better if more attention had been given to the worlds themselves.

Sometimes the author does not even have this choice of whether to do a lot with the scientific elements or to relegate them to the distant background. The Clement stories are a good case in point. I find myself presently confronting another one—a story very much about people, but set against an all-pervasive background of changing environmental conditions totally unlike any in past experience. The situation in question is a projected sequel to *The Sins of the Fathers,*[18] which will take place during an attempt to move the Earth to a neighboring galaxy. So much can be worked out about the changes that would occur during this trip (I have described some of them in the *Analog* article already cited) that I would not dare even attempt this story without first doing a lot of that working-out. Even with a reasonable ability to do so, the prospect is intimidating—but I'll probably do it anyway. (This, incidentally, is a good illustration of something I hinted at earlier: scientific background is actually more essential to a writer [or reader] in cases of relatively close-to-home extrapolation than in far-out innovation.)

Which sciences are most important, in those cases where science is really essential to a story? Again, it depends. To write (or understand) a short story or novelette based on a single idea, only a single science may be vital—but that one may be anything. One of the more intriguing things I've found about science-fiction writing is that virtually nothing is irrelevant to it. Researching stories has at one time or another led me into almost any field you can name—not only "hard sciences" like physics and astronomy, but "soft sciences" like ecology and anthropology and linguistics, and even "nonsciences" like music and sculpture.

But in certain types of story, including some very broad, widely recurrent ones, certain fundamentals are central and indispensable. A great many science-fiction stories, for example, are set at least partly in other worlds. It seems to me that any writer or careful reader of such stories owes it to himself to be at least reasonably familiar with the basics of reasonably up-to-date astronomy—and astronomy has been growing and changing explosively in the last several decades. Any attempt to absorb modern astronomy will lead inevitably into certain areas of physics. Quite often these worlds will have native life, and rational consideration of what forms that might take requires certain rudiments of chemistry and biology. Moreover—and this is particularly true when a whole world is to be created and made real, as in an Anderson novel—all these "separate" sciences tend to become inextricably entwined in each other. Possible evolutions of life forms, for example, are very much shaped by astronomical factors. The bridge between these two seemingly unrelated sets of phenomena is "general planetology," a sort of generalized alloy of astrophysics, geophysics, meteorology, and oceanography—in other words, the study of what forms planets themselves may take.

Happily, there exist several books which gather the most pertinent parts of these interrelated sciences together in forms which are potentiallly very useful to science-fiction writers and readers. A few of these (all with the additional virtue of being readable) are suggested below.[19]

Ultimately, it all comes back to Sturgeon's dictum with which I began: "A science fiction story is a story built around human beings . . . which would not have happened at all without its scientific content." That leaves room for tremendous variation in the amount, kind, and role of the scientific content. And that content deserves as much attention and care as the particular story demands. The writer *must* give it that attention and care—and the reader will very likely find it worth his while as well.

NOTES

1. Sam J. Lundwall, *Science Fiction; What It's All About* (New York: Ace Books, 1971), p. 117.
2. Bob Shaw, "Light of Other Days," in Brian W. Aldiss and Harry Harrison, eds., *Nebula Award Stories, Number Two* (New York: Pocket Books, 1968).
3. John W. Campbell, ed., *Analog 1* (New York: Doubleday & Co., 1963), p. xv.
4. Lester del Rey, "The Day is Done," in Isaac Asimov, ed., *Where Do We Go From Here?* (Greenwich, Conn.: Fawcett Publications, 1971).
5. Frederik Pohl, ed., *The Second* If *Reader of Science Fiction* (New York: Ace Books, 1968), p. 1.
6. Thomas N. Scortia, "Science Fiction as the Imaginary Experiment," in Reginald Bretnor, ed., *Science Fiction, Today and Tomorrow* (New York: Harper & Row, 1974), p. 174.
7. Poul Anderson, "The Creation of Imaginary Worlds: The World Builder's Handbook and Pocket Companion," in Bretnor, pp. 235-58; Hal Clement, "The Creation of Imaginary Beings," in Bretnor, pp. 259-77.
8. Stanley Schmidt, "How to Move the Earth," *Analog*, 96 (May 1976), 59-72.
9. But "easier and safer" often go hand in hand with "less interesting." In my own experience, my most challenging story potentials have grown out of pursuing logical consequences of assumed explanations. Such pursuits have alarming moments, though. Once, a couple of weeks into backgrounding a story, I was horrified to discover what I thought was a 30,000-year discrepancy in my chronology. But I found a way to modify the theory to fix it, and that, in turn, generated vital elements of the plot.
10. Alistair Cooke, "A Firebell in the Night," in *Alistair Cooke's America* (New York: Alfred A. Knopf, 1973), chapter 6.
11. Isaac Asimov, ed., *Before the Golden Age* (New York: Doubleday and Company, 1974).
12. Isaac Asimov, "Introduction," *The Best of Stanley G. Weinbaum,* (New York: Ballantine Books, 1974), p. xi.
13. John W. Campbell, Jr., ed., *The Astounding Science Fiction Anthology* (New York: Simon and Schuster, 1952).
14. Raymond J. Healy and J. Francis McComas, eds., *Famous Science Fiction Stories: Adventures in Time and Space* (New York: Modern Library, 1957).
15. Tom Godwin, "The Cold Equations," in Robert Silverberg, ed., *The Science Fiction Hall of Fame* (New York: Avon Books, 1970), vol. 1.
16. Gordon Dickson, "Call Him Lord," in *Nebula Award Stories, Number Two.*
17. Stephen E. Whitfield and Gene Roddenberry, *The Making of Star Trek* (New York: Ballantine Books, 1968).
18. Stanley Schmidt, "The Sins of the Fathers," *Analog,* 22 (November 1973-January 1974).
19. I. S. Shklovskii and Carl Sagan, *Intelligent Life in the Universe* (San Francisco: Holden-Day, 1966); Poul Anderson, *Is There Life on Other Worlds?* (New York: Collier Books, 1963); Stephen H. Dole, *Habitable Planets for Man* (New York: American Elsevier, 1970).

Revivals of Ancient Mythologies in Current Science Fiction and Fantasy

S. C. Fredericks

In his recent study, *Mythology in the Modern Novel,* John B. White has effectively characterized the problem of myth-criticism in contemporary literary studies, and I find his general assessment applicable to the specific field of science fiction and fantasy:

> One is often left uncertain whether the notion [of a 'return to myth' by a modern creative writer] denotes a return to specific mythologies, such as Greek, Roman or Sumerian, or whether it refers to the revival of certain archaically mythical qualities in modern literature.[1]

Though it remains a common tendency among myth critics, certainly with justification, to apply the second and more comprehensive of White's two types—"the revival of archaic qualities"—it is my purpose here to explore only revivals of myth in the first, or literal and specific, sense that White describes; that is, explicit revivifications of pre-existing myths. Consequently, the following paper is a study of those authors in the field of science fiction and fantasy who have deliberately and self-consciously based their stories on famous world myths in order to extend their own personal creativity and the literary possibilities inherent in the themes of science fiction and fantasy.

By way of historical introduction, I want to mention some older classics of science fiction and fantasy that are mythological in this narrow sense of the word and which anticipate more recent developments. The first instance is a group of short stories by Stanley G. Weinbaum, all of which have metaphorical titles based on the *Odyssey* of Homer: "A Martian Odyssey" (*Wonder Stories,* 1934), "The Lotus Eaters," (*Astounding Stories,* 1935), and "Proteus Island" (*Astounding Stories,* 1936).[2] Yet the stories are all pure science fiction and the contents are Odyssean mostly by analogy—that is, because their heroes have to survive, like Odysseus, through the use of their wits and intellectual capability. In these stories, too, the planets Mars and Venus, filled with alien and unpredictable life-forms, ripe for exploration and adventure, provide a displacement in science-fiction terms of the ancient *Odyssey's* fairy-tale lands. As a second example, no revival of a specific myth is better known than C. S. Lewis's *Perelandra* (1943), the second volume of the famous trilogy. In this story, Lewis transfers without displacement the entire myth of the Garden of Eden from the Old Testament book of Genesis onto Perelandra, the real name of the planet we call Venus; this time the story of Eden has a happy conclusion thanks to an Earthman with the suspiciously allegorical name of Ransom, who is present to throttle the spirit of deception when he whispers his sweet nothings into the first woman's ears. Perelandra remains unfallen.

I will also mention—as a parallel to Lewis—the first novelette in Fletcher Pratt and L. Sprague de Camp's *Incomplete Enchanter* (1941), "The Roaring Trumpet," in which an experiment with a new form of symbolic logic plunges the hero into the mythical age of Snorri Sturluson's *Prose Edda,* Norse mythology complete with an impending Ragnarok and all the sword and sorcery imaginable.

Finally, Charles L. Harness provides an important example of the theme in his novelette, "The New Reality" (1953).[3] The intellectual basis for this story is Immanuel Kant's distinction between reality as we humans know it—the "phenomena," or world of appearances—and reality as it is "in itself"—the "noumena," or world of essences, amenable only to divine knowledge. An evil scientist named Luce performs the ultimate experiment on our phenomenological reality by successfully splitting a photon of light, thereby creating a scientific paradox which destroys our world and plunges only three survivors out of all mankind into a noumenal universe. Ironically, of course, this "new reality" turns out to be the Garden of Eden, two of the survivors ending up as Adam and Eve; the other, the scientist Luce, as Lucifer, Satan himself.

It is in the last fifteen years or so that the quality of mythological science fiction and fantasy—mythological in the specific sense I have just described—has become extensive enough to indicate a literary mannerism. I wish to consider these more recent examples in detail and perhaps suggest that the characteristics of these mythological novels warrant the interpretation that we have here a more or less deliberate and conscious literary program.

The first type of mythological revival is one that is both narratively complete and thoroughly obvious: the revival of an *entire* ancient mythology, with detailed correspondence in characters, themes, and atmosphere. The paradigmatic author for this type is Roger Zelazny. His *This Immortal* (1966),[4] Zelazny's first Hugo Award winning novel, combines themes from both ancient Greek mythology and modern Greek folklore with a science-fiction rationale. At some unspecified time in the future, after Earth has devastated itself in an atomic war and much of mankind has consequently evolved into a mutant species, our planet remains only a museum. Most humans, in fact, no longer live here but have migrated to distant planets where they remain indolently under the tutelage of an extraterrestrial race, the Vegans, who are now the absentee landlords of the planet and who use it only for a resort.

This Immortal is therefore a study of our human birthright, for its Greek-born hero, Conrad Nomikos, is at once the guardian of our past and guarantor of our future. Officially, he is Commissioner of Arts, Monuments, and Archives on the planet, and his assignment is to conduct a guided tour for the Vegan, Cort Myshtigo, whose clan owns the planet. On the other hand, he is really the folk hero, Kallikanzaros, once the leader of the revolutionary forces known as Radpol, an invincible fighter, a mutant who seemingly will never age or die, and an avatar of Hercules, the ancient Greek monster-slayer.

The tour on which Conrad takes Myshtigo is one that is supposed to retrace human history up to the moment when the Three Day War brought a cataclysmic end. There is a visit to Egypt, though the entire second half of the novel deals only with Greece, a land that the hero calls "Lousy with myth" (p. 156). Hence, Conrad must recapitulate the trials of the ancient Greek heroes and regain the Earth for its own species, for this mutant, post-atomic world has plunged the remnant of mankind into a time when heroism of the ancient Greek type is both possible and necessary. Conrad's words suggest that it is this mutant landscape that contains the revival of the ancient mythology:

> Centaurs, too, have been seen here—and there are vampire flowers, and horses with vestigial wings. There are sea serpents in every sea. Imported spider-bats plow our skies. There are even sworn statements by persons who have seen the Black Beast of Thessaly, an eater of men, bones and all—and all sorts of other legends are coming alive. . . . The age of strange beasts *is* come upon us again. Also, the age of heroes, demigods.
>
> —pp. 94, 98

In our human past, in this Greek museum of our myths and legends, is conserved the latent energy to guarantee our future. Though the catastrophic future hurls us into a dark age, it is the temporal continuity inherent in the past that allows the human species a future and produces in Conrad a source of heroic redemption.

Similarly, one of the perfections of *Lord of Light* (1967) lies in the correspondence between ancient Hindu mythology (and the revolution of the Buddha) and a science-fiction universe. The hero is known as Sam—short for Mahasamatman, variously termed Siddhartha, Kalkin, Lord of Light, Binder of the Demons.[5] He is, in fact, one of the First; that is, one of the original members of the crew of the starship that colonized this new world ages ago. He once locked up the Rakashi Demons, the high energy beings who were this planet's original inhabitants, though he has long been a lone wolf and a nonconformist, going his own way and ignoring the history of the planet he helped found.

But mankind as a whole has actually regressed after several generations, for a combination of genetic mutations, advanced technology, and developed psychic powers has promoted one group of men to superhuman godhead while the general mass of humanity lives in subjection with all science, political freedom, and, above all, immortality (as a technological achievement) withheld from them by the gods.

No progress is possible in this state of affairs, so Sam takes it upon himself to foment revolution at almost every level—failing in his first attempt but succeeding in the second. In religious terms he becomes the second Buddha and leads men away from the crude and bloodthirsty Hindu pantheon which includes horrible "deities" like Kali, goddess of death; Agni, god of fire; Yama, Death himself; and Shiva, god of destruction. There is political revolution, too, for Sam is determined to wreck the rigid caste system that preserves the karma-machines for the gods and their favorites. Hence the powers of the Masters are broken once and for all; now humanity can progress as it was supposed to when this world was first colonized.

This novel is clearly in the tradition of superman literature developed by such authors as H. G. Wells, Olaf Stapledon, and Stanley G. Weinbaum. Yet, although the future of man has in it the possibility for immortality and the other attributes of divinity, the moral character of man as superman still seems less than satisfactory. Hence, as in *This Immortal,* Zelazny's theme is again redemption. Sam, as Buddha, must redeem a world by bringing its gods back to the fold of common humanity. This suggests an inversion of Christian redemption— bringing the gods back to man rather than vice versa.

A second novel which describes godlike beings—variously termed "Immortals" and "Angels"—is *Creatures of Light and Darkness* (1969).[6] In this instance, Zelazny works with ancient Egyptian mythology, though it is primarily the names themselves that act as inspiration for the Immortals in the science-fiction story. The cosmos of Zelazny's novel is a flawed one, perhaps even "fallen." A group of "Middle Worlds" inhabited by six intelligent but mortal races is the seething battleground for an absolutely polarized combat between the two groups of gods: the House of the Dead, led by the dog-headed Anubis; and the House of Life, led by the bird-headed Osiris and his son, Horus, the god of vengeance. It is the cosmological function of these two Mafia-like Houses (or "Stations," as they are sometimes termed) to regulate and balance the forces of life and death in the Middle Worlds, regardless of the horrible consequences that the mortal races often must suffer.

It was not always like this. Once Thoth, the Prince of a Thousand, had regulated the various energies and forces of this universe in a more tranquil fashion, and all the Immortals and Stations followed his benign and orderly decrees. But a monstrous and alien power (Set once describes it as "an old god"), called "the Nameless," arose and disrupted the cosmic organization. Since that time Thoth has had to use all his own powers to coerce this Thing, and, in the process, he has also lost his two warrior sons, Set the Destroyer and Typhon,[7] while the Angels have revolted and abandoned their proper Stations. Thus, the rebel Houses of Life and Death share the mastery of the universe, and only their Stations maintain their regulatory functions (pp. 95-102). Now both rebel Houses are trying to preserve this status quo and to liquidate Thoth. Yet Thoth's original order is restored when Typhon returns unexpectedly from Chaos and Set the Destroyer is reborn from the House of the Dead as Wakim, a victim of total amnesia and a would-be agent of Anubis. One major plot line of *Creatures of Light and Darkness,* consequently, lies in Set's reacquisition of his original name, identity, and powers; his successful conquest of the Nameless; the defeat of the rebel Houses of Thoth and Typhon; and the restoration of the more orderly cosmos under the rule of the Prince of a Thousand.

And it is in this cosmological theme—the recurrent theme of the victory of the royal forces of order over the rebel forces of chaos—that *Creatures of Light and Darkness* is a revival of ancient Egyptian mythology on the large scale. As Henri Frankfort has written in *Kingship and the Gods,* in the ancient Egyptian cosmological myths enemies and rebels represent chaos, while it is the function of royal authority to maintain order at all costs.[8] This is *the* theme of both the ancient myths and Zelazny's novel.

We encounter a structually different type of revival in the next two examples, which are retellings of specific myths rather than recapitulations of entire mythological systems. The first of these, Michael Moorcock's irreverent masterpiece, *Behold the Man* (1968), a Nebula Award winner, takes up the life and mission of Jesus Christ considered as a myth.[9] The hero, Karl Glogauer, is a psychiatrist manque whose sexual biography from early childhood on forms the background to his story, and his checkered career is a textbook case-history in neurosis. It combines masturbatory fantasies, homosexual interludes, heterosexual love-hate relationships, a mother fixation, and an obsession with crosses; added to these are alcoholism, migraine headaches, and epileptic seizures until Christian mysticism and Jungian psychology complete the picture of this garbled personality. Glogauer is, on the one hand, an absolute masochist; on the other, a would-be Messiah. He is one who must suffer frustration in a world in which God is dead, as his mistress, a psychiatric social worker named Monica, keeps telling him (pp. 68, 98). Whereas modern man, to Glogauer's mind, has destroyed "the myths that make the world go round" (p. 80), Glogauer wants the myths to be true; he needs God (p. 98).

When Monica leaves him for another woman, masochist Glogauer's ego endures its last rebuff from the modern world, and he becomes a willing participant in a time machine experiment conducted by one of his homosexual acquaintances, Sir James Headington. The machine itself, shaped like a womb and insulated with fluid to reduce the shock of travel, constitutes a second birth for the hero (p. 13). He successfully reaches the shores of the Dead Sea in A.D. 28 in time to join John the Baptist and his group of Essenes.

From this point on, all the themes coalesce perfectly as Glogauer, calling himself Emmanuel (Hebrew for "God is with us," an ironic choice in view of Glogauer's fate), takes up a quest to locate the Christ who has provided the only meaning for his neurotic life. It is during one of his seizures that he wanders away from the Essenes through the desert and finally makes his way to Nazareth, only to discover things are not quite what he expected. He encounters Jesus as a congenital imbecile and Mary as a lusty, if overweight, wench who tries to seduce him (pp. 107-13). His god-seeking seems to have reached a dismal conclusion.

However, Glogauer despairs of faith only momentarily—after all, more than anything in the world he "wanted the New Testament to be true" (p. 45). He therefore executes the mission of Christ himself, pretending he is Jesus, the son of Mary and Joseph, preaching to the poor, healing the sick, performing other miracles, and finally dying on the cross. This is a most successful, if perverted, *imitatio dei*:[10]

> But it was not his life he would be leading now. He was bringing a myth to life, a generation before that myth would be born. He was completing a certain kind of psychic circuit.
>
> —p. 132

The cycle is indeed perfect. In terms of the science-fiction theme of a time-paradox, Glogauer merely fulfills what will become history when he plays out the role of Jesus. It is psychiatrically complete, too, because he is by the time-paradox the source of his own Christian neurosis, but he also becomes its solution when he dies on the cross and satisfies his own masochism.

In this perfect circle there is a potentially compelling statement about our myths: that even when they are inadequate models for reality, in living them out, we make them work anyway; or as Glogauer says, "Jung knew that the myth can also create the reality" (p. 80). Indeed, the irony of the novel may be summed up in the argument between Monica and Glogauer (p. 68): "The *idea* preceded the *actuality* of Christ" (Glogauer); "The *actuality* of *Jesus* preceded the idea of *Christ*" (Monica). Given Moorcock's use of the time-paradox, both statements are accurate!

Although John C. Gardner is in every sense a mainstream author, his ironic retelling of *Beowulf* has been attracted into the orbit of readers of fantasy and science fiction.[11] Perversely, the novel is entitled *Grendel* (1971), and it is told completely in first person narrative form, this time from the monster's point of view and with his voice. Grendel is an existential anti-hero, and through his eyes—those of a creature lost, alone, and turned into a gruesome fiend out of his own loneliness—men appear to be the real monsters. As he remarks about his loathing of man at first sight:

> Some of them had shiny domes (as it seemed to me then) with horns coming out, like the bull's. They were small, these creatures, with dead-looking eyes and gray-white faces, and yet in some ways they were like us, except ridiculous and, at the same time, mysteriously irritating, like rats.
>
> —p. 18

As a corollary to the shift in perspective, what were heroes in *Beowulf* become swinish, drunken thugs in *Grendel,* where men are crueler to one another than animals could ever be (p. 27), crueler even than the monster who devours them half in sport.

It is the word "hero" that is most irritating to Grendel, for the poet named Shaper is always creating illusions by altering events to make meaningless and arbitrary acts of stupidity and villainy into ones of glory and valor.[12] Thus the monster conducts a personal vendetta, lasting twelve horrible years, against the Scyldings and their king, Hrothgar, in order to destroy human society and to prove to men that there are no heroes:

> I understood that the world was nothing: a mechanical chaos of casual, brute enmity on which we stupidly impose our hopes and fears.
>
> — p. 16

Indeed, most of the novel is Grendel's pursuit of his quest-ideal: his humiliation of the would-be hero, Unferth (chapter 6); his destruction of the ideal of beauty with his assault on the lovely young queen, Wealtheow (chapter 7); his ridicule of the priests and their belief in the gods (chapter 9).

The ending of this story, which has so much of the atmosphere of Black Humor about it, moves off even further into ambiguity and irony. An unnamed "stranger" arrives (chapters 11 and 12), no ordinary man as Grendel comes to admit, for the monster must acknowledge that he has finally encountered an authentic hero who can break his arm and tear it off at the shoulder. The hero does exist:

> *Heroism is more than noble language, dignity. Except in the life of the hero the whole world's meaningless.*
>
> —p. 143

If *Grendel* is the ultimate statement of the anti-heroic predicament and of the jaundiced perspective that accompanies it in the monster's outlook on life, then I believe Gardner has taken the concept of anti-hero to the point where it becomes inverted and returns to the original image of herohood in Grendel's final dismemberment by the hero. The topsy-turvy perspective has been carried to a conclusion where, with Northrop Frye at the end of his essay on irony and satire in *Anatomy of Criticism,* we "pass a dead center, and finally see the gentlemanly Prince of Darkness bottom side up."[13] This myth of an "anti-anti-hero" restores the world of proper heroism, and the hero whispers his own rebirth to the dying monster:

> *Though you murder the world, turn plains to stone, transmogrify life into I and it, strong searching roots will crack your cave and rain will cleanse it: The world will burn green, sperm build again. My promise. Time is the mind, the hand that makes (fingers on harpstrings, hero-swords, the acts, the eyes of queens). By that I kill you.*
>
> —pp. 149-50

In contrast, two recent productions, one a short story and the other a novel, transfer the relationship between myth and science fiction onto a completely different critical level since these two stories are imaginative explorations of the meaning and purpose of the great myths of mankind. In each of them it does seem as if one purpose is a re-interpretation of mythology itself, and that in itself may explain why groups of myths are revived in them.

Samuel R. Delany's *The Einstein Intersection* (1967, Nebula Award, 1968)[14] is set is a phase of Earth's history which is discontinuous with our own. Perhaps the time is some future post-atomic world, for the gene pool of this future race has indeed been permanently damaged. The title itself is perplexing enough, but in simple terms it means that the world described by Einstein's cosmology—a world of rational science pushed by human technology to its limits—has been superceded by an irrational world of unlimited possibility described by Kurt Goedel's theorem.[15] After the Einstein intersection as a fact of cosmology and history, in other words, the recognizable world of our humanity has been abandoned altogether, and the populace of this new universe is a different species. One evidence of this is that the normal categories of "physical" and "spiritual" no longer retain their original meaning, and even the distinction between life and death is less significant because some characters can be returned to life after they have been killed.

Hence, the problem for the quest-hero of the novel, a male normal named Lo Lobey, is to uncover the nature of himself and his race. In his intellectual odyssey through this world, then, it is the great myths of mankind that help him achieve not just this sense of self-indentity, but in fact a sense of the real. From our world, only myth remains to this new post-human race of creatures who have inherited our earth. And it is reasonable, given the presuppositions of this world—its radical "difference" from ours—that only our myths could be useful to them because only myths are free and uncategorical enough to be of use in a world that operates under laws that are completely at odds with our own.

Hence, just to give a few examples, Lo Lobey is in some sense Orpheus because he goes on a quest to recover his dead beloved La Friza, and because he plays a flute that has power over nature—and, in fact—as we find out in the course of the novel—over life and death, too. But the flute, representing a "coincidence of opposites" (combining good and evil, creativity and destruction) is also a machete, a valuable weapon;[16] and in one of the first of Lo Lobey's confrontations with his heroic destiny, he has to become Theseus and defeat a mutant, minotaur-like bull in the labyrinthine source-caves. At this point he receives further knowledge from a computer there called PHAEDRA—Psychic Harmony Entanglements and Deranged Response Association—which once belonged to the old humanity. Hence, the confrontation in the caverns with a minotaur and the computer is the hero's experience of old humanity's Collective Unconscious. Other examples along the same lines include Kid Death, who is at once Hades, Satan, and Billy the Kid; the four-armed dragon-master, Spider, who is both Pat Garrett and Judas Iscariot; Green-Eye, a transmutated Christ; Le Dove (a hermaphrodite), who combines Jean Harlow, the Great Mother archetype, and the Holy Ghost. In all of this is the basic idea that only by living out myths can this ghostly and unreal race of post-human creatures become *real,* yet in this universe, because it operates under irrational Goedelian laws and not under rational Einsteinian ones, there will be differences. the reality which will ensue for Lo Lobey and his comrades will be a different world from ours because our mankind is itself a myth to this future race.

A reciprocal example is presented in Robert Silverberg's short story "After the Myths Went Home" (*The Magazine of Fantasy & Science Fiction,* 1969).[17] The story begins in the middle centuries of the twelfth millennium of our era when mankind is already long bored with its technological power. For a century now these men could call up from the past for their own amusement such great figures of human history as Caesar and Cleopatra, Freud and Marx. So Leor, the inventor, devises a new and more powerful machine which can recreate the great mythical personages of older mankind in physical form. Some of these are products of pure imagination; others are figures who were once real men but after their deaths were transfigured and acclimatized to pre-existing archetypes and so became more than men. John Kennedy is one of these, for the manner of his glorious young life and tragic early death caused him to fall into the mythological category of Osiris, Attis, and Balder as a dying god of the spring fertility.

Silverberg's story, of course, plays with the paradise myth by altering the relationship between gods and men, for the men of the twelfth millennium are almost serene gods in their own world, and as long as they are entertained by the talents, powers, and tricks of these old gods and heroes, they let them enjoy a new life. But then the boredom soon sets in again; after half a century the mythfolk are gathered up one by one and stuffed inexorably back into the machine. Only Cassandra, the last to go, provides a prophetic comment:

> 'You should have kept us,' Cassandra said. 'People who have no myths of their own would do well to borrow those of others, and not just as sport. Who will comfort your souls in the dark times ahead? Who will guide your spirits when the suffering begins? Who will explain the woe that will befall you? Woe! Woe!'

The first person narrator only replies:

> 'The Woes of Earth lie in Earth's past. We need no myths.'
>
> Cassandra smiled and stepped into the machine. And was gone.
>
> And then the age of fire and turmoil opened, for when the myths went home, the invaders came, bursting from the sky. And our towers toppled and our moons fell. And the cold-eyed strangers went among us, doing as they wished.
>
> And those of us who survived cried out to the old gods, the vanished heroes.
>
> Loki, come!
>
> Achilles, defend us!
>
> Shiva, release us!
>
> Heracles! Thor! Gawain!
>
> But the gods are silent, and the heroes do not come. The machine that glittered in the Hall of Man is broken. Leor its maker is gone from this world. Jackals run through our gardens, and our masters stride in our streets, and we are made slaves. And we are alone beneath the frightful sky. And we are alone.
>
> —pp. 44-45

For Silverberg, myth lies between man and the unknown; man is still not an omniscient species, so he cannot exercise full mythical powers yet. Man needs the mythfolk lest he isolate himself from an understanding of his own world. The loss of myth is the loss of effective control over his own universe. Even in the technological Eden of a distant future, the presence of the gods and demi-gods remains a requirement for paradise.

Certainly the German novelist Hermann Broch was correct when he characterized the twentieth century as "the mythical age," meaning by that specifically "a return to myth in its ancient forms."[18] Since the revolutionary work of imaginative anthropologists like Frazer, Lang, and Taylor, the importance of the ancient myths to modern literature has continued to become more obvious, and recent critical works by Angela Belli on modern drama, Lillian Feder on modern poetry, and John White on the novel indicate the extent of the revivals as a literary process.[19] Since Northrop Frye's definition of science fiction as "a mode of romance with a strong inherent tendency to myth,"[20] the last decade and a half has seen science fiction and fantasy move in the direction of overt retellings of ancient mythology, as is the case of literature in general.

Perhaps this is due primarily to the universalizing power of myth, for the traditional narratives and themes of science fiction have enough *imaginative* appeal in their own right, but mythology can provide a ready-made dimension of universality and absoluteness. In the words of T. H. Gaster from his *Thespis*: "The function of myth is to translate the real into terms of the ideal, the punctual into terms of the durative and transcendental."[21] In these terms, even the future can share in eternity, however much change that future will bring.

No doubt there is a danger here. By concentrating on this quasi-religious, eternal aspect, science fiction may lose its progressive, free-thinking quality, which has been its distinguishing characteristic as a popular literature. It might become just another form of mainstream literature that deals with the timeless, "archetypal" nature of man and his role in the world, and for that reason merely repeat what has been said too often in much the same way. But—at least from all the examples I have discussed in this paper—the mythological elements have so far in no way limited the proper themes and interests of the science-fiction writer. On the contrary, because of the undisguised excellence of every one of these books they maintain their dual nature to perfection, balanced between the futuristic themes of science fiction—space and time travel, technological advances not yet available to the present world, and the implications of *change in general*—and the ancient, perhaps even "archetypal," interests of mankind in mythological themes like the loss of paradise, the descent of the gods to men, the redemption of fallen mankind, and life after death. It must be concluded that every one of the authors has accomplished a creative synthesis of the universal and timeless element represented in the ancient myths and the equal and opposite necessity of "future shock" that has been studied by science fiction as its proper object.

NOTES

1. John B. White, *Mythology in the Modern Novel* (Princeton: Princeton University Press, 1971).
2. These stories have been reprinted often. All three are available in Isaac Asimov, ed., *The Best of Stanley G. Weinbaum* (New York: Ballantine Books, 1974).
3. Charles L. Harness, "The New Reality," in *The Rose* (New York: Berkley Medallion, 1969).
4. Roger Zelazny, *This Immortal* (New York: Ace Books, 1967).
5. Roger Zelazny, *Lord of Light* (New York: Avon Books, 1969). As background reading for Hindu mythology and the origins of Buddhism, I follow Joseph Campbell, *Oriental Mythology,* volume two of *The Masks of Gods* (New York: The Viking Press, Inc., 1962). Zelazny has told me that Campbell's book was basic reading material for his novel.
6. Roger Zelazny, *Creatures of Light and Darkness* (New York: Avon Books, 1969).
7. Typhon was the name the ancient Greeks applied to Set (cf. Plutarch's essay, *Isis and Osiris*); hence Zelazny presents us with a split representation by making the two of them brothers. He also inverts the intention of the original myth by characterizing Osiris and Horus as the traitors and rebels (in ancient Egyptian mythology they are the mythological prototypes, respectively, of the deceased and living king, father and son).

8. Henri Frankfort, *Kingship and the Gods* (Chicago: University of Chicago Press, 1948), p. 9. This point is re-emphasized at length throughout Frankfort's *Ancient Egyptian Religion* (New York: Columbia University Press, 1948).
9. Michael Moorcock, *Behold the Man* (New York: Avon Books, 1970). All references are to this rather than the 1968 edition.
10. White discusses examples in mythological novels where the re-enactment of myth is a form of insanity (p. 239). Moorcock cites Jung (*Modern Man in Search of a Soul,* 1939) on the idea that even identification with Christ as a model might lead to insanity if carried out in absolute terms (p. 81). A converse example, where re-enactment of myth is used as a form of psychotherapy, is presented in Zelazny's *The Dream Master* (New York: Ace Books, 1966), though here, too, living out a myth finally leads to insanity at the novel's end.
11. See the brief but valuable review by Veronica Kennedy, in *SFRA Newsletter,* no. 12 (June 1972), p. 4.
12. Grendel loathes the transformational power of song as much as he does the Shaper. John Gardner, *Grendel* (New York: Ballantine Books, 1972), pp. 9, 29, 35, 39-48.
13. Northrop Frye, *The Anatomy of Criticism* (Princeton: Princeton University Press, 1957), p. 239.
14. Samuel R. Delany, *The Einstein Intersection* (New York: Ace Books, 1967). I must also acknowledge my debt to Stephen Scobie, "Different Mazes: Mythology in Samuel R. Delany's 'The Einstein Intersection,'" *Riverside Quarterly,* 5 (1971), 12-18. I take as my point of departure Scobie's remark: "The central subject of the book is myth" (p. 71). Delany also interlaces his narrative of Lo Lobey's quest with pages from his own autobiographical journal, and since many of the author's adventures take place in Greece, there is more than a suggestion that he is identifying himself as a quest hero, too. Since every one of these passages may be juxtaposed to some theme in the science-fiction narrative, there is purpose in Delany's statement that "Endings to be useful must be inconclusive" (p. 125).
15. I wish to thank Douglas Barbour for informing me—at second hand from the author himself—that Delany originally had entitled the work "A fabulous formless chaos" after a line of William Butler Yeats, and I report it as important evidence that "myth" in this novel means a search for form in a chaotic world, though, indeed, Lo Lobey's quest remains inconclusive to the last.
16. For the "coincidence of opposites," which is a Jungian idea, see C. G. Jung and C. Karenyi, *Essays on a Science of Mythology* (Princeton: Princeton University Press, 1963), p. 93.
17. Robert Silverberg, "After the Myths Went Home," in Donald A. Wollheim and Terry Carr, eds., *The World's Best Science Fiction 1970* (New York: Ace Books, 1971), pp. 36-45. I wish to thank Judy Sigsbee for bringing this story to my attention.
18. Cited by White, p. 3.
19. Angela Belli, *Ancient Greek Myths and Modern Drama: A Study in Continuity* (New York: New York University Press, 1969); Lillian Feder, *Ancient Myths in Modern Poetry* (Princeton: Princeton University Press, 1971).
20. Frye, p. 49. "Romance" is Frye's term for that literature which is primarily concerned with an idealized world as opposed to a realized one (p. 362, a definition from the glossary).
21. T. H. Gasper, *Thespis* (New York: Harper Torchbooks, 1966), p. 25. The book is subtitled *Ritual, Myth and Drama in the Ancient Near East.*

Tyranny By Computer: Automated Data Processing and Oppressive Government in Science Fiction

Carolyn Rhodes

Many of the unresolved problems of our troubled final quarter of the twentieth century center around the need for safeguards to prevent our technological wonders from turning into terrors. One such problem is the records which computers can keep about us all—the automation of the storage and retrieval of facts and sometimes fictions about everyone. Massive data banks hold public and private information, including hearsay. Critics of society raise disturbing questions about just how much data and pseudodata is being collected, who can analyze it for what purposes, and what decisions are being made on the basis of interpretations of such quantifiable data.[1]

Since the 1950s, science-fiction writers have been trying to warn their readers of these very problems. They foresaw the potential abuses of computerized record-keeping and decision-making, particularly in government. They recognized that the opinion-tapping and opinion-shaping skills developed by advertisers and politicians would be very dangerous if government-controlled. And they dramatized the power of computers as adjuncts to the surveillance which so well abets thought-control.

The earliest world of tyranny by computer appears in Kurt Vonnegut's *Player Piano* (1952).[2] The place is the United States of America; the time is a decade after a future third world war, and the controlling computer is EPICAC XIV. Technology has solved many problems, particularly material problems, but has created other social and ethical problems which the author develops with antic bitterness. Automation dominates all industry, whether planning or manufacture and distribution of products, as well as the entire educational and job-placement system of the country. The elite minority who rule the country are managers and engineers; they are the machine-inventors and machine-programmers who do not realize that they also have become the tools of their tools. Delighted with their power and privileges, they truly believe that they have brought America into a new golden age, and they refuse to recognize how mechanization has blighted the lives of the majority.

The controlling computer is a fourteenth generation device so huge that it sprawls throughout the Carlsbad Caverns, incorporating its own electronic ancestry—EPICACs I through XIII. Even the first of the series had been "intelligent enough, dispassionate enough, retentive enough to convince men that he, rather than they, had better do the planning for the war" (p. 116). The planning of EPICAC XIV includes the policy-making decisions which have split American society into three classes: the managers and the engineers at the top, the civil servants and professional people a step below, and, at the bottom and markedly isolated from the ruling groups, the great majority of people. College graduates (the two upper groups) are indoctrinated to consider themselves superior, while the masses bitterly resent the limitations of their lives and the practices which separate them from the privileged. A college education is the means to enter the class of the elite, the managerial class, and the National General Classification Tests determine who may go to college. The ratio is less than one person in twenty; production is so efficient and so fully automated that these few highly educated people supply all the skills needed. Those who do not qualify for college have so few options for work that they must join the army or the public-works service, officially termed the Reconstruction and Reclamation Corps, but familiarly called the "Reeks and Wrecks" (p. 31).

The happiness and efficiency of the nation derive entirely from EPICAC XIV, the gigantic electronic computing machine through whose skills all decisions are made:

> . . . how many refrigerators, how many lamps, how many turbine-generators, how many hub caps, how many dinner plates, how many door knobs, . . . how many everything America and her customers could have and how much they would cost. And it was EPICAC XIV who would decide for the coming years how many engineers and managers and research men and civil servants and of what skills, would be needed in order to deliver the goods.
>
> —p. 117

The visiting Shah of Bratpuhr grasps the essential problems of this dystopian world. To him, EPICAC XIV is a "baku," or false god, comparable to the straw and mud figures once worshipped by a now-extinct tribe in Bratpuhr; it is a man-made object to whom godlike powers are wrongly attributed; it could not save its worshippers from destruction (pp. 121-22). The Shah can neither speak nor understand a single word of English, yet he can observe the true nature of the relationship of the Americans to their machines, and make pragmatic piercing comments. No matter how often he is assured that the ordinary people whom he meets are citizens, he continues to call them a word that means slaves. Finally, after his nationwide tour, seeing "what he could learn in the most powerful nation on earth for the good of his people" (p. 26), the Shah is offered free assistance in transforming his country:

> America will send engineers and managers, skilled in all fields, to study your resources, blueprint your modernization, get it started, test and classify your people, arrange credit, set up the machinery
>
> —p. 302.

The Shah's response (in translation) is a question: "Before we take this step, please, would you ask EPICAC what people are for?" (p. 302).

Vonnegut treats the lesser computers, which manage personnel, with even more distaste than he shows for the EPICAC series. These personnel machines evaluate people's qualifications for work, classify them, and constantly re-evaluate them, making reclassification when new information is received. The author shows these computers as oppressive, in that they implement a too-rigid set of standards, overvalue I.Q. scores, and cannot weigh information sensibly, but only act on it automatically, even if certain bits of its data are misleading. For example, a man's A.B., M.A., and Ph.D. are cancelled after a lifetime of successful work for the State Department, when it is discovered that he never finished his college undergraduate requirement for physical education credit:

> The State Department's personnel machines, automatically, with respect for law and order never achieved by human beings, had started fraud proceedings against him, since he had never been entitled to his Ph.D., his classification numbers, or, more to the point, his pay check.
>
> —p. 301

Many episodes illustrate lives that are needlessly frustrated because machines treat qualitative and variable data as if these were quantitative and fixed. In Vonnegut's view, total dependence upon these machines is responsible for his society's ignoring the truth that many valuable human traits involve subtleties which defy measurement. Record-storage tends, Vonnegut suggests, to make pseudo-facts permanent, whereas human personality changes. The machines, the computers, in *Player Piano* do not recognize intellectual and personality changes for better or for worse. And when these devices meet facts which they have not predicted, they react to them by increasing surveillance; the machines are programmed to suspect the unexpected, but they are incapable of appreciating, assimilating, and utilizing it.

Vonnegut stresses many other negative aspects of automation. Workers have a complete "security package," paid by installments automatically deducted from their R & RC paychecks; the package includes all insurance (health, life, old age) and all commodities (furniture, house, car). But the workers have few options among insurance plans or among models of houses and furnishings. They automatically receive the latest ones allowable for their income. The calculators are said to be protecting both the consumer and the nation "from the old economic ups and downs by the orderly predictable consumer habits the payroll machines give him. Used to be he'd buy on impulse, illogically, and industry would go nutty trying to figure out what he was going to buy next" (p. 161). Thus people have little choice in matters that affect the quality of family life. Also automation has narrowed and warped the range of other choices. For example, all the book publication is done by the various book-of-the-month-clubs (like Dog Story of the Month), and economy dictates that no book be published unless it will attract a mass of readers, enough to make profitable use of the machinery—"the electronic billers, the electronic addressers, the electronic wrappers, the electronic presses, and the electronic dividend computers" (p. 231). So the economics of computerized processing set limits on the quality of products, and art and education are treated as products.

The author of *Player Piano* particularly exposes the failure of one aspect of the dream of automation, the hope that it would free people from dreary, repetitive tasks. Here the nightmare has occurred—workers, skilled and unskilled, have been freed to fill their time with more menial work, more pointless made-work, drudgery, or boredom. The title, *Player Piano,* underlines stark recognition of the possibility that full automation may displace even the relatively skilled, leaving them with nothing to do. In the scene which gives the book its title Vonnegut parallels two instances of man rendered superfluous by his own skills. The former machinist, Rudy Hertz, kills much of his time in a saloon. There he watches a player piano with great delight in the way that the keys produce the touch of a skilled pianist. The irony of his pleasure in the musical device lies in the fact that neither he nor any other machinists nor any workers whatsoever are now needed at the plant where Rudy once worked, because every worker's motions have been recorded on tape, and the tapes now run the machines. Rudy is naively proud to have been the machinist chosen for the honor of having his superior skills immortalized in this way. At the same time, the author shows that Rudy is dimly aware of what automation has done to him when he says:

> Makes you feel kind of creepy, don't it, Doctor, watching them keys go up and down? You can almost see a ghost sitting there playing his heart out.
>
> —p. 38

Player Piano presents a dystopian society deliberately designed by its author to dramatize the dangers of certain trends, then foreseeable (1952), which he feared would diminish the quality of American life unless controlled. And the dystopian author is not very concerned with doing justice to the positive aspects of customs or institutions which he attacks. Nor does he take the responsibility of the utopian writer, to demonstrate how an improved society would function. The dystopian points out hazards, but does not feel obligated to offer a fully developed ideal society as substitute for his flawed one.

Thus, when the benefits of computerization are shown in the much-automated meritocracy of *Player Piano,* they are shown from a wry viewpoint. Questioners of the society concede its material prosperity, and the conforming elite shrug off the indignities of lower class lives by assuming that the common people should be grateful not to be starving (p. 43). Even the rebels recognize that minimal education, health care, jobs, welfare protection, cars, houses, and the like, are easily attainable for all. But the critics of society are aroused because the automation necessary to spread these benefits so widely has meant the loss of private choice in all of these areas.

The speeches of the protagonist, Paul Proteus, are straightforward summaries of the author's sense that Americans should reject the domination of machines. Near the end of the book, Paul is on trial for conspiracy to commit sabotage, and he defends the rebels' plans. One point he makes is that not all new scientific knowledge serves the good of humanity; he insists that humanity's "main business . . . is to do a good job of being human beings, not to serve as appendages to machines, institutions, and systems" (p. 297). Paul's rebellion was motivated by a sincere wish for reform, and he insists that his goals are not treasonable but patriotic, ways to return sovereignty to the people:

> The machines . . . have exceeded the personal sovereignty willingly surrendered to them by the American people for good government. Machines and organization and pursuit of efficiency have robbed the American people of liberty and the pursuit of happiness.
>
> —p. 296

In summary, then, the dismal world of *Player Piano* diminishes the lives of its citizens in three major ways: first, loss of meaningful work for the majority of citizens; second, alienation of the people from the elite; and third, pervasive loss of freedoms, partly through centralized decision making and partly through the surveillance which inhibits all variations in behavior, preventing actions that are inconvenient for automated supervision, as well as actions which raise doubts about the socio-economic system. The pride and the pleasure of elite status blind the engineers and managers to the abuses which they enforce, while the security and distractions offered to the common people keep them trapped, resentful but pacified by shallow consumerism. The manifesto of the rebels says that the machines must be deposed. Just as people of earlier ages rejected the notion of the divine right of kings, they should now reject "the divine right of machines, efficiency, and organization" (p. 284).

In asking readers to look where they are headed and warning against one likely destination, Vonnegut does not tell how to get to that better place, some true utopia. But he insists that Americans ought to have better sense than to stay on a downward path. If we're so smart, he demands, can't we figure out a way to have self-respect and dignity along with all those material benefits of technology? Vonnegut asks his readers to remember the emotional security which people also need—jobs that they are proud to do; choices that they make on their own, not dictated by machines; freedom either to take risks beyond their measurable capacities or to relax and ignore progress.

For Vonnegut and for most of his fellow dystopian writers, static good is impossible. Any supposedly good world which does not encourage questioning and dynamic change soon is revealed as a bad world. Unchanging happiness amounts to complacency, at best, and complacency inevitably declines into oppression. The healthy society must actively encourage eccentric viewpoints, because they are vital sources of creative change.

Poul Anderson in "Sam Hall" (1953)[3] imagines a computer as the prime device for totalitarian surveillance in a future U.S.A., and ends his tale with a rebellion which promises to stop the government record-keeping on all citizens. In this story, three hundred million Americans must carry their constantly up-dated, punched cards at all times, and they must use them to receive clearance for such routine activities as attending school, joining any organization, or staying at a hotel. Anderson describes the intricate process of Citizen Blank Blank's registration at a hotel for a span of two pages in the story, detailing the registry machine's aluminum jaws closing on the card, teeth feeling the holes, and electronic tongue tasting the life of Blank Blank. This machine then sends out eighteen separate categories of information to "the sorter unit of Central Records. Click. Click. Bzzz. Whrrr. Wink and glow. A scanner sweeps through the memory circuits" (p. 294) and, with this new information on his night's lodging neatly added, the citizen's spool is returned to the memory bank. "The machine has swallowed and digested another day. It is content" (p. 294).

The central computer, Matilda, has been functioning from her safe cool place in the Rocky Mountains for twenty-five years and attains absolute power by combining all records of various kinds under a single ID number for each citizen. The two-letter and nine-digit identification mark must also be tattooed on each person's right shoulder. Among Matilda's programmers, who are officers of the Security Police, is the secretly rebellious hero of the story, the character who voices the author's concerns. He thinks back over the machine's encroachments on privacy and liberty and wonders bitterly why the intellectuals have not protested the record-keeping policies from their inception. They should have been outraged over this "Europeanization of America: government control, a military caste, nationalism, and racism" (p. 296). He also feels that he has become some sort of high priest of a machine tending cult; he goes through the ritual of entering "the temple of Matilda" and surveys her majesty:

> She crouched hugely before him, tier upon tier of control panels, instruments, blinking lights, like an Aztec pyramid. The gods murmured within her and winked red eyes at the tiny man who crawled over her monstrous flanks.
>
> —p. 293

The author connects Matilda's power with the post-World War III domination of America by the military, as well as with some extrapolated methods for psychological testing and control (called psychotyping—one's type is a bit of data on every punched card—and hypnoquizzing).

When the Army of Liberation triumphs over Matilda, they decide that she will remain in use only temporarily as an aid in their reorganization of the country, and then be destroyed: "She's too powerful an instrument. It's time to loosen the strings of government" (p. 322).

Kendell Foster Crossen's novel *Year of Consent* (1954)[4] shows an American superstate of the near future, governed entirely by social engineers. This book, though a less realistic extrapolation than Vonnegut's, involves a thoroughgoing picture of the dangers of a ramified version of national information storage and retrieval. The villains in *Year of Consent* are the data-processers who run the electronic computer which keeps track of all citizens. They are also manipulators who exert their power through intricate secret methods. While they apparently serve the politicians and businessmen, they actually direct them, along with all the other citizens.

Year of Consent dramatizes a fantastic conspiracy in a far-fetched version of a future United States, yet it also warns of repressions and cruelties which Crossen connects with abusive uses of computer technology. The master computer, SOCIAC, monitors daily life extensively in addition to processing many other kinds of information. Other computers also serve to enforce conformity, particularly one which lobotomizes people who show signs of questioning or dissent.

Crossen's novel dramatizes a pragmatic alliance between businessmen, politicians, and advertising or public-relations men until it becomes finally a psychologically-controlled arrangement, one in which the social engineers entirely dominate the other powerful groups and in effect have total control. The ruthless practices of the consent engineers are extensions of the methods of public relations men combined with those of behavioral scientists—all facilitated by the intensive use of electronic calculators. The novel demonstrates how many dystopian abuses might result from such methods and goals.

Consent engineers are the elite of Crossen's dystopia. By 1990, the United States of Americas has become a nation of nearly 380 million people in 74 states, including all of the territory of North and South America and some outlying areas. The planet is dominated by two opposing superstates, the American and the Russian, and both of them have outlawed agitators known as Uns. The Uns rebels call for a return to the principles of the United Nations in international government, and they seek to re-establish rights which have been suppressed in both superstates, particularly the rights to individuality, privacy, and the free exchange of ideas. Both superstates control mass communications, and both use giant electronic brains for oppressive social engineering. The main setting of the book is in Washington, D.C., and all the incidents which dramatize computerized opinion-molding and computerized surveillance of the citizenry occur in familiar cities of the United States. Consent engineering is applied in every institution of American life without the awareness of those whose choices are manipulated; the people live out their lives uncritically in agreement with the plans of their controllers, the hierarchy of the Bureau of Security and Consent, or SAC.

Crossen elaborately develops a three-class system. The Producers are at the top, called Pros and made up of wealthy businessmen and others with corporate interests—all of whom seem to control lawmaking. The Consumers, called Cons, form the mass of docile wage-earners. The Nonproducers, called Nulls, are the intellectuals and the esthetic or spiritual outsiders; some Nulls have their status clearly identified as "second class citizen"—stamped on their identity card (p. 203). The true elite and rulers are the social scientists of SAC, who manipulate unwitting consent from all three classes by setting up the school systems to teach what they approve, by controlling all advertising to sell what products they please, and by shaping opinion effectively, whether political or social in its impact. Thus SAC readily can lead people to hate and fear Uns and Commies, or it can control the birth rate by introducing contraception or fertility hormones in diet pills whose sales they control by effective advertising. They take pride in having abolished the "old slipshod methods of governing" (p. 25).

Automation is used in Crossen's novel to enforce SAC's both routine and horrible methods of thought control. The gigantic electronic brain, SOCIAC, manages both the opinion-shaping and the surveillance which dominate this society. While it serves all government planning and record-keeping and data processing, it is shown in use primarily in its role as monitor of all public activities and most private ones. Cameras are present almost everywhere; travel permits require the computer's approval, and devices for analyzing all telephone conversations are linked to Herbie, as SOCIAC is familiarly called (after Herbert Hoover, p. 16). Persuasive manipulation through the use of computerized data is just as important to SAC's power as spying, and both are vital to constant coercion of the public with minimal risk of rebellion. All the propaganda techniques (whether commercial or political) depend upon full and accurate information-gathering:

> The administration wanted to know as much as possible about what everyone thought and felt. What people ate, where they spent their vacations, what they talked about—all these things were added up and passed through Herbie [SOCIAC] to produce complete pictures of individuals and groups. Thus when the administration wanted to make a new move, they knew exactly how to condition the people so that it would be backed. Or they knew exactly what sort of man to put up to win a popular election. This, then, was government by consent.
>
> —p. 32

When the hero broods about the power of the SAC system, he feels that SOCIAC is as much an enemy to his Uns group as the human agents who employ the calculator for their goals:

> Creativity versus science. It was an old argument, but one which science had been winning steadily for a good many years. On one side the handful of human brains, on the other an army of giant mechanical brains presided over by Herbie—whose brain occupied ten floors and an annex.
>
> —p. 114

Electronic calculating devices appear in other coercive and oppressive roles in *Year of Consent,* always connected with SOCIAC; that is, Herbie. Two extrapolations of computer use are machines which are employed by the Clinic Squad of SAC. One of them is a "psychotherapy calculator" (p. 46) which has been designed as an aid to diagnosis,[5] but has developed into a flawed substitute for psychiatric care, particularly liable to abuse in this dystopia where disagreement with the current government by consent is "automatically diagnosed as a communication block; a psychological illness" (p. 47). A patient under treatment by the psycho-calculator suffers a new form of torture, since the machine is programmed to persist in requiring acceptable answers:

> It has instructions to cure you and it won't stop probing and treating until you are cured or until your responses make the electronic tube

> conclude you're incurable and the machine spits out a neatly-typed tape which recommends pre-frontal lobotomy. . . . there weren't many who survived the ordeal and continued to function.
>
> —p. 47

The other computerized machine in frequent use by the Clinic Squad is a device for performing psychosurgery on the human brain. The patients whom it lobotomizes are, of course, largely the actual or potential opponents of SAC rather than people who would need such severe treatment in a free society.

Another extension of technology for mind-control occurs in the episodes concerning Depth Interview Day. Every SAC agent must affirm his loyalty to the secret elite in this testing process once a year. For twenty-four hours, he undergoes questioning while having his physiological as well as his verbal responses recorded. He must wear portable devices which transmit his physiological responses—skin moisture, blood pressure, pulse rate, temperature—for computer analysis. A camera records all that he sees during the day, and at times he receives special broadcasts or taped questions that must be answered immediately. Obviously, the author is extrapolating a perfected form of a lie-detector. Crossen particularly stresses the use of SOCIAC's data-banks on the agent's life-history and normal patterns of responding, as well as SOCIAC's sophistication in detecting any signs of deviation.

Crossen's computer technology closely resembles the police-state surveillance devices made famous by George Orwell's *1984,* published five years earlier in 1949.[6] For instance, in Orwell's oppressive superstate, omnipresent cameras are presumably manned by human observers, while in Crossen's America similar omnipresent cameras are linked electronically to SOCIAC. The author does not explain how SOCIAC detects suspicious behavior on the films and on taped telephone conversations, leaving the reader to imagine that the voiceprints of every citizen could be filed like fingerprints, and copies of phone calls kept for review. He merely assumes that the popularly-known methods of electronic spying would be improved in his imaginary future, to the point that an oppressive government would employ automation to add speed and thoroughness to its monitoring of citizens. Crossen's psychotherapeutic and psychosurgical machines are no more than automated variants of the brainwashing imposed on Winston Smith by O'Brien. Orwell stresses the conversion of Winston to final adoration of the dictator, Big Brother, while Crossen stresses the dulling of the minds of those who question the system. Many other parallels and partial contrasts could be traced, but it suffices to say that Crossen adapted the successful Orwellian formulas to trends in America in 1954 which he deplored: opinion-shaping against the best interests of the public and increasing use of illicit spying devices, combined with scare stories about presumptive foreign-based spying. Crossen extends such trends into a future where electronic brains serve the "bad guys," and serve them with terrifying effectiveness.

If efficiency as a value could be separated from the purpose which it serves, Crossen could be said to demonstrate the amazing utility of automated personal data systems in *Year of Consent.* The various classes of citizens are satisfied with the system because they are deceived about how it really works, and they fear other political and economic systems. The Producers or Pros think that they rule, since they know that the public elections of legislators are managed by opinion-shaping techniques, and all members of Congress represent interests. All citizens, including loyal SAC agents who realize how the secret inner party works, praise the efficiency of their national system: "the government operates smoothly and with little waste. The healthy people of the nation are satisfied and happy" (p. 25).

Crossen's central governing computer is used to enforce every kind of miseducation, to limit and to warp the academic, the political, the social and the commercial choices and attitudes of every citizen. Unlike Vonnegut, Crossen does not consider the benefits of automation worth discussing except as illustrations of how unsympathetic characters are deceived by the social engineers. The final episodes feature plans for confounding the calculators, that is, making SOCIAC ineffective.

In summary, all of the effects of automation are treated as liabilities, since the stressed functions of SOCIAC and of the lesser psycho-manipulative calculators consist entirely of oppressive human engineering. Computers provide the speedy, sure, multifaceted and automated guardianship needed by a gigantic totalitarian system, and they can prevent dissent without making many people feel threatened, so that a group favoring rebellion rarely forms.

Crossen envisions the safeguards against the thought-control that can be exerted by mass communication techniques as either preventive—not letting governments sway the opinions of citizens—or reactive—the sort of rebellion which ends the book. The author is, like so many dystopians, writing what he hopes will be a self-defeating prophecy. His sympathetic hero reviews the events of the fictional future in the twentieth century, and concludes that both communism and democracy have lost their meaning and been replaced by governments run by social engineers and giant calculators. Then he decides that nonconformity is the solution to such control. Thoreau is often cited as the guiding spirit of the Uns, the rebels in Crossen's *Year of Consent,* with references to him as symbolic of that sort of individualism which distrusts all governments; doubtless some of Crossen's readers would see little practicality in such abstract safeguards as an admiration of Thoreau; but it should be noted that two readers of "Civil Disobedience," Mohandas Gandhi and Martin Luther King, found it something of a practical guide.

Only rarely is the reader reminded in *Year of Consent* that computers can, and ought to, serve human needs. Much of the novel glories in the sabotage of electronic calculators and fails to suggest the possibility of programming the machines to accommodate diversity rather than suppress it. One of the author's rare observations about the potential of the machine for beneficial uses may, therefore, be worth quoting: "Even the electronic brains can be good things, if they're used to serve individuals and not to create a mass man" (p. 198).

A whimsical version of a highly-computerized dystopia based on manipulations by advertisers is Shepherd Mead's *The Big Ball of Wax* (1954).[7] Just as in the previous dystopias of consumerism, the business corporations who control a future America use automated methods for gathering, storing, and analyzing data so as to influence purchasing habits. But the tone of the novel is lighter, without the starkness that underlies Crossen's warnings of the totalitarian thrust of the taste-makers. Mead's America comically extrapolates both Huxley's feelies and real-life TV watching, as he satirically exaggerates the absorption of some viewers in second-hand experience. Mead's future is dominated by the imaginary process XP, which is transmitted experience on a much fuller scale than merely viewing. A member of the audience undergoes the full range of sensations that were taped during the original subject's experience. The author has a good deal of fun with the effects of XP on such matters as the declining sales rate of foods and declining spending on holidays and even declining birth rate, once people can cheaply buy pseudoexperience that has been recorded by connoisseurs. But he also treats the computerization of many facets of life, and always shows the effects as diminishing the quality of life. Like other dystopian authors, he makes clear to his readers that when full records are gathered on popular reactions, and when people are then given what sixty percent want, with choices limited to the middle or best-selling range in art or products or ideas, "then your standards will go down, almost as fast as your techniques go up" (p. 82). *The Big Ball of Wax* also incorporates a lighter version of computerized mental therapy than the one in *Year of Consent*. A patient's problems are coded onto an IBM card, which is then fed into a machine that both analyzes the profile of symptoms or complaints and selects an appropriate tape-recorded movie of consolation and advice (pp. 57-59). Such episodes, and many more relating to the fields of personnel work and advertising, all serve to show the reader that automated analysis of data enables those who would want to manipulate others to do so more efficiently. Thus computerization tends to encourage the treatment of human beings as less and less unique, to shape people toward some mass standard that forever shrinks. People assume less responsibility and endure more insanity. Electronic monitoring also disrupts privacy in some episodes in Mead's book.

Isaac Asimov treats a nationalized computer with wistful irony, probably suggesting the sense of helplessness of the voter in a mass society, rather than attempting a literal prediction about the future of the polling trends. His story "Franchise" (1955),[8] projects a United States which has simplified the electoral process to the selection of a single voter, the most typical person, one who is located by the national computer Multivac. The story playfully traces the tension felt by the selected man, who is humorously named Norman. As he fulfills his responsibility to be the single representative voter on November 4, 2008, his fears focus on the possibility that he will be remembered as the man who chose an unpopular president. In two particularly witty episodes, Asimov points up ironies within this future "Electronic Democracy." First, Norman does not directly name his political choices, but instead replies to a series of questions on special issues. The senior Computer, Multivac's human agent, explains the process to the voter:

> Multivac already has most of the information it needs to decide all the elections, national, state and local. It needs only to check certain imponderable attitudes of mind and it will use you [Norman] for that. We can't predict what questions it will ask, but they may not make much sense to you, or even to us. It may ask you how you feel about garbage disposal in your town; whether you favor central incinerators. It might ask you whether you have a doctor of your own or whether you make use of National Medicine, Inc.
>
> —p. 170

Then, after his three hour session of answering questions, Norman is disappointed that he will learn the results no sooner than any other member of the electorate. Nonetheless, he feels intense pride—

> In this imperfect world, the sovereign citizens of the first and greatest Electronic Democracy had, through Norman Muller (through *him*!), exercised once again its free, untrammelled franchise.
>
> —p. 173

Far more painful versions of computerized decision making appear in two other American science-fiction works of the 1950s. These two novels present computer-augmented control by governments which are fearfully oppressive, and both authors connect the horrors that they describe with excessive emphasis on military power.

Two computers, EMSIACs, make all the military decisions in Bernard Wolfe's *Limbo* (1952).[9] The computer-aided control is represented as abhorrent and as a contributing factor in a disgustingly warped world where the sense of human worth is literally as well as figuratively crippled. A major horror in the 1990s here depicted is the custom of deliberate amputation of limbs in order to have them replaced by supposedly superior prosthetic devices—devices that enable men to wield weapons more efficiently. In his treatment of many topics in his book, Wolfe reiterates his fear that the mechanistic image of man encourages dehumanized attitudes. Among these topics are brain surgery (pp. 51-53 and passim) and scientific management in industry (p. 95), as well as the book's central subject, planet-wide warfare, coolly waged as a game (p. 209) between the EMSIACs (Electronic Military Strategy Integrators and Computers, p. 26).

In Mordecai Roshwald's *Level 7* (1959),[10] the characters all have numbernames, coded to their work, and they are robot-like in being helplessly enslaved to a computerized machine of war. The setting is the fully-automated bottom level of a complex of shelters, and the characters are the tenders of a computerized system which will bomb the enemy superstate, Russia, if war should begin. At the end of the novel, the planet is in radioactive ruins after the two great superstates have destroyed all life on earth.

The narrator, X-127, keeps a diary during the sequence of events which leads to the cataclysm. One significant note is the author's ironic awareness that people can come to praise their own helplessness in a technologically dominated world of violence. The programmed system defines all the inhabitant's roles, delivers their synthetic foods, and propagandizes them with taped lectures. They have no longer any contact with the rest of mankind except through their instructions, designed before level 7 was sealed off. The philosopher among them, Ph-107, eulogizes their circumstances as "perfect, absolute democracy . . . there is no personal authority here. . . . We obey only impersonal commands. . . . We acknowledge only the authority of the loudspeaker—the impersonal, the suprapersonal personification of all of us" (p. 43).

The author shows the dehumanization of the caretaker of the machine as he yearns to become more machine-like:

> What is the difference between men and an electronic brain? It can calculate far better, work more efficiently; it makes no mistakes. It cannot get fond of anybody. Neither can I. . . . Are we really monsters, or merely miserable creatures who deserve pity? . . . How deep does it go? Oh, I wish I could stop fretting about it. If I were a real machine I should be much happier. A happy gadget!
>
> —p. 48

Finally, the narrator becomes a part of the machine. He pushes the button that destroys thousands of millions but is baffled by the suicide of one of his fellow button pushers. He concludes that the suicide resulted from brooding over the killings initiated from level 7. And he finally decides that automated destruction is far less distressing than, say, being a hangman:

> No, I still do not believe I could be a hangman. . . . But to push a button, to operate a 'typewriter'—that is a very different thing. It is smooth, clean, mechanical. That is where X-117 went wrong. For him it was the same thing. He could even talk about strangling P and me with his bare hands! Maybe this inability to distinguish between killing with the bare hands and pushing a button was the source of his mental trouble.
>
> —p. 112

Roshwald is of course bitterly ironic. He wants the readers of the diary to see how X-127 has developed a terrifying indifference to human emotions, a loss of connection with the natural. The entire thrust of the novel is to awaken people to what the author perceives as the imminent dangers of man's ability to see himself as machine and to abstract himself from the implications of his destructive powers, powers so dreadfully enlarged by technology.

Negative treatments of computers in government were obviously prominent in science fiction in the 1950s. Alarm about mechanization has a long history in this literature, and it is no wonder that, at the time when actual computer potentialities were becoming more apparent, many dystopian writers would exploit them. Such depictions of the future risks inherent in technology have always merged readily with whimsical or fantastic or Gothic effects. For example, Samuel Butler in *Erewhon* (1872)[11] playfully asks a somber question—have humans abandoned their human responsibilities when they allow machines to become increasingly dominant in society? The myth of the machine gone wrong is doubtless as old as machinery; we all know why the sea is salt and what became of the sorcerer's apprentice. Science fiction has continued to play in countless ways with the truism that a machine which can perform logical processes, although created to serve, may harm rather than help its master. Ambrose Bierce told a fine, scary tale in "Moxon's Master" (1893).[12] A chess-playing automaton feels such rage when its inventor wins games that it destroys him.

In its development of self-awareness, Moxon's calculator is not only a literary descendant of Frankenstein's monster, but a mechanical antecedent of all of the robots and computers who develop personal consciousness and personal needs, whether they revolt or obey. Some do turn against their creators, like the rebellious workers in Karel Čapek's *R.U.R.* (1921).[13] Some frustrate their masters simply because they have concerns of their own, like the data-processing machine in Murray Leinster's "A Logic Named Joe" (1946).[14] Others are cooperative, at least with scientists, like the mind-reading Engineers who tend the city of dreams in Arthur C. Clarke's *The Lion of Comarre* (1949).[15] Best of all, many are dedicated to obedience, even when it requires all of their ingenuity. Isaac Asimov's Three Laws of Robotics became famous in the magazines of the 1940s, and epitomize the cheerful prospect of the thinking machine.[16]

We are concerned here with only those devices which are identified as computers and put to use for data-processing and decision making in government. Even so, certain memorable writings are worth noting briefly for the way in which they have dramatized the awesome capacities of computers in controlling intricate systems. Ray Bradbury's poignant short story, "There Will Come Soft Rains" (1950)[17] describes the running down and then the collapse of a fully-automated home after its occupants have died in an atomic war. The house is a wonderland of media: wall-sized films, music, poetry on tape, and even a speaking clock. It is almost entirely work-free, with the cooking and cleaning and the running of baths done on schedule, without troubling the inhabitants even to push buttons to start the services. Entire cities are computer-controlled in "Dumb Waiter" (1952) by Walter M. Miller, Jr.,[18] in *A Torrent of Faces* (1967) by James Blish and Norman L. Knight,[19] and in *Cybernia* (1972) by Lou Cameron.[20] Computers begin to be taken for granted as tools, typically very reliable tools, in works about space travel, for example. Often the author's treatment of the machine has no more elaboration of detail than a typewriter would receive in a novel about Madison Avenue intrigues. Arthur C. Clarke counters this trend and re-enlivens the concept of the machine-gone-wrong with HAL in *2001: A Space Odyssey* (1968).[21] Like HAL, many of the most accomplished computers of recent years have been developed by their authors into personalities too far-fetched to be relevant for this study, even though the basic computer does share in government. No less than three such governing but personally fantastic computers appeared in 1966, in Robert Heinlein's *The Moon Is a Harsh Mistress*,[22] in D. F. Jones's *Colossus*,[23] and in Roger Zelazny's "For a Breath I Tarry."[24] Then John Brunner created Shalmaneser in *Stand on Zanzibar* (1968)[25] and David Gerrold continued the trend to Godlike machines in *When HARLIE Was One* (1972).[26]

Returning to the more realistic extrapolations of automated data-processing for government, we find one further full-scale depiction of a computer-controlled dystopia in Ira Levin's *This Perfect Day* (1970).[27] The time is a few centuries in the future, when Earth has become a single peaceful community whose eight billion people call themselves the Family. The gentle, happy, healthy members of the Family depend on UniComp, a massive central computer, to allot to each of them an equitable portion of the world's goods and privileges. Each one wears his nameber (that is, name-number) on a bracelet which serves many purposes. Scanners are placed everywhere to read these bracelet-namebers so that UniComp can keep track of the activities of all citizens and approve or reject requests. The identity bracelets function as keys and charge-plates to enter into public or private places, to process a phone call, or pay for goods when leaving a store. If UniComp rejects the member's "claim" of an object or a service, such as a holiday trip, the member waits patiently and later repeats the claim, confident that he will have a fair share of what the Family can afford. One of the most familiar sayings is "Uni knows best" (p. 48).

UniComp presides like a god over the docile members who are constantly reminded that the computer is omniscient and benevolent. Little children who hear of unexpected sorrow in existence are told, "We've got UniComp looking out for us everywhere on earth" (pp. 13 and 15), and are comforted. Members who fail to follow routine feel guilty toward Uni later, and think, "Forgive my offense, Uni who knows everything" (p. 77). Rather than "You're welcome," people say, "Thank Uni." And when adult members of the society come to learn that a few rebels do exist and fight against UniComp's controls, they are sickened and frightened. Their advisers, who relate to them like parents, priests, and psychologists, then must admit that some facts of existence are beyond human explanation, although still somehow within UniComp's grasp. One adviser says, "I don't know. But

Uni does. I told you before . . . trust Uni" (p. 151). Nobody ever need feel any guilt or responsibility, because all decisions are left to Uni:

> the machine that's going to classify you and give you your assignments, that's going to decide where you'll live and whether or not you'll marry the girl you want to marry; and if you do, whether or not you'll have children and what they'll be named if you have them.
> —p. 21

UniComp is also pragmatically awesome in the variety of data it gathers and manipulates. It not only determines and monitors the activities of the eight billion people, but also processes the planning and control of every material aspect of life, from the design of cities to weather control.

Levin particularly emphasizes the tendency to assign numbers whenever possible, presumably at least in part as an aid to automated handling of data. All place names throughout the planet have been reduced to an eight-unit code, three letters for the continent and five numbers for the spot, comparable to zip coding. When the building number is also known, one member has all the necessary information to find another, as when the hero traces his lost beloved in North Africa: she is at Afr14509, building P51. It is even easier to reach her by phone, assuming Uni grants the privilege of calling when he places his identity-bracelet at the phone scanner, because everyone can be dialed by his nameber. All jobs are also coded on a system of digits and letters, and citizens are classified and assigned their lifetime work while they are still teenagers. Levin suggests that the convenience of quantification joins with other shallow or oppressive goals to make lives duller and social patterns more rigid.

In the world of *This Perfect Day* everyone must be humble, docile, and conformist. Every member has been taught about the horrors of the bad old Pre-Unification days, and is grateful for the "freedoms" provided through UniComp's efficient distribution of goods and surveillance against irregularities—"free of war and want and hunger, free of crime, violence, aggressiveness" (p. 142).

Life is very fully scheduled, with chimes ringing to indicate mealtime, worktime, bedtime, and some leisure; weekly sexual activity is encouraged (Saturday nights); clothing and food are in plentiful supply (coveralls in colors keyed to occupations, and synthetic meals of totalcake, washed down with totalcoke).

A healthy member of the Family functions within routine patterns which are taken to show his normality and contentments:

> He did his work well, took part in house athletic and recreational programs, had weekly sexual activity, made monthly phone calls and bi-yearly visits to his parents, was in place and on time for TV and treatments and adviser meetings. He had no discomfort to report, either physical or mental.
>
> —p. 56

Humility consists largely in gratitude for Uni's gifts, while goodness means nonaggression, unselfishness, and mutual guardianship. The Family fears all signs of anger or of competitiveness, connecting these traits with greed and warfare.

Readers familiar with Aldous Huxley's *Brave New World* (1932)[28] will by now have recognized the tradition within which Levin writes. *This Perfect Day* is a complacent dystopia, a world in which the citizens are indoctrinated, soothed, and distracted from inconvenient behavior, whether criminal or creative. Huxley's World Controller was dedicated to turning people into "nice tame animals," and Huxley's dystopia featured many methods which Levin uses: drugs, distractions, and genetic manipulations. Both emphasize propaganda in teaching, and art reduced to the level of advertising and community singing. In short, the quality of life is diminished to the lowest common denominator; citizens are satisfied because they can imagine no other life-styles, constantly being told that things were worse in former ages. In both worlds, some few members become aware of the horror of being manipulated, and break out of their complacency to raise the questions which are the authors' deepest concerns: What is happiness? What is freedom? What are people for?

At the end of Levin's book, a new revelation alters the nature of the dystopia, when the truly oppressive rulers are revealed as the programmers of UniComp. Uni, it turns out, has only been the highly efficient tool for the plots of a dictator and his cohorts. These clever, ruthless, and greedy programmers live in sensual excess while they keep the mass of humanity in the static dullness of regimented lives: "chemotherapy plus computerization equals no change" (p. 119).

Because Levin reveals the secret elite who control UniComp only in the last section of the novel, it is difficult to say how seriously a reader is expected to recall the anti-automation feelings which the would-be rebels have expressed in the bulk of the story. But some of the hostility to computer-monitored life is equally memorable, whether the computer has become the god-like self-sustaining being it seems to those it has tamed, or whether it is exposed as a device employed by the vicious elite. And it should not be forgotten that the elite are the programmers, people who came to their immoral power in association with an amoral machine of massive powers. At any rate, in *This Perfect Day,* the reader again meets that familiar pairing of efficiency and freedom as opposites which tend to negate each other.

When authors like Vonnegut, Crossen, and Levin attack efficiency as a danger, they are of course pointing out the potential abuses of efficient automated personal record-keeping by governments. In their computer-controlled worlds, the mass of people lead miserable lives. Their lives are materially adequate, since nobody starves, but dulled and tormented by ever-present surveillance and sloganizing, by leveling in education, by inanity in art and pastime, and by exclusion from the privileged and condescending elite. Computers help to impose all of these indignities, particularly the computers which record, survey, analyze, and predict personal data about the citizens. These authors usually grant that the machines at their best are amazingly thorough, accurate, fast, and cheap. But when computers serve dystopian values, the better they are in expanding efficiency, the worse they are in shrinking individuality.

Are these authors unfair to computers in their steady attack upon them? It seems at times even a personal attack, since the computers have names whereas the people are reduced to numbers, and since the enraged sympathetic characters finally make physical assaults upon the machines. Anyone committed to the hopeful prospects of technology would argue that the underlying problems are mistaken cultural priorities, that the computers are mere tools. But these authors, like Emerson, know that we can become the tools of our tools. They show how computers act not only as agents but also as causes of narrowness and suppression. The very nature of massive processing of data is to warp the recognition of intricate qualities, to define eccentricity as potential criminality, and to encourage reductionism: that is, to focus on the presumed needs and capabilities of the majority so exclusively that all but the average are neglected or even harmed.

Perhaps the question is meaningless, as to whether the calculating machines are agents or principals among the forces which lead to dystopia. The evolution of the machine is a threatening progress, as Samuel Butler insisted over a century ago. Dystopian authors who depict computers as part of government suggest that we humans take on mechanical qualities as we depend more on machines. Both the chicken and the egg keep the species going, no matter which comes first. As automation increases, so does indifference to the special case, emphasis on quantifiable rather than qualitative, and rejection of the human.

NOTES

1. For an early example of such concern, see Norbert Wiener's *The Human Use of Human Beings* (Boston: Houghton Mifflin, 1954). For a recent study, including an extensive bibliography, see *Records, Computers, and the Rights of Citizens, Report of the Secretary's Advisory Committee on Automated Personal Data Systems* (Washington, D.C.: U.S. Department of Health, Education & Welfare, 1973).
2. Kurt Vonnegut, Jr., *Player Piano* (New York: Avon Books, 1971).
3. Poul Anderson, "Sam Hall," in Groff Conklin, ed., *Science Fiction Thinking Machines: Robots, Androids, Computers* (New York: Vanguard Press, 1954).
4. Kendell Foster Crossen, *Year of Consent* (New York: Dell Publishing Company, 1954).

5. Crossen emphasizes the practicality of this extrapolated imaginary device by noting that one specialist working with giant mechanical brains foresaw the possibility of such a use for them as early as 1949 (p. 46). Through the fictional psycho-calculator Crossen starkly delineates the intrinsically dangerous inhumanity of relying on mechanical methods for handling human problems, and he adds a new twist of horror to that familiar dystopian motif, the threat, for dissenters, of mental crippling. The psycho-calculator is a literary descendent of O'Brien's pain-machine, used in the brainwashing of Winston Smith in Orwell's dystopia.
6. George Orwell, *Nineteen Eighty-four* (New York: Harcourt, Brace, 1949).
7. Shepherd Mead, *The Big Ball of Wax: A Story of Tomorrow's Happy World* (New York: Avon Books, 1954).
8. Isaac Asimov, "Franchise," in Richard Ofshe, ed., *The Sociology of the Possible* (Englewood Cliffs, N.J.: Prentice-Hall, Inc., 1970), pp. 163-73.
9. Bernard Wolfe, *Limbo* (New York: Ace Books, 1952).
10. Mordecai Roshwald, *Level 7* (New York: Signet Books, 1961). The topical nature of this novel, written when America and Russia were competing for records in super-bomb output, is indicated by its dedication: "To Dwight and Nikita" (p. 4).
11. Samuel Butler, *Erewhon* (New York: Signet Books, 1961). Erewhonian philosophy insists that people must give up using machinery because machines show evidence of undergoing Darwinian evolution. Thus machines, unless suppressed, can be expected to develop consciousness and the power to reproduce themselves and the will to over-master their inventors. Butler had first published such satirical speculations in 1863.
12. Ambrose Bierce, "Moxon's Master," in *Can Such Things Be?, The Works of Ambrose Bierce* (New York & Washington: The Neale Publishing Company, 1910), vol. 3.
13. Karel Čapek, *R.U.R. (Rossum's Universal Robots),* in Arthur O. Lewis, Jr., ed., *Of Men and Machines* (New York: E. P. Dutton & Co., Inc., 1963).
14. Murray Leinster, "A Logic Named Joe," in Sam Moskowitz, ed., *Modern Master-pieces of Science Fiction* (Cleveland and New York: World Publishing Company, 1965), pp. 69-88.
15. Arthur C. Clarke, *The Lion of Comarre* (New York: Harcourt, Brace & World, 1968).
16. Isaac Asimov, *I, Robot* (Garden City, N.Y.: Doubleday & Company, Inc., 1950). This first collection of his robot stories is dedicated "To John W. Campbell, Jr., who grandfathered the robots."
17. Ray Bradbury, "There Will Come Soft Rains," in J. W. Johnson, ed., *Utopian Literature* (New York: The Modern Library, 1968).
18. Walter M. Miller, Jr., "Dumb Waiter," in Conklin, *Science Fiction Thinking Machines.*
19. James Blish and Norman F. Knight, *A Torrent of Faces* (New York: Ace Books, 1968).
20. Lou Cameron, *Cybernia* (Greenwich, Conn.: Fawcett Publications, Inc., 1972).
21. Arthur C. Clarke, *2001: A Space Odyssey* (New York: Signet Books, 1968).
22. Robert A. Heinlein, *The Moon Is a Harsh Mistress* (New York: G. P. Putnam's Sons, 1966).
23. D. F. Jones, *Colossus* (New York: G. P. Putnam's Sons, 1966). Jones's sequel, *The Fall of Colossus* (New York: G. P. Putnam's Sons, 1974), dramatizes the continuing oppressive government of the Earth by the computer, until it is finally confounded by Martians—who may be machines themselves—not the hoped-for liberators.
24. Roger Zelazny, "For a Breath I Tarry," in *Survival Printout: Science Fact: Science Fiction* (New York: Vintage Books, Inc., 1973), pp. 68-107.

25. John Brunner, *Stand on Zanzibar* (Garden City, N.Y.: Doubleday & Company, 1968).
26. David Gerrold, *When HARLIE Was One* (New York: Ballantine Books, 1972).
27. Ira Levin, *This Perfect Day* (New York: Fawcett Publications, 1971).
28. Aldous Huxley, *Brave New World* (New York: Harper & Row, 1969). Huxley depicts a complacent dystopia: the citizens are kept busy with shallow customs. Two later dystopian works satirize consumerism in ways reminiscent of *Brave New World,* and both show number-naming of citizens—coded unique identification of the sort which we now associate with computers. These works are: "The Unknown Citizen," a poem by W. H. Auden (1940) and *The Space Merchants,* a science-fiction novel by Frederik Pohl and C. M. Kornbluth (New York: Ballantine Books, 1953). Readers can infer from both that dossier-keeping by human clerks could be as great an aid to dystopian government as records stored and retrieved by automation. Levin's computer-manipulated processes incorporate some of the literary motifs of dystopias, as well as some cautionary satire on the abuse of computer skills.

The Known and the Unknown: Structure and Image in Science Fiction

Gary K. Wolfe

Perhaps the most frequently made claim concerning science fiction as a genre of literature and film is that it serves the function of a modern mythology. As early as 1930, Olaf Stapledon wrote, "We must achieve neither mere history, nor mere fiction, but myth,"[1] and since then this notion has been reiterated countless times by both writers and critics of the genre. It is a difficult proposition either to challenge or defend, because both of its major terms—science fiction and myth—lack clear and widely accepted definitions. One could probably take a list of definitions of myth and another list of definitions of science fiction and pick out the ones that match, but this would be largely an exercise in semantics, unacceptable to students of both fields in the long run. Furthermore, any student of myth soon becomes so confused by the plethora of theoretical approaches that it comes as a relief to find someone as knowledgeable as Stith Thompson asking, "But why should myth be accurately defined? Is there actually any need to differentiate, for example, between such concepts as mythology and hero tales?"[2] Similar questions might be asked of science fiction. Is it really necessary to have a formulaic definition in order to explore how this kind of narrative works?

This does not mean that we ignore the question of science fiction as myth, but it does shift our focus from asking what is meant by each of these terms to asking why the comparison is made in the first place. And here we come up against yet another ill-defined term: science fiction is often called a kind of myth because it produces in the reader a "sense of wonder," that feeling of awe and slightly elevated consciousness that myth is supposed to have produced in earlier cultures. "Sense of wonder" is a commonplace enough term in science fiction, but serious discussion of its meaning is scarce.[3] What causes wonder? What are its sources, and how does it contribute to one's overall response to a work? Such questions go far beyond the scope of science fiction, but in this paper I will try to demonstrate at least one way in which the sense of wonder arises from and is associated with certain recurring structures in science-fiction narratives, and how it is often symbolized by almost ritualistic images or "icons"—such as the spaceship, the creature, and the city.

C. S. Lewis speaks of certain stories that retain their peculiar power over the reader or listener no matter what the version or the retelling, such as the myth of Orpheus.[4] It is in such works that the sense of wonder is perhaps at its strongest, and such works are nearly always characterized by recurrent emblematic or iconic images that act as cultural triggers to a certain kind of emotional response. Neither as private as literary symbols nor as universal as archetypes, such icons are easily recognized by the audience for which they are intended. The dragon, for example, once carried a specific emblematic meaning not unlike that carried by representations of the head of Christ in early Christian iconography—in both cases the image transcended symbolic values to become a stimulus to the sense of mystery and wonder in those familiar with it. Apart from its specific iconographic meanings in art and literature, the image of the dragon became a kind of aesthetic shorthand for something terrible which had to be overcome.

Such icons, I suggest, also exist in science fiction, and examples of them can be found prominently throughout the history of the genre—the spaceship in "space operas" of the 1930s, the Bomb during the postwar period, the monster in the so-called "creature cycle" of 1950s films, and the city in much recent science fiction. Such images, like the dragons of romance, serve to initiate, however subliminally, the "sense of wonder" that gives science fiction much of its mythic impact. They are more than cliches and stereotypes by virtue of their systematic relationship to other elements in the work and to what Gombrich calls "the invisible world of ideas"[5] implied by the work. More importantly, I believe they draw their power from their pivotal relationship in one of the key oppositions of all science fiction, the opposition between the known and the unknown.

It is this key structural opposition or antinomy and the way it is represented in science fiction that is my concern in this paper. The idea of the known-unknown opposition should not be a startling one to any reader of science fiction, and indeed the importance of this opposition has been implied without being directly stated by a number of critics. Ketterer, for example, talks about the symbolic destruction of the "real" world (the known) by the creation of new ones (the unknown) by the "apocalyptic" writer.[6] Suvin has written of the importance of defamiliarization and estrangement—making the known seem unknown—in science fiction.[7] Todorov has similarly noted that science fiction often confronts the reader with an unknown or "supernatural" event, but that the reader "ends by acknowledging its 'naturalness.'"[8] And Scholes speaks of the necessity for a "radical discontinuity" in which extrapolations "must depart from what we know."[9] In each of these cases, the critic sees fantastic literature in general and science fiction in particular as bringing together the known or familiar with the unknown or bizarre. It is the particular way that science fiction brings these opposing elements together that I propose to treat next. Much science-fiction narrative, I believe, is constructed on the principle of recurring assimilation of the unknown into the known, and a resulting recurrent redefinition of these terms.

It is not difficult to see how the various symbols I have mentioned stand between the universe of the known and the universe of the unknown. The spaceship, for example, nearly always fills the role of the vessel of the known or the vessel of the unknown. It is, in fact, a closed universe, with its own life-support systems, its own ecology, and its own social structure. In stories dealing with the exploration of space by people from earth, the interior of the ship is an image of the known world and the exterior an image of the unknown world, with its threatening and fearful associations. The ship itself stands between the two, and the crossing of the barrier of the ship's hull is what precipitates the action in a great many science-fiction stories. Conversely, in stories dealing with spaceships visiting earth from other planets, the polarities are reversed, and the interior of the ship becomes the image of the unknown universe while the exterior is the known. Again, the crossing of the barrier is what precipitates the action. All this may seem rather simplistic, but the fact that science-fiction writers are aware of this opposition and are capable of making sophisticated use of it is evidenced by a number of stories, two notable examples of which are Theodore Sturgeon's "Bulkhead" (1955) and Murray Leinster's "First Contact" (1944). In each of these stories, a kind of conundrum is established by constructing a narrative in which the spaceship represents simultaneously the worlds of the known and the unknown. In "Bulkhead," Sturgeon speaks of the transition the space traveler makes from being on the "inside looking out" to "inside looking on;"[10] in other words, the transition from the opposition of known-unknown to the resolution of the more acceptable "scientific" opposition of observer-observed. As we shall see later, this process of resolving oppositions into acceptable modes is not uncommon in science fiction, nor for that matter in cultural myth in general.

The central device in this story is the bulkhead between the two compartments occupied by the two members of the exploration team. The bulkhead is there ostensibly because of the tensions that inevitably result in sometimes deadly clashes when two people are so closely confined for years on end; "reduce a world to two separate nations and see what happens." The oppositions of known and unknown thus become doubly complex; not only is there the conventional interior (known)-exterior (unknown) tension, but for each member of the crew the opposite half of the ship becomes the unknown as well. As far as that other compartment is concerned, the opposition becomes interior (unknown)-exterior (known). The action in the story is precipitated when the two crew members begin to communicate and to care for each other via the intercom. In order for the starship to succeed on its mission, this breaking down of the internal barrier must first take place, thus creating a unit which then can function in terms of the primary opposition between the interior and exterior of the ship. The two characters finally decide they would like to go on another mission together, which presumably indicates that the bulkhead can be removed in subsequent missions. But the real meaning of the barrier, and to some extent I think the central meaning of this known-unknown opposition for all science fiction, is not revealed until the end of the story. We discover that the two astronauts are in fact one, space-age doppelgangers of a sort, and the reason for the separation is a psychological experiment involving the reintegration of a trained spaceman with his earlier childlike self. During the grueling training period, all memories of that younger self had been suppressed, in order not to interfere with the training. The implication, of course, is that the childlike sense of wonder and devotion must be able to work in concert with the highly trained adult technician in order for space exploration to be a success. The opposition of known and unknown, then, is really an opposition that exists within the human mind. "Bulkhead" is one of the clearest examples I can think of to illustrate this important point, although science-fiction readers may recognize a similar structure in Cordwainer Smith's "Scanners Live in Vain" in which the "scanners" are robotized humans who have been rebuilt to function in the "up-and-out" of space—the unknown—and who must "cranch," or become temporarily human again, in order to experience the known—the appetites and emotions of the human world. As both these examples illustrate, the opposition of known and unknown is fundamentally artificial, and what is known in one set of relations may become unknown in another.

In Leinster's "First Contact," the interior of the human spaceship functions as an image of the known, and the exterior is the unknown. But in relationship to the alien ship, the exterior of space becomes the relatively known and the interior of the alien ship the unknown. Contact is made between the two ships, and the resulting problem—perhaps reflective of the political spirit of the time the story was written—is that the crew of each ship is afraid to return home for fear the aliens will follow and invade the home planet. On another level, however, the problem is essentially the same as that in Sturgeon's "Bulkhead": this new set of oppositions must be resolved in such a way that each crew can continue to function in terms of the larger mission of exploration. After much agonizing over whether or not the alien ship must be destroyed, a resolution is finally reached which satisfies all necessary conditions: each ship is programmed in such a way that it cannot return home or follow the other ship, and the crews then exchange ships. In this way the interior of the alien ship becomes the known, and the mission can continue.

Like the spaceship, the icon of the creature stands at the border of the known and the unknown. In the case of creatures which are themselves the result of a transformation process (such as the vivisection experiments in Wells's *Island of Dr. Moreau*), the creature may literally represent the sometimes ill-defined boundary between the known of human experience (represented by the state of normality from which the creature has passed) and the unknown (represented by the transformed state). Here I am not talking about every alien being that occurs in science fiction, by any means. The closely realized aliens of a writer such as Hal Clement, for example, hardly fall into this category. What I am talking about is the popular icon which I mentioned earlier, using as an example the *Creature from the Black Lagoon*. These stories, too, generally consist of three elements: the known, the unknown, and the barrier separating the two. Again also, action is precipitated when the barrier is crossed.

In the case of the film *The Creature from the Black Lagoon,* we have several such barriers established between the known and the unknown. First, there is the barrier of time, established when we learn that the creature is an anachronism apparently produced by some ancient aberration of the laws of evolution. Secondly, there is the barrier whose crossing provides the suspense in the early sequences of the film, that of the frontier of civilization: the creature inhabits an unexplored area of the Amazon basin which an anthropological expedition enters in order to conduct research (this barrier is one of the most familiar means of separating the known from the unknown and is essential to almost all "lost world" stories from Haggard on). Third, there is the all-too-familiar barrier between darkness and light, in this case represented not only by day and night (as it is in almost all horror films), but also by the contrast between the shadowy depths of the lagoon itself and its sunlit, mirror-like surface. Related to this, and highly important to the film's visual structure, is the barrier represented by the surface of the water in the lagoon, with the human community represented as the crew of a boat which rests on the surface while the underwater world (depicted by some effective underwater photography) is the realm of the creature, or the unknown. One sequence of the film which has been noted by more than one commentator especially points up the importance of this latter barrier, and has been called by John Baxter "the key scene in the film." The heroine goes for an innocent swim in the lagoon, unaware that the creature is swimming just beneath her, mocking her movements on the surface with his own exaggeratedly sexual movements underwater. The scene is mostly shot with an underwater camera, so that we see the girl as the creature sees her, "penetrating a Cocteau-like mirror," as Baxter writes, or in other words penetrating the barrier between known and unknown that is represented by the surface. By thus penetrating this final barrier, she attracts the sexual attention of the creature, and establishes the situation for the remainder of the action of the film. Later in the film the creature actually constructs a physical barrier to prevent the boat from leaving "his" lagoon, again emphasizing the barrier theme; this final barrier must be crossed by the crew before they can return to the known world of civilization.

Such images of barriers are important to a great many films of science fiction and fantasy. *King Kong,* for another example, presents us with two very substantial and literal barriers in the story itself: the thick fog that surrounds the island on which Kong lives, and the immense wooden wall that the natives have constructed to keep him away—these in addition to the barrier of time which, as in *Creature from the Black Lagoon,* separates Kong's prehistoric world from our own.

The literal image of the barrier occurs in science-fiction literature as well. Blish's "Surface Tension" makes the barrier between known and unknown the surface of a puddle of water that microsopic humans must penetrate. In a story which reduces the barrier to almost purely iconic terms, "Arena" (1944), Frederic Brown seems to be very much aware of the known-unknown opposition that such a barrier represents. Not only does the invisible barrier of that story separate the human spaceman from his alien counterpart, but it also provides the means of education by which the battle may be won, and the process by which the barrier is finally penetrated is an analogue of the scientific method itself. The protagonist discovers early on that the barrier may be penetrated by inorganic objects, and this first penetration of the barrier provides him with his first important discovery. Later the barrier is penetrated by dead organic matter; this penetration, too, adds to the protagonist's knowledge. Finally, by discovering that the barrier in fact affects only conscious life, he is able to penetrate the barrier by making himself unconscious and thus win the victory. The action depends on a series of increasingly significant penetrations of the barrier and the knowledge gained from each of these penetrations: the known steadily impinging on the unknown until conquest is achieved. During all this, the two antagonists are further separated from the rest of the universe by a trick of time engineered by the superior beings who set up the contest: in the rest of the universe, time is at a standstill until this contest can be resolved. A kind of chain reaction of oppositions is thus set up: by penetrating the invisible barrier and destroying his enemy, the protagonist is able to cross the barrier that separates him from the normal time-flow of the universe. Once he crosses this barrier, the opposition represented by the warring cultures (of which he represents one, the alien the other) is resolved by the annihilation of the enemy forces, and a kind of equilibrium is restored, as it was in Leinster's "First Contact."

Ursula LeGuin, in *The Dispossessed* (1974)—and to a lesser extent in *The Left Hand of Darkness* (1969)—sets up the barrier between known and unknown in a more complex and, I think, more richly rewarding way. The first important image to occur in *The Dispossessed* is the fence which separates the utopian communist colony of Anarres from the landing dock for ships from the sister planet Urras. The colonists on Anarres have long enforced the barrier between the two planets in order to prevent what they regard as ideological contamination from the society from which they fled generations earlier. Spaceships from Urras, then, serve much the same function as spaceships in invasion-of-Earth stories: they represent the unknown of Urras, which the residents of Anarres would just as soon keep unknown. The action of the novel is caused by the penetration of this barrier by Shevek, a physicist who wants to break down all the barriers between the two cultures. Alternate chapters are told from the point of view of the citizens of Urras, to whom the spaceship serves much the same function it does in exploration-of-space stories: it contains the known world, and Anarres—beyond the barrier—is the unknown. But when the spaceship returns to Urras bearing Shevek on board, the polarities are reversed; it now contains an alien, and thus its interior represents the unknown. The contrasts between the urban, capitalistic, sexist society of Urras and the agrarian, communistic, egalitarian society of Anarres are pointed up repeatedly in the book. Shevek, in attempting to cross these barriers, discovers that each side of the opposition contains an element of the other, as in the yang-yin, and that the basis of this opposition finally exists within the individual as much as between cultures. As in Sturgeon's "Bulkhead," the opposition between the manifestly known and unknown is transformed into the more fundamental opposition between elements of the human mind. A cultural opposition is thus transformed into a characterological one, as Shevek finds that the two cultures are in effect parts of the same larger culture, that there can be no political solutions to this antinomy, and with this realization the narrative ends.

The ways in which these barriers between the known and the unknown may be manifested in science fiction are as numerous as the imaginary situations available to the genre—in other words, almost limitless. But there seem to be a number of key images representative of this barrier that recur often enough, and are familiar enough to readers and viewers of science fiction, to constitute veritable icons of this opposition. By serving this function, such icons become the structural pivot of many works of science fiction, and the examination of the structural relationships to other elements in the work may enable us to discern recurrent patterns in works of science fiction that are widely disparate in surface content. The spaceship, the surface of the Black Lagoon, the fog in *King Kong,* the invisible barrier in "Arena" are all widely different in terms of their meaning to the content of the various stories they function in, but they all fulfill the same structural role in terms of the opposition between known and unknown which is vital to all these stories.

An icon or pattern of iconography need not always be simple, of course, and the full extent of meaning of such a pattern can only be revealed by examining one in somewhat more detail than I have so far done. I earlier mentioned the importance of the city as such an icon, and though this image for sheer complexity of meaning strains the use of the term "icon," it is one of the most persistent and significant such images in all science fiction, especially that of recent years. One need only think of Simak's *City* (1952), in which the city itself looms as an unseen presence knitting together the various threads of the narrative; of Brunner's *Stand on Zanzibar* (1968) and *The Sheep Look Up* (1972); of Delany's *The Fall of the Towers* trilogy (1961-1964); of John

Christopher's *City of Gold and Lead* trilogy (1971); of Cooper's *The Overman Culture* (1972); of Silverberg's *The World Inside* (1971); of Blish's *Cities in Flight* novels (1970), in which the icon of the city is ingeniously merged with the icon of the spaceship; of Asimov's *Foundation* trilogy (1951-1953), with its planet-wide cities such as Trantor—the list might go on and on. In addition, one should not disregard the importance of cities in such works as Herbert's *Dune* (1965) or the novels of Ursula LeGuin.

Arthur C. Clarke's *The City and the Stars* (1956), though admittedly in many ways a flawed novel, itself looms as one that I think clearly demonstrates the iconic value of the city and the structural importance of this higher opposition, much in the manner that Levi-Strauss describes the transformations which myth works upon the antinomies of culture.[12] As a result, the novel gives us the opportunity not only to explore the city as icon, but also to examine a number of other such icons as, one by one, they supplant the image of the city in the narrative. These other images are all familiar ones, and some we have discussed briefly already. Spaceships, robots, alien creatures, computers—each at some point in *The City and the Stars* stands at the border of the known and the unknown and in each case the crossing of that border carries the narrative action forward.

The basic narrative is rather simple. Alvin, a young man just coming of age, finds that he is the only citizen of the ancient walled city of Diaspar who seems to have any curiosity about what lies on the outside. His tutor Jeserac can provide him with some information, but it is not until he meets Khedron, or the Jester, that he begins to find means to really answer his questions.[13] With the aid of Khedron, Alvin finds his way out of the mechanized city and visits the more pastoral society of Lys, the only other remaining human community on Earth—which, like Diaspar, has kept an enforced isolation. Here he meets Hilvar, with whose aid he visits a nearby legendary fortress, Shalmirane, according to tradition the site of the last great battle defending Earth from mysterious invaders who had driven mankind from the stars. In Shalmirane, a giant alien polyp is found, the last disciple of an ancient messiah known as the Master.[14] Alvin persuades the polyp to allow one of its three service robots to return with him to Diaspar, where Alvin interrogates the robot with the aid of Diaspar's massive central computer. What Alvin learns from the robot allows him to raise an ancient spaceship from beneath the desert floor where it has lain for centuries. Returning with the ship to Lys, he picks up Hilvar and they journey to an artificial star system known as the Seven Suns, once the hub of an immense galactic civilization. The Seven Suns are now deserted, but there they attract the attention of a vast, incorporeal intelligence known as Vanamonde, who enables them to reconstruct the true history of Earth. There had, in fact, been no invaders. Earth had not been able to achieve interstellar travel at the time it came in contact with superior civilizations, and more or less shamed by its own lack of development, human society began to concentrate on engineering human evolution, with the goal of joining this galactic civilization, but the evolutionary goal of creating a bodiless intelligence remained. When such a mind was created, it was either insane or hostile to matter, and it wreaked havoc on the universe until it was imprisoned in an artificial sun. Other, more benign intelligences were later created, of which Vanamonde was one. Finally, the galaxy—in fact, the entire known universe—was abandoned when the galactic civilization decided to join an even more advanced and more massive civilization in another universe. Left behind were only the most provincial elements of the galactic civilization, and Diaspar and Lys were the surviving societies of those who remained behind on Earth. Now, because of Alvin's discoveries, they would try to re-establish contact with the civilization that had left them behind millions of years earlier.

From the point of view of our known-unknown oppositions, it is easy to see that Clarke's narrative moves in ever-widening circles. Initially, the city functions as it does in much science fiction: it is the total human community, isolated from the mysterious outside by a barrier of towers and by generations of psychological conditioning. This is the first major opposition in the book, and it is much like the opposition at work in the imagery of spaceships: the interior is the known, the exterior the unknown. All of the traditional oppositions that once characterized life on Earth have been resolved into this single great opposition of inside-outside. There is no longer day or night, heat or cold, calm or wind—even life or death, since all of the city's inhabitants are periodically "reborn" into a new life. All oppositions are kept in stasis by the central computer, and the only opposition over which this computer does not have absolute control is that of inside-outside. Hence this is the only barrier between the known and the unknown in this part of the narrative, and it is the one that must be breached if the story is to move forward.

The first part of the narrative, then, consists of events leading up to the breaking of this barrier and the transformation of this first opposition into a higher one. Very early in the narrative, oppositions are set up which are analogues of this basic opposition. The novel opens with an image of the opposition between illusion and reality: Alvin and his friends are enjoying a "total experience" kind of "saga" that has them undergoing elaborate adventures that are frankly pulpish—perhaps an indication of the artistic decadence of Diaspar and very probably an allusion by Clarke to an earlier era of science fiction. Alvin's inquisitiveness threatens the integrity of the illusion, however: ". . . it seemed as if the structure of reality trembled for an instant, and that behind the world of the senses he caught a glimpse of another and totally different universe. . . ."[15] This "other universe" is of course the reality of Diaspar, glimpsed through the veil of sensory illusion set up by the saga. The structure of the saga is an analogue of the structure of Diasparan life itself: Alvin and his friends are pretending to be part of a subterranean culture whose entire universe is the interior of a planet. As in the real Diaspar, the outside is taboo, and when Alvin suggests they explore the outside, his violation of the taboo destroys the illusion, abruptly bringing the saga to an end. Alvin's friends berate him for thus interrupting the saga (the third time he has done so), and Alvin realizes that "here was the barrier that sundered him from all the people of his world, and which might doom him to a life of frustration. He was always wanting to go outside, both in reality and in dream" (p. 11). Here, then, is another opposition, another barrier: Alvin is an "outsider" in terms of the psychological norms of his people. There is a social inside-outside opposition within Diasparan society, and it is apparent that Alvin has already breached this social barrier.

We learn that Alvin is on the verge of crossing yet another cultural barrier. He has reached the age of twenty, and his guardianship is coming to an end. He is now outside the family unit, an independent agent. Alvin's father further tells him that he is unique, the first child born on Earth in more than ten million years. (All other Diasparans are resurrections, with edited memories, of citizens who had lived before). Thus, even physiologically, Alvin finds himself on the outside of his society.

The editing of personal memories before a Diasparan is reconstituted, and the general suppression of human history before Diaspar, call to mind the two aspects of the astronaut's mind in Sturgeon's "Bulkhead." Yet another barrier is thus created, this one in time rather than space, separating the limited history of Diaspar from the vastly larger history that preceded it. Alvin can learn all he wants of the history of Diaspar with the guidance of his tutor Jeserac, but Jeserac, too, has an opposite in the figure of the Jester Khedron, whose function is to "introduce calculated amounts of disorder into the city" (p. 35). Khedron becomes Alvin's alternate teacher, the apostle of the unknown as Jeserac is the apostle of the known. It is with Khedron's aid that Alvin discovers the true nature of the stasis of Diaspar, a stasis maintained by the central computer, which allows only limited change within preset patterns. In a sense, then, Diaspar has been outside of time for millions of years; all history has been a restructuring and rearranging of these patterns. The real meaning of Jeserac's earlier discouraging warning becomes clear: in Alvin's quest to leave Diaspar, "'the physical barriers are the least important ones'" (p. 24).

By now, the pattern that controls the first third of the novel is clear. The central opposition to be resolved, or transformed, is that between the interior and exterior of Diaspar. But in order to achieve this transformation by leaving Diaspar, Alvin must first resolve lesser oppositions contained within this larger one. He must overcome the psychological agoraphobia of his people, the cultural narrowness of his family and his education, the historical block imposed by his society, and the logical and mechanistic block imposed by the central computer. When all this is achieved, Alvin can complete the crossing of the first great barrier by leaving Diaspar. Once Alvin has metaphorically broken out of his society by transgressing its taboos, he is ready to physically break out.

In the second part of the narrative, the opposition of the interior and exterior of Diaspar is transformed into the opposition between Diaspar and Lys. Clarke points up a number of oppositions between the two societies: Diaspar is urban and mechanized; Lys is pastoral and more dependent on highly developed human powers such as telepathy. The citizens of Diaspar choose a kind of controlled immortality programmed by the central computer; the Lysians choose to grow old and die. Diasparan art is utilitarian, serving the psychological need for escape and variety; the art of Lys is expressive and creative. Even the names are suggestive: Diaspar of the Babylonian exile, with its associations of defeat and decline and its hint of the dispersion that has happened to the rest of humanity; Lys of the more optimistic Elysium. (One might even carry this a step further and suggest the two cities represent Hebraic and Hellenistic culture.) But what they have in common is more important—a forced provincialism and xenophobia and a general disinterest in the unknown. Clarke's explanation of the stasis of Lys is less satisfactory than his account of Diaspar, since the Lysians know of Diaspar and do not have to contend with the problem of immortality. In fact, the entire opposition between the two cultures is in some sense a false one, and although it seems to occupy a central place in the narrative, it really does little more than serve as a secondary structure of oppositions designed to carry the narrative from the inside-outside opposition of Diaspar to the larger but parallel opposition of Earth-galaxy.

It might be noted, however, that the Diaspar-Lys opposition points up some key structural parallels between this novel and Ursula LeGuin's later *The Dispossessed,* which I have already discussed briefly. Both works deal with societies of opposing ideologies, separated by generations-old self-imposed barriers. In each novel, one society is urban and mechanized, the other rural and communistic. In both cases a single individual transgresses cultural taboos by crossing the barrier that separates the societies, and in both cases this action reveals that the two societies are in fact parts of a larger whole. The societal opposition thus becomes transformed into a more fundamental one—but here is where the parallel ends. LeGuin, like many modern science-fiction writers, is concerned with character, and the transformations of her novel turn inward, toward problems of human psychology. Clarke's transformations, on the other hand, lead outward, toward vast (if finally somewhat fuzzy) speculations on human destiny and the nature of the universe.

This direction becomes manifest in the third major opposition in *The City and the Stars.* This opposition—the provincialism of the Earth societies vs. the expansiveness of the galaxy—is introduced in the Shalmirane episode, and the image that introduces it is yet another science-fiction icon: the creature, in this case a massive polyp with its servant robots. In the first part of the novel, Alvin had to overcome barriers relating to information about Diaspar and the "outside"; in this part, he must overcome barriers relating to Earth and the galaxy. He does this with the aid of the memory of one of the service robots from Shalmirane. With the information thus gained, and with the discovery and raising of the interstellar spaceship as a result of that information, Alvin finally assumes the role of representative of the unknown. He now possesses information that makes him an outsider to both Diaspar and Lys, and the opposition between the cultures of Earth and the culture of the universe (and Earth's own past) is the next he must overcome.

The spaceship then becomes the next icon of the unknown. Alvin guides it to the largest planet of the central sun of the Seven

Suns and finds there an obelisk which may well be the forerunner of the obelisks in *2001,* and which in that film are deliberately treated as icons of the unknown.[16] Also on this planet he encounters a mysterious barrier of immense proportions, some sort of corral whose inhabitant had long ago escaped. The barrier isn't fully explained, but it does serve to reinforce the barrier imagery that is central to the novel. It is perhaps significant that the discovery of this most massive of all physical barriers is followed immediately by the appearance of Vanamonde, who represents the final breaking down of the barrier of physical being, the resolution of the basic opposition of mind and matter.

Vanamonde's story, which is presented only in synoptic form at the end of the novel, reveals that the final opposition of the narrative exists on an even broader scale than that of Earth-galaxy. The discovery that the galactic civilization had abandoned this universe for another altogether sets up the final barrier for Alvin to try to cross. To this end, Alvin sends the spaceship off to find the galactic civilization and re-establish contact, rather like the proverbial note in a bottle cast into the sea. Then he turns his attention to rebuilding the society of Earth in terms of the new values he has discovered—the values inherent in seeking the unknown, or, put more simply, the values of scientific progress.

In the most simple terms, the novel is a study in two contrasting attitudes toward the opposition of known-unknown, two attitudes which have come in conflict in our cultural history. Diaspar and Lys represent the belief that this opposition should remain in stasis; Alvin represents the attitude more common to modern culture and obviously shared by Clarke (and most science-fiction writers) that the oppositon should be in a continuous state of resolution or transformation into higher oppositions, a kind of dialectic of scientific progress. The movement of the narrative as I have just discussed it, with its widening circles of inquiry, represents one of transformations that demonstrates Clarke's belief in the virtue of this dialectic. Another set of transformations is revealed by examining the novel not in terms of its plot, but in terms of the chronology of earth history that is gradually revealed. This history begins with earth in an opposition to the rest of the galaxy: man has achieved space travel only to discover that far superior intelligences control the galaxy, leaving man on the outside. This spatial opposition is transformed into a temporal one when man decides to concentrate on engineering his evolution in order to eventually gain entry into the community of advanced civilizations. Once this evolutionary barrier is overcome, the attempt of the galactic civilizations, including earth, to overcome the problem of physical intelligence leads to the opposition of matter and mind. This barrier in turn is overcome by the creation of incorporeal intelligences such as Vanamonde, seemingly the ultimate in scientific and evolutionary progress. But still two more oppositions come of this, and each of them effectively goes beyond the limits of rational extrapolation into areas of mysticism and morality. The first of these is the opposition of Vanamonde and his insane prototype, the Mad Mind. This is left unresolved at the end of the novel, although we are told that the day of confrontation will come (Judgment Day, in effect). With the Mad Mind and Vanamonde, Clarke has reached an opposition that cannot be resolved through extrapolation: the opposition of good and evil, a subject which Clarke pretty much avoids, but which brings the narrative to an acceptable conclusion by leaving us with a traditionally accepted antinomy. The other opposition that Clarke leaves us with is equally mystical but somewhat less satisfactory: this is the opposition of the galactic civilization, representing ultimate scientific progress, with that mysterious "other" that is so attractive over in the next universe. To speculate on what this "other" might be would be to get into almost theological questions, which Clarke also avoids, but since this opposition is less clearly defined and less traditionally acceptable than that between Vanamonde and the Mad Mind, it is also less satisfactory. We could perhaps regard this as a culturally acceptable antinomy by viewing it as a variant of the myth of the Golden Age, but Clarke does not specifically invite such an interpretation.

By choosing to structure his narrative in a series of ever-widening circles, Clarke inevitably ends up with this kind of mystical situation that cannot be resolved by rational extrapolation. Clarke himself seems to realize this in his well-known statement that sufficiently advanced technology is indistinguishable from magic; purely rational extrapolation, in other words, has its limits. The problem is not unique to Clarke, and one of the best examples of this widening-gyre kind of structure is the work of Olaf Stapledon, who virtually ignores narrative suspense in favor of the kind of synoptic history that Clarke gives us in the story of Vanamonde. The opposition of known-unknown does not always have to lead in this direction, however. As LeGuin's *The Dispossessed* shows, the movement may be inward rather than outward, revelatory of individual character rather than of galactic history. In LeGuin, Clarke, and Stapledon, however, we see characters crossing barriers into the unknown, and in each case we see these barriers represented by means of a convenient and easily understood iconography of cities, planets, and spaceships.

All this may seem a rather schematic way of dealing with a novel, but such an approach may prove useful in a genre that so often employs a schematic use of the imagination to achieve the "sense of wonder." It is interesting to note how analogous the structural movement of *The City and the Stars* is to the manner in which Levi-Strauss and others see myth as functioning to resolve cultural antinomies. As summarized by Geoffrey Hartman, "the original problem is made to expand its context until it is brought into association with other problems which are moral and social rather than metaphysical—in short, for which a socially structured solution exists."[17] Similarly, Clarke repeatedly transforms what are initially rather mechanical oppositions into ever higher ones until he arrives at such virtually irreducible oppositions as good and evil. And this process, which is essentially the structure of what we call extrapolation, is not confined to *The City and the Stars* among Clarke's work. Among all major science-fiction writers, Clarke perhaps most consistently pushes the process of extrapolation to the limits of rationality and beyond. *Childhood's End* (1953), "The Nine Billion Names of God" (1953), *Rendezvous with Rama* (1973), and a number of his other works follow this pattern of moving, through a series of transformations, from the known to the unknown to the unknowable. And characteristically, when he reaches this third level, he ends the story, knowing that this is as far as extrapolation can take him.

I should perhaps not close without a final note about the icon of the city. Diaspar is the archetypal science-fiction city. Like other such cities in science fiction, it immediately strikes us with that "sense of wonder" of which I spoke earlier. If such icons as the spaceship and the creature work because they signal the unknown, the icon of the city works because of its very rationality; it is the only icon of these three that seems to represent the known and familiar. It stands in the midst of the unknown just as humanity exists in the wilderness of space and time, and its wonder comes not only from the implication of the waste beyond, but also from the awe at what might be accomplished with human knowledge. It is the icon which alone most nearly suggests the extrapolative element of science fiction, since its power is located in familiarity and rationality rather than in "otherness." At the same time, it draws power from subrational fears: the unknown is represented not only by the "world outside" but also by the labyrinth within. It may be a supremely rational image, but like the supremely rational structure of modern science itself, it threatens to overwhelm the individual; it cannot all be comprehended at once, and one never feels quite in control. Because of its iconic value, it can be adapted for a variety of rhetorical or poetic ends. One thinks of the social parable of Lang's *Metropolis,* of science fiction's many urban satires, of recent ecology-oriented novels and films. One might also note that this value of the city is exploited in such non-science-fiction works as Robbe-Grillet's *In the Labyrinth* or certain of the short stories of Borges.

One conclusion that may be drawn from all this is that the intellectual basis of much science fiction—this kind of dialectical extrapolation—is more closely related to the emotional basis (the "sense of wonder") than is generally suspected. The process may be summarized somewhat as follows: the known exists in opposition to the unknown, with a barrier of some sort separating them. The barrier is crossed, and the unknown becomes the known. But the crossing of the barrier reveals new problems, and this sets the stage for a further opposition of known and unknown. This barrier is crossed, yet another opposition is set up, and so on. The "sense of wonder" grows in part out of the tension generated by awareness of this opposition, and the images of the sense of wonder are those which most strongly reinforce this tension, images that stand at the barrier. The transformations continue until an opposition is arrived at that requires no further transformation or resolution. In the case of Clarke, this is often some realm of mystical "unknowableness"; in other writers, it may be a stasis of good and evil; and in still others, such as LeGuin, it may reduce itself to problems of character and human nature. The iconography of science fiction is the pattern of imagery that carries this movement forward.

Such an approach, as I have said, will not account for all science fiction and hardly even constitutes a theory of science fiction. But it can illuminate a substantial number of individual works, and it may help to reveal vital connections between science fiction and fantasy, between science-fiction literature and film, and between sub-genres and historical periods within science-fiction works for a popular audience, and to provide concrete evidence for the frequently made assertion that science fiction is indeed a kind of modern mythology.

NOTES

1. Olaf Stapledon, "Preface," *Last and First Men* (New York: Dover Publications, Inc., 1968), p. 9.
2. Stith Thompson, "Myth and Folktales," in Thomas A. Sebeok, ed., *Myth: A Symposium* (Bloomington: Indiana University Press, 1965), p. 172.

3. Reginald Bretnor, in the "Introduction" to *Science Fiction: Today and Tomorrow* (New York: Harper & Row, 1974), simply describes the sense of wonder as "this elusive quality" and adds that "science fiction tries to induce a sense of wonder about the physical universe and man's own interior private universe" (p. 11). Sam Lundwall, in *Science Fiction: What It's All About* (New York: Ace Books, 1971), suggests that this is what attracts readers to the genre: "Exactly what this Something is, no one has succeeded in finding out, even though the phenomenon has been given a name: Sense of Wonder. If you have Sense of Wonder, then you can appreciate science fiction" (p. 24). Other writers on this subject are hardly more revealing.
4. "There is, then, a particular kind of story which has a value in itself—a value independent of its embodiment in any literary work." C. S. Lewis, *An Experiment in Criticism* (Cambridge: Cambridge University Press, 1961), p. 41. The particular kind of story that Lewis refers to, of course, is myth, and it is interesting to note that Claude Levi-Strauss, working from a quite different perspective, arrived at essentially the same conclusion, writing that "the mythical value of myth remains preserved, even through the worst translation." Claude Levi-Strauss, "The Structural Study of Myth," in Sebeok, p. 85.
5. E. H. Gombrich, *Art and Illusion* (Princeton, N.J.: Princeton University Press, 1969), p. 9.
6. David Ketterer, *New Worlds for Old* (New York: Doubleday Anchor, 1974), p. 13.
7. Darko Suvin, "On the Poetics of the Science Fiction Genre," *College English,* 34, (December 1972), 372-82.
8. Tzvetan Todorov, *The Fantastic: A Structural Approach to a Literary Genre,* trans. Richard Howard (Ithaca, N.Y.: Cornell University Press, 1975), p. 172.
9. Robert Scholes, *Structural Fabulation* (Notre Dame: University of Notre Dame Press, 1975), p. 43.
10. Theodore Sturgeon,"Bulkhead," in *A Way Home* (New York: Pyramid Publications, Inc., 1961), p. 34.
11. John Baxter, *Science Fiction in the Cinema* (New York: Paperback Library, 1970), p. 119.
12. Levi-Strauss, in Sebeok.
13. In the earlier version of the novel, *Against the Fall of Night* (New York: Gnome Press, 1953), Alvin's quest is conducted under the posthumous tutelage of an ancient named Alaine of Lyndar, who had provocatively left clues all over the city for Alvin, or someone like him, to find. Alaine is partly replaced by Khedron in the later novel, but partly also by the near-mythical figure of Yarlan Zey, the city's founder, who had anticipated a quest such as Alvin's and thus deliberately left loopholes in programming safeguards in the central computer. When Alvin finds these loopholes, the logical questions arises as to why they were put there in the first place. As in many good mysteries, Alvin deepens the overall puzzle by solving the first part of it.
14. In *Against the Fall of Night,* this role is filled by an old man rather than a polyp. The old man, like the beast, is a kind of icon, but one more associated with fairy tales than science fiction, and one whose presence is never satisfactorily explained in the earlier novel. By replacing him with a polyp, Clarke not only can take advantage of the iconic value of the beast-image, but can provide a biological explanation of the creature's presence and its immense age. The explanation provides a curious analogue with Diaspar: the creature is immortal, but lives in cycles, with its cellular structure dispersing and restructuring at the end of each cycle according to a genetic "program"—much as Diaspar's inhabitants are eternally "recycled" by the computer.
15. Arthur C. Clarke, *The City and the Stars* (New York: New American Library, 1957), p. 9.
16. Since this paper was originally written, it has been pointed out to me by Thomas Clareson and others that such images as these are common in Clarke's fiction, and that

together they constitute yet another important icon of the known and the unknown: the sentinel. The most familiar example of this icon is, of course, in Clarke's story of the title, which provided the basis for *2001: A Space Odyssey*. There are a number of sentinels in *The City and the Stars*: the spaceship, waiting in the desert; the central computer, waiting for its secret to be discovered; the polyp, waiting for its Messiah; and, in the end, Alvin himself, waiting for the unknown.

17. Geoffrey Hartmann, "Structuralism: the Anglo-American Adventure,"in *Beyond Formalism: Literary Essays* 1958-1970 (New Haven: Yale University Press, 1970), p. 18.

Lost Lands, Lost Races: A Pagan Princess of Their Very Own

Thomas D. Clareson

Because in America, at least, science fiction has been so closely associated with the pulp magazines from 1926 onward, we too often think of it as a recent phenomenon confined to the last half-century and limited in content to technological gimmicks, space-ships, distant planets, and oozing Bug-Eyed Monsters. The brief and happily ill-fated name "space fiction" illustrates that short-sightedness, while the movies have perpetuated the error. Granted that such writers as Mary Shelley, Poe, Verne, and Wells have been acknowledged as precursors of the field, most academic and critical attention has been confined either to such individuals or to the recent, if not immediately contemporary, period. In like manner, because the utopia has long received attention, the movement from utopian vision to dystopian nightmare has supplied the most respectable axis for serious consideration of science fiction as a whole.

A briefer form of this article was published in *The Journal of Popular Culture*, 8 (Spring 1975), 714-23.

To indulge in such arbitrary limitations is a mistake, a simplification that keeps us from giving needed attention to a vast body of fiction written from the 1870s onward and intended for an adult, not juvenile, audience. Even more important, this body of popular fiction helps to join science fiction to the central, ongoing literary tradition by providing a much-needed link between the imaginary voyages to the ends of the Earth, so frequent in the eighteenth century, and the interstellar flights of recent decades. The result emphasizes an unbroken chain of imaginary societies—in a sense, symbolic worlds—extending back at least to the medieval travel books, if not farther. It is a chain modified as each historical period—each generation—gave voice to its own interests and concerns.

Especially in both Britain and America, during those years between the 1870s and the 1930s, by far the most popular kind of imaginary voyage took the form of the so-called "lost race" novel. Most simply, that type of story reflected the impact of three interrelated areas upon the literary and public imaginations of the period: first, the renewed vigor of the explorations which sought to map the interiors of Africa, Asia, and South America, as well, of course, as both polar regions; secondly, the cumulative impact of geological discoveries and theories which expanded the past almost immeasurably and populated it with such creatures as Tyrannosaurus Rex, Pithecanthropus Erectus, and Neanderthal Man; and finally, the impact of archaeological discoveries and theories which—from the valley of the Indus to the depths of Africa and Pre-Columbian America—raised civilizations in the past more spectacular and mysterious than legendary El Dorado or the Kingdom of Prester John. In a sense, the appearance of the "lost race" novel measures the degree to which ideas and phenomena known to intellectual circles for some time finally became public property. And though some students of modern science fiction would dismiss that type of story as so much fantasy, one can argue that inasmuch as it reflected current knowledge and theory in geology and archaeology, at least, it was the most popular form of the science fiction of its period.

The impact of geology on these writers may perhaps be best illustrated by the rather plaintive wish of one of the characters in James DeMille's *A Strange Manuscript Found in a Copper Cylinder* (1888):

> The so-called fossil animals may not be extinct. There are fossil specimens of animals that still have living representatives. There is no reason why many of those supposed to be extinct may not be alive now. . . . Who can tell but that the moa or the dodo may yet be lurking somewhere here in the interior of Madagascar, or Borneo, or Papua.[1]

Many of the writers decorated their settings with "strange survivals of a bygone geologic age," as did Frank Cowan in *Revi-Lona* (undated).[2] The practice reached perhaps its greatest absurdity in Frank Savile's *Beyond the Great South Wall* (1901); once the expedition has penetrated deep into Antarctica, it finds a single "Beast . . . like nothing known outside the frenzy of a delirium. Swarthy green was his huge, lizard-like body, and covered with excrecences of a livid hue. His neck was like the lithe neck of a boa-constrictor."[3] Once discovered, this Beast pursues sundry members of the expedition throughout the remainder of the narrative. Because the heroine has paused to snatch her "puppy dog" from his oncoming path, the Beast pins the hero and heroine in a cave; there, instead of fainting, the heroine confesses her love, the Beast is killed by a sudden earthquake, enabling the couple to return happily to England to be married. He was, of course, "*Brontosaurus excelsus,* remains of which have been found in the Jurassic formation of Colorado" (p. 216). So fascinated was Savile with him that once he was introduced, Savile ignored the ancient Mayan manuscripts which had lured his explorers to the Antarctic and the ice-encased ruins of a Mayan temple which they found there. In contrast, the finest creation of a remnant of the prehistoric world occurred in Conan Doyle's *The Lost World* (1912).

Such survivors, be they one or many, provided little more than stage trappings. The basic formula of the "lost race" novel was easily identifiable: an explorer, scientist, or naval lieutenant, either by chance or intentional quest, found a lost colony or a lost homeland of some vanished or little-known civilization. In a sense, in the early years at least, the "lost race" novel was little more than a modification of the traditional utopia, and its evolution during the late nineteenth and early twentieth centuries provides a number of insights into the period. In its earliest form, which did persist, although in ever-diminishing numbers, throughout the period, its protagonist did find an ideal society. Such discoveries provided the writers with opportunity to debate a wide variety of topical concerns, perhaps best illustrated by enumerating a number of typical novels.

Will N. Harben's *The Land of the Changing Sun* (1894)[4] pictures a vast subterranean cavern lighted by a man-made electrical sun and peopled by the descendants of a group of men who arbitrarily colonized it in order to enjoy without restrictions the wealth of its gold mines. The novel becomes a platform from which Harben argues in favor of a harsh eugenics allowing no imperfection in anyone.

John Uri Lloyd's *Etidorhpa* (1895, 1914)[5] becomes a violent attack against current theories of biology, particularly that of evolution.

Henry S. Drayton's *In Oudemon* (1900)[6] proposes a kind of Christian Socialism rather than the Marxist dialectic, idealizing the natural man and a fundamentalistic religion based solely on the "effort to follow the teaching of the Bible" (p. 177).

Robert Ames Bennet's *Thyra: A Romance of the Polar Pit* (1901)[7] portrays a lost clan of Vikings living in a "full-fledged social democracy" 'p. 80)—Marxist in nature.

David M. Parry's *The Scarlet Empire* (1906) amounts to little more than a series of dialogues attacking Bellamy and destroying the protagonist's belief in socialism.

Richard Hatfield's *Geyserland: 9262 B.C.* (1908)[9] again argues in favor of Marxism, while in the same year Willis George Emerson's *The Smoky God* draws upon mythology, the Bible, and current scientific theory to find the Edenic homeland of mankind in a Symmesian inner world located in the Arctic. God had intended man to live in the interior of the hollow Earth, he declared, and only after Adam's fall was man exiled to the external surface, where he lives "like the lichen on the mountain side, clinging determinedly for bare existence."[10] Louis P. Gratacap, who had realized *The Certainty of a Future Life on Mars* in 1903, also declared in favor of the Edenic homeland in the Arctic in *The New Northland* (1915).[11]

Perhaps these few examples will suffice to indicate that such novels became the forum—the intellectual battleground—for the burning issues of the day. Many of them continued the Bellamy-inspired debate on socialism, but with a difference. Whether Marxian or not, even when the societies portrayed had the use of an advanced technology, as in Henry Drayton's *In Oudemon,* the writers insisted that a perfect society can exist only when man lives close to nature. Others emphasized an attempt to reconcile the new discoveries and theories with established religious beliefs. Indeed, after Ignatius Donnelly published *Atlantis: The Antediluvian World* (1882), an increasing number of mystics turned to that legendary continent as the Edenic homeland of mankind. When that concept faltered, they turned to the Pacific, to Lemuria. (An examination of the changes in the fiction suggests that not until after increasingly sophisticated knowledge lessened the possibility of such prehistoric, earthly paradises, did science fiction and fantasy turn outward *quantitatively* to the planets and the stars.)

One can interpret all of this as part of a new primitivism, a rejection of the increasingly complex urban-technological society being spawned by the new century. One of the most telling expressions of this pervasive theme came from the biographer of Mark Twain. In *The Great White Way* (1901), Albert Bigelow Paine took his expedition deep into Antarctica, where its members saw "stretching [before them] away to the farthest horizon limits a thick, yielding carpet of wonderful Purple Violets."[12] The protagonist—a young man who is both a scientist and a mystic—chooses to remain with the primitive people found there because:

> Ambition and achievement—of such kind as we know and prize—seemed foreign to their lives. . . . They regard with sorrowful distrust

> our various mechanical contrivances. . . . Here, shut away from the greed and struggle of the life we know the lives of the people have linked themselves with the sun and stars, with the woods and fields, with the winds and waters, and with each other [telepathically], in one rare, universal chord. . . . It was truly a 'Land of Heart's Desire.'
>
> —pp. 236, 243, 258

The mysticism remained, but as the period progressed, the essay-like topical debates gave way increasingly to story. The first significant modification had occurred as early as Jules Verne's *Five Weeks in a Balloon* (American edition, 1869), in which his explorers use a balloon to voyage across the interior of Africa. The narrative mixes together lengthy accounts of the history of balloonry and African geography with innumerable, essentially disconnected pursuits and threats of capture by various natives and animals in a loose, episodic structure. This was to be the basic formula for the juvenile audience, lasting well into the twentieth century.

But the individual who transformed the imaginary voyage and gave the "lost race" novel its lasting identity was Sir H. Rider Haggard. Having begun with *King Solomon's Mines* (1885)—a panorama of African life as well as a search for treasure—he turned to *She* (1887) and *Allan Quatermain* (1887). Within a year five parodies had been published: *He, It, King Solomon's Wives, King Solomon's Treasures,* and *Bess.* By the 1920s Haggard himself had published some forty novels, while the number of his imitators, both British and American, runs at least to a thousand. Somehow, then, Haggard seemed to trigger a dominant, popular literary response to the period, one that was more significant in many ways than that begun by Edward Bellamy.

Drawing upon personal experience in Africa, he created the Valley of Kor in the unknown heart of the continent. There, amid the ruins of a once beautiful city, the descendants of Egyptians live in caves, cut off from the mainstream of civilization since the time of the pharaohs. To rule them he created the immortal queen, Ayesha, who waited impatiently for the reincarnation of her beloved Kallikrates. She dies at the end of the novel—

withering and aging in the "Flame of Life," which had theretofore given her immortality, a plot device echoed as late as James Hilton's *Lost Horizon* (1933).[13] Sexuality may once again have motivated Anglo-American literature when McTeague kissed Trina as she sat in his dentist's chair, but high romance reasserted itself when Ayesha, "She-who-must-be-obeyed," loved Leo Vincey—described as "a statue of Apollo come to life . . . the handsomest man in the University, and one of the nicest too."[14] The only ingredient absent from *She,* Haggard added to *Allan Quatermain,* in which the narrator, Henry Curtis, remained in Africa, taking as his wife the beautiful Nyleptha, queen of the sun-worshipping Zu-Vendis, who soon presented him with a son and heir: "a regular curly-haired, blue-eyed young Englishman in looks . . . destined to inherit the throne of the Zu-Vendis."[15] In short, obviously, for Haggard and his imitators, whatever else it might be, the "lost race" novel was a love story.

To say this is inadequate; here is Haggard as he describes the first on-stage appearance of his heroine, "She-who-must-be-obeyed":

> At length the curtain began to stir. Who could be behind it?—some naked savage queen, a languishing Oriental beauty, or a nineteenth-century young woman, drinking afternoon tea? I had not the slightest idea, and should not have been astonished at seeing any of the three. Indeed, I was beyond astonishment. Presently the hanging agitated itself, then from behind its folds there appeared a most beautiful white hand, white as snow, and with long tapering fingers, ending in the pinkest nails. This hand grasped the curtain, drawing it aside, and a voice spoke, I think the softest and yet most silvery voice that I have ever heard. It reminded me of the murmur of a brook.
>
> —pp. 107-08

> . . . a tall figure stood before us. I say a figure, for not only the body, but also the face, was wrapped with a soft white and gauzy material in such a way as at first sight to remind me most forcibly of a corpse in its grave-clothes. And yet I do not know why it should have given me this idea, seeing that the wrappings were so thin that I could distinctly see the gleam of pink flesh beneath them. . . . a tall and lovely woman, instinct with beauty in every part, and also with a certain snake-like

> grace which heretofore I had never seen anything to equal. When she moved a hand or foot her entire frame seemed to undulate, and the neck did not bend, it curved.
>
> —p. 108

Soon Ayesha "unveils" after a rather lengthy dialogue in which she asks if the Messiah of the Jews has yet come and denounces them for crucifying him:

> She lifted her white and rounded arms—never had I seen such arms before—and slowly, very slowly, she withdrew some fastening behind her hair. Then of a sudden the long, corpse-like wrappings fell from her to the ground, and my eyes travelled up her form, now robed only in a garb of clinging white that did but serve to show its rich and imperial shape, instinct with a life that was more than life, and with a certain serpent-like grace which was more than human. On her little feet were sandals fastened with studs of gold. Then came ankle more perfect than ever sculptor dreamed of. About the waist her white kirtle was fastened by a double-headed snake of solid gold, above which her generous form swelled up in lines as pure as they were lovely, till the kirtle ended at the snowy argent of her breast, whereon her arms were folded. I gazed above them at her face, and—I do not romance—shrank back blinded and amazed. I have heard of the beauty of celestial beings, now I saw it; only this beauty, with all its awful loveliness and purity was evil—or rather, at the time, it impressed me as evil. . . . The man does not live whose pen can convey a sense of what I saw. I might talk of the great changing eyes of deepest, softest black, of the tinted face, of the broad and noble brow, on which the hair grew low, and delicate, straight features. But beautiful, surpassingly beautiful as were all these, her loveliness did not lie in them. It lay rather . . . in a visible majesty, in an imperial grace, in a godlike stamp of softened power, which shone upon that living countenance like a living halo. Never before had I guessed what beauty made sublime could be—and yet, the sublimity was a dark one—the glory was not all of heaven—but nonetheless it was glorious.
>
> —pp. 117-18

Yet the narrator perceives in her "first flush of ripened beauty" some "deep acquaintance with grief and passion." Neither the "dimples of her mouth" nor "those glorious eyes" are able to "hide this shadow of sin and sorrow." It seems to say to the narrator:

> 'Behold me, lovely as no woman was or is, undying and half-divine; memory haunts me from age to age, and passion leads me by the hand—evil have I done, and with sorrow have I made acquaintance from age to age, and from age to age evil shall I do, and sorrow shall I know till my redemption comes.'
>
> —p. 118

She laughs—"ah, how musically!"—and nods her head "with an air of sublime coquetry that would have been worthy of the Venus Victrix": then she asks, "Rash man! . . . Say, hast thou seen enough?" Good Englishman that he is, the narrator can only reply "hoarsely":

> 'I have looked on beauty, and I am blinded.'
>
> —p. 119

Needless to say, a variety of critics could make much of such a passage, as has Margaret Atwood in "Superwoman Drawn and Quartered: The Early Forms of *She*."[16]

After the entrance of Ayesha, that of Nyleptha in *Allan Quatermain* may seem anticlimactic; yet Nyleptha proved to be the true prototype of the "lost race" heroines:

> I have seen beautiful women in my day and am no longer thrown into transports at the sight of a beautiful face; but language fails me when I try to give some idea of the blaze of loveliness that then broke upon us in the persons of these sister Queens. Both were young—perhaps five and twenty years—both were tall and exquisitely formed; but there the likeness stopped. One, Nyleptha, was a woman of dazzling fairness; her right arm and breast, bare after the custom of her people, showed like snow against her white and gold-embroidered 'kaf,' or toga. And as for her sweet face, all I can say is, that it was one that few men could look on and forget. Her hair, a veritable crown of gold, clustered in short ringlets over her shapely head, half hiding the ivory brow, beneath which eyes of deep and glorious gray flashed out in tender majesty. I cannot attempt to describe her other features, only the mouth was very sweet, and curved like Cupid's bow, and over the whole countenance there shown an indescribable look of loving kindness. . . .
>
> —pp. 525-26

After noticing her brunette sister, whose "figure, like [Nyleptha's], was almost perfect in its curves and outlines," the narrator observes that the woman "of dazzling fairness" looks upon him and his party:

> . . . I saw the swift blood run up beneath Nyleptha's skin as the pink lights run up the morning sky. Red grew her fair bosom and shapely arm, red the swanlike neck; the rounded cheek blushed red as the petal of a rose. . . .
>
> —p. 527

Love had come to the African queen; her feminine instincts had been overwhelmed by the mere appearance of the Englishman.

Once begun, this type of love story—modern man (be he British or American; naval lieutenant, scientist, or explorer) and his primitive beauty—spread like wildfire. The most obvious indebtedness to Haggard occurs in such titles as Mabel Fuller Blodgett's *At the Queen's Mercy* (1897),[17] whose supernaturally-endowed queen rules a city in Africa, and Sidney J. Marshall's *The King of Kor* (1903),[18] which is a deliberate sequel to *She*.

Other notable early examples would include the following. In *A Strange Discovery* (1899)[19] Charles Romyn Dake attempted a sequel to Poe's *The Narrative of A. Gordon Pym*. Pym finds a Roman colony in the Antarctic and, of course, falls in love with a princess as beautiful as Helen of Troy: "the episode of Romeo and Juliet sinks into insignificance by the side of the story of their love" (p. 156). Although they marry, "a strange thermal phenomenon" brings on a terrible blizzard (p. 270), and the princess Lilama dies of starvation although Pym goes out to seek supplies. He, in turn, flees to Montevideo, Uruguay, and disappears.

In Duffield Osborne's *The Secret of the Crater* (1900)[20] an American naval officer discovers Phoenicians in the Pacific and spends much of the remainder of the narrative saving his beloved princess, who is to be the virginal sacrifice to the volcanic gods of the dark-skinned native priests. They live happily ever after, for he refuses to return to service. In the prologue to the novel Osborne may well reveal something of the explanation for the widespread appeal of this new romance when he wrote:

> I wonder how soon the time will come when the world shall be so thoroughly explored and its people so cosmopolitanized that adventure and discovery will be things of the past. . . . No more Odysseys; no more Circe; no Lotos-eaters; no more travels of Sir John Mandeville; no Prester Johns, with their mysterious courts. Even the wanderings of Captain Cook had [before the narrator's recent adventure] begun to read like the works of the modern story tellers whose very inventions bade fair soon to reach a limit, and then the world would have nothing to do but settle down to the dead level of studying humdrum facts and natural improvements.
>
> —pp. 1-2

This opinion is echoed in John Reed Scott's *The Duke of Oblivion* (1914),[21] in which eighteenth-century French and English are found in the Caribbean. Its protagonist asserts:

> There is little enough to discover. Amundsen and Scott have found the South Pole, and Peary and Cook the North; Africa is as open as a moving-picture show; the Grand Lama has a British Resident. There remains only the known to be discovered.
>
> —p. 9

Whatever sense of ennui may have accounted for the popularity of the motif, and whatever the setting of the individual works, the necessary ingredient was the bewitchingly lovely maid. In Edward T. Bouve's *Centuries Apart* (1894),[22] in which descendants of sixteenth-century British and French inhabit two islands in the Antarctic, she is Kate Percy. Promising to come back, her American lover returns to the States to be killed in the Civil War; she, too, dies. (Within its narrative frame, the novel reads like an inferior historical romance—perhaps important as a sign that many writers sought to take advantage of the "lost race" formula.) Viking women proved a favorite, as in William H. Wilson's *Rafnaland* (1900),[23] and the seemingly ardent Marxist Robert Ames Bennet named his first novel for Thyra, blonde princess of the polar pit. Even by the 1890s, however, the formula was not confined to those narratives dealing with some unexplored corner of the world, for Gustavus W. Pope permitted his protagonist, Lieutenant Hamilton, of *A Journey to Mars* (1894) and its sequel, *Wonderful Adventures on Venus* (1895)[24], to woo and wed a Martian princess so that they might adventure romantically upon the three worlds. Yet she might well be a creation of Haggard's:

> The Princess Suhlamia was rather above the middle height; her form exquisitely graceful and symmetrical. . . . Her complexion was of the most delicate aureate hue, combined with the soft, rich, creamy tint of the tropical magnolia. Her luxuriant hair—which if loosed, would have flowed to the ground in wavy masses—was a deep, rich purple, verging on a glossy blackness, mingled with a tinge of red gold, and shimmered with a sparkling lustre like the dust of sapphires; her hands and feet were small for her height and beautifully moulded. Her eyes were magnificent, their color indescribable, resembling that abysmal darkness seen in the fathomless gulfs of the celestial heavens. . . . She was attired in a simple robe of pure white, scarce concealing the exquisite outlines of her form and without ornament save for a little budding flower on her breast.[25]
>
> Suhlamia bent forward and laid her hand almost caressingly on my head;—her warm and delicious breath fanned my cheek;—I raised my face to hers;—one ravishing glance from her resplendent eyes met my ardent gaze;—one bright smile that thrilled my soul with ineffable joy, a faint blush mantled in her cheek,—she kissed my brow and softly murmured—'Dear Frederick;—'tis the seal of our friendship.'
>
> —p. 252

Because the dates of the examples cited thus far cluster at the turn of the century, one may fail to realize the persistence with which the "lost race" formula survived in the twentieth century—probably because of the reinforcement Edgar Rice Burroughs gave to the original impact of Haggard. By 1926 in *The Glory of Egypt* by L. Moresby (the pseudonym of L. Adams Beck)[26] the scene has shifted to the mountains of Tibet, where British officers find both Egyptian ruins and a lovely virgin princess about to be sacrificed to Osiris:

> How shall I describe her? She was certainly more beautiful than any dream I had made of her—pearl-pale with suffering, with heavy clouds of midnight hair about her brows, the only colour in her face the great dark eyes and the crimson of lovely lips. . . .
>
> —p. 196

She loves the narrator at once and at one point accedes to his insistent urging that the "way in which a woman can help a man is obedience. It is but like a child to act hastily and violently. Be patient if you would have my gratitude" (p. 252). But she will be satisfied only with his love. By 1935 in T. A. Willard's *The Wizard of Zacna,*[27] perhaps to gain credibility, an envelope structure portrays the triangle of a young American and the two daughters of a wealthy Mexican, while the Mayan whom he saves recounts the discovery of an ancient city where he, too, had to choose between two beautiful women:

> But she who sat on the king's right held my gaze firmly. Of dazzling fairness, like the faint light of a new dawn. . . .
>
> The dark princess, who was equally beautiful, was of the opposite type; with olive skin set off by the deep color of her lips . . . and wide brown eyes with lashes as black as night. Her hair, smooth and shining as polished jet. . . .
>
> —pp. 120-22

He initially favors the "fair maid," who suggests that he might become her Prince Consort when she rules the city. Of her appearance on one occasion, he wrote;

> She was clad in a long filmy robe of white, plain save for the embroidery of the counted threads at the neck and sleeves—which was in gold. The light from the hanging lamp threw upon it a faint shade of pink, like the color that nature had painted upon her face. Of such thinness was it that, from where I stood, the light from behind the curtains drew an outline of her glorious form beneath the robe. Like some draped statue of the goddess of beauty did she appear.
>
> —p. 166

One characteristic of the formula is well illustrated by two early works of Edison Marshall. In *Ogden's Strange Story* (1934),[28] in an attempt to dramatize the theory of evolution, he echoed such earlier writers as Jack London and Stanley Waterloo by allowing his protagonist, Ogden Rutherford, to suffer amnesia after an airplane crash in the Yukon and to revert atavistically into "Og, the brute man, the hunter of the ancient forest."[29] During the year or so before he is rescued he kidnaps and weds an Indian girl who commits suicide after realizing that they will be separated. In *Dian of the Lost Land* (1935),[30] however, the hero finds the blond, halfcaste daughter of an Englishman who was supposedly lost during a 1908 polar expedition; she is the priestess-goddess of the last surviving group of Cro-Magnon men. And she is beautiful:

> Her only garment was a gorgeous wild animal fur, silvery in hue, from her waist to midway on her thighs. Her legs were bare, her feet clad in sandals of a pattern Adam had never seen before. About the upper part of her body, just under her arms, was a gold band, four inches broad, fastening two metal cups or bowls worn over her breasts. . . .
>
> These lost people whom she ruled worshipped physical perfection. . . . Dian herself was the embodiment of a physical ideal, the product of centuries of mate-selecting by the tribal queens. She was a tall girl, hardly four inches less than six feet, deep-bosomed, finely formed. Her straight bare limbs flashed ivory-white in the firelight. She was athletic rather than buxom; she looked as if she could run like a deer.
>
> Her English blood had refined her beauty without taking away the pagan look native to her race. . . . Now, beholding her splendid body, he thought of her as a Gothic princess beyond the uttermost sway of Rome, perhaps a daughter of Vercingetorix on a forest throne.
>
> —pp. 34-35

The protagonist chooses not to return to civilization but to stay with her: "Adam, the youth, the primal man, had entered into his heritage" (p. 148).

Be she Assyrian, Egyptian, Viking, Carthaginian, Phoenician, or a cavewoman, so long as she might somehow be accepted as part of a bloodstock which had contributed to modern Europe and America, she was eligible for a happily-ever-after marriage or mating. On the other hand, seemingly increasingly so as the period progressed, the storytellers avoided miscegenation. Ogden's Indian wife—named "She-Who-Laughs" and described as being "extremely dark" (p. 49)—deliberately walked off the edge of a mountain cliff because she apparently *knew* that she could not remain with him after his rescue. Nevertheless, he dreams of her even after his marriage to a "pale" wife. In Clifford Smyth's *The Gilded Man* (1918)[31] another Indian maid, the comely Sajipona, princess of a people descended from the Incas, throws herself into a pool of radium because the protagonist must return to the blond Una. Moresby did not permit the Egyptian princess to live in *The Glory of Egypt*; his Englishman must return to Joan Boston, surely the coquette of British India. Nor did James Hilton allow Lo-Tsen to survive her emergence from Shangri-la into the outside world.

Perhaps these examples will be sufficient to indicate the scope and durability of the "lost race" novel. This fiction is important to the study of popular culture in a number of ways. First—and earliest—it provided a podium from which to argue controversial issues of the day. Secondly, it emphasized those aspects of various areas of science which had the greatest impact upon, and greatest appeal to, the literary and popular imaginations. Thirdly—perhaps most important thematically—it rejected the new urban-technological society in favor of a primitivism. In doing this, it paralleled such other popular fiction as that of James Oliver Curwood, Zane Grey, and Gene Stratton Porter. But there was a difference, because more than any other group of novels, the "lost race" novels provided their readers with the acceptable erotica of the period.

No single treatment of the motif better illustrates this erotic quality than does Robert Ames Bennet's *The Bowl of Baal,* first issued as a serial in *All Around Magazine* in 1916.[32] It also measures the evolution of this kind of story, for Bennet proves to be an erstwhile Marxist. He abandons all causes in favor of a love triangle acted out in the depths of the Arabian peninsula against a background of a blind saurian monster, a barbaric race of cave dwellers, and the rivalry of two beautiful women. And, of course, the protagonist is attracted to both of them:

> . . . O'Brien was struck with admiration for [Tigra's] beauty. The perfect oval of her face was tinted the rich cream-white of a Spanish lady's. Her full, alluringly arched lips were as scarlet as the bloom of a

> pomegranate tree. . . . In her large and black oval eyes was all the fire, the passion, and the languor of the Orient. The coils of her abundant, jet-black hair . . .
>
> —p. 52

> . . . There was no sensuous enticement in the beauty of the [fair Istara]. . . .
>
> —p. 122

From more than three hundred pages O'Brien proclaims his love for Istara, kisses her "with a tender ardor" as she hides "her scarlet face on his shoulder" (p. 215), and rescues her from a variety of threats, including the schemes of the "stately sorceress," Tigra (p. 55). Tigra dupes him into an unconsummated marriage and generally demands his attention:

> . . . A rosy glow in her cream-white cheeks added no little to the Oriental beauty of her features. Her midnight eyes flashed with proud fire, yet at the same time melted with tender allurement. . . . Her satiny robes and simple jewels redoubled the charm of her rich beauty by their suggestion of maidenly softness. O'Brien drew in a deep breath and wisely grasped the chance to look away when the sultana's salaam forced her to break the spell of her fascinating gaze.
>
> —pp. 95-96

> . . . she started to dance. Swaying and bowing and flexing with a seductive grace, she glided slowly around the American. Subtly, imperceptibly, Tigra began to weave a spell about him, a spell of beauty and grace and enticement. Her jet-black hair with its blue sheen, her amorous, black eyes and the rich loveliness of her face, her lithe, rounded form, her exquisitely graceful, sinuous bendings and turnings of limbs and head and body—all combined to fascinate and enravish him.
>
> —p. 129

> O'Brien saw that she loved him with the absolute, fundamental, primeval passion that will stop at nothing however high or low to win the mate. She was the mate woman—unmoral, remorseless, alluringly beautiful, and, in her way, as pure as the soft-eyed Istara.
>
> —p. 197

> . . . She danced with her flexing body and gesturing arms, scarcely moving her feet. Presently she freed the outer drape from her lissome

body. It wafted overhead in her pink fingertips and drifted away on the light breeze like a diaphanous cloud. She loosed another drape, and another—

O'Brien divined that he was witnessing that most ancient of all Oriental dances, the Dance of the Seven Veils. Still other drapes were freed and permitted to float away. The creamy whitness of the sultana's form began to gleam through the lessened thicknesses of gauze. The dancer loosened her hair so that it fell about her in a black maze. O'Brien put out his hand in a gesture that forbade the continuance of the dance.

—p. 235

And so it goes until, in the best tradition of discovery, O'Brien understands that he really loves Tigra—"beautiful beyond all other women—more alluring than the houri of paradise" (p. 238). It is too late. They fight side-by-side against the barbarian cavemen until she is wounded; they flee toward civilization in his monoplane; but they must land in the desert, where she dies in his arms.

Although Bennet's language—and his concern for the dance—may give something of a unique flavor to his treatment of established conventions in *The Bowl of Baal,* he was never original. In a sense, all of these writers simply rework the grounds marked out by Haggard. Among Americans only Edgar Rice Burroughs proved to be of the stature of Rider Haggard in shaping the motif. His most famous creation was, of course, Tarzan of the Apes, who gave up his identity as Lord Greystoke in effete modern society to live in the jungles of Africa with Jane Porter, formerly of Baltimore. In that first novel of the Tarzan series (1912), the apeman saves Jane from a lioness and writes a note in which he declares his love for her, but not until he rescues her from the ape Terkoz, who has seized her and begun to carry her into the jungle, do hero and heroine really become acquainted. Tarzan kills the great ape in hand-to-hand combat as Jane watches; then,

When the long knife drank deep a dozen times of Terkoz' heart's blood, and the great carcass rolled lifeless upon the ground, it was a

> primeval woman who sprang forward with outstretched arms toward a primeval man who had fought for her and won her.
>
> And Tarzan?
>
> He did what no red-blooded man needs lessons in doing. He took his woman in his arms and smothered her upturned, panting lips with kisses.
>
> For a moment Jane Porter lay there with half-closed eyes. For a moment—the first in her young life—she knew the meaning of love.
>
> But as suddenly as the veil had been withdrawn, it dropped again, and an outraged conscience suffused her face with its scarlet mantle, and a mortified woman thrust Tarzan of the Apes from her and buried her face in her hands.[33]

Tarzan cannot understand why she resists him:

> . . . Tarzan of the Apes had felt a warm, lithe form close pressed to his. Hot, sweet breath against his cheek and mouth had fanned a new flame of life within his breast, and perfect lips had clung to his in burning kisses that had seared a deep brand into his soul—a brand which marked a new Tarzan.
>
> Again he laid his hand upon her arm. Again she repulsed him. And then Tarzan of the Apes did just what his first ancestor would have done.
>
> He took his woman in his arms and carried her into the jungle.
>
> Early the following morning . . .
>
> —p. 142

Thus began one of the immortal love affairs of the twentieth century.

One might follow Tarzan through his other adventures. In *The Return of Tarzan* (1915)[34] and *Tarzan and the Jewels of Opar* (1918),[35] La, high priestess of Opar—the last outpost of Atlantis—the city whose jewels and gold provide him with his wealth, is bewitched by his strength, as is the impulsive Nemone, queen of Cathne, in *Tarzan and the City of Gold* (1933).[36] When he himself is not beloved, he may assist others, as in the instance of James Blake and the Princess Guinalda, descendant of medieval knights whose city, Nimmr, provides the backdrop for *Tarzan Lord of the Jungle* (1928).[37]

If one tires of Africa, he may go with John Carter to Barsoom where Dejah Thoris awaited his love; one may plunge with David

Innes into Pellucidar, that prehistoric world within the hollow Earth; or one may join Carson Napier, "Earth's first astronaut,"[38] as he voyages to Venus to find the Princess Duare and, again, a primitive world.

One may argue that Haggard's achievement came from his creation of a new context for the femme fatale and love goddess so important to the pre-Raphaelite, Aesthetic, and Decadent Movements—Swinburne and Flaubert's *Salammbo* come immediately to mind. Similarly, Burroughs's achievement may well have lain in his ability to infuse a new vitality into the conventions established by Haggard at a time when imitators of Haggard were beginning to voice their despair at the idea that soon there would be no unknown lands to discover. This would explain, at least in part, the homage paid to his four principal series, and it would also suggest why his indebtedness to the "lost race" formula is most apparent in single works such as *Jungle Girl* (1931), recently re-issued as *The Land of Hidden Men.*[39]

Although trained as a medical man, the protagonist of *The Land of Hidden Men,* Gordon King, has chosen to search for ruined cities in Cambodia, and, of course, he finds instead lost cities. Very early in the narrative, perhaps to prepare for what will occur in the jungle, Burroughs permits King to reflect upon his relationship with an American girl:

> . . . What a peach of a girl Susan Anne was! It seemed strange to him that she had never married, for there were certainly enough eligible fellows always hanging around her. He was rather glad that she had not, for he realized that he should feel lost without the promise of her companionship when he returned home. He had known Susan Anne as far back as he could remember, and they had always been pals. . . .
>
> —pp. 22-23

Such an attitude only heightens his reaction after he has rescued the girl, Fou Tan, from a tiger:

> As they seated themselves, King became acutely conscious of the marked physical attraction that this girl of a forgotten age exercised over him. Every movement of her lithe body, every gesture of her graceful arms and hands, each changing expression of her beautiful

> eyes were provocative. She radiated magnetism. He sensed it in the reaction of his skin, his eyes, his nostrils. It was as though ages of careful selection had produced her for the purpose of arousing in man the desire of possession, and yet there enveloped her a divine halo of chastity that aroused within his breast the protective instinct that governs the attitude of a normal man toward a woman that Fate has thrown into his keeping. Never in his life had King been similarly attracted to any woman.
>
> —p. 60

King learns immediately that Fou Tan has escaped from a city where she was forced to serve as a dancer in the court of a leprous king, whose "sore[s] upon his repulsive body seemed to reach out to seize and contaminate me. It was with difficulty that, half fainting, I went through the ritual of the dance" (p. 62). She fled into the dangers of the jungle after being told that the king had noticed her beauty and that in three nights' time she was to be his newest concubine. It is a basic characteristic of Burroughs's work that the erotic is developed by a tension between the hero's awareness of the heroine's physical beauty and a threat—usually explicit—to her virtue. In this case the remainder of the novel is made up of a series of captures and escapes as King saves Fou Tan from a fate worse than death. He remains with her to rule her city.

The pattern is crystallized clearly in *The People That Time Forgot* (1918),[40] in which the protagonist loves a cave girl on a lost island in the Pacific. When he kills a hulking apeman, the girl reacts:

> . . . Once again the girl smiled her slow smile and stepping closer caressed the barrel of my automatic. As she did so, her fingers came in contact with mine, and a sudden thrill ran through me. . . .
>
> —p. 28

He finds pleasure in the company of "this half-naked little savage . . . a new pleasure that was entirely distinct from any that I ever had experienced. When she touched me, I thrilled as I had never before thrilled in contact with another woman" (pp. 29-30).

Again, she is "this beautiful animal" (p. 33). He remains in the prehistoric world with her instead of returning to America.

Some of these writers were racists; all of them, from Haggard to Burroughs, were male chauvinists, for whom these primitive beauties were only sex objects. Surprisingly, perhaps, this attitude increases as the period progresses. A passage which measures how justifiable a basis women's lib has occurs in Burroughs's *Land of Terror* (1944),[41] one of the last tales of Pellucidar. The protagonist has become separated from his queen, the red-headed Dian the Beautiful. Captured by Amazons, he watches two of them fight; they are large, heavy-muscled, apparently bearded, and perhaps as much as two hundred pounds in weight:

> . . . They pounded, kicked, clawed, scratched and bit each other like two furies. The brutality of it sickened me. If these women were the result of taking women out of slavery and attempting to give them equality with men, then I think that they and the world would be better off if they were returned to slavery. One of the sexes must rule; and man seems temperamentally better suited for the job than woman. Certainly if all power over man has resulted in debauching and brutalizing women to such an extent, then we should see that they remain always subservient to man, whose overlordship is, more often than not, tempered by gentleness and sympathy.
>
> —pp. 21-22

A yearning for the past stood behind the popularity of the "lost race" novel. Its writers emphasized primitivism and sought to reconcile old beliefs and ideals with the facts and theories of the period. When their use of the past did not answer their questions nor solve their problems, under the influence of Rider Haggard they created a new, erotic escapism. Their narratives became increasingly a proving ground for the protagonists' masculinity: survival in a hostile world; physical victory over sundry opponents; and the devotion of a sensuous and primitive woman. Burroughs, Haggard, and their imitators wrote in the idiom and erotic code of another generation. To say that idiom no longer has an effect, or to mistake that code for prudery because its expression is not that of the contemporary generation—both are naive judgments and ignore the basis of its popularity, then and now. Such views also ignore that their code, if one may continue to call it that, became a part of both fantasy and science fiction in general during the 1920s and 1930s in novels ranging from A. Merritt's *The Face in the Abyss* (1931) to Stanley G. Weinbaum's *The Black Flame* (1939).

In the naturalistic world of *An American Tragedy,* Clyde Griffiths could only wish for a pagan girl, but in the "lost race" novels, the protagonists and readers may still possess a pagan princess of their very own.

NOTES

1. James DeMille, *A Strange Manuscript Found in a Copper Cylinder* (New York & London: Harper & Brothers, 1888), p. 9.
2. Frank Cowan, *Revi-Lona* (Greensburgh, Pa.: Tribune Press, n.d.), p. iii.
3. Frank Savile, *Beyond the Great South Wall* (New York: New Amsterdam Book Company, 1901), p. 184.
4. Will N. Harben, *The Land of the Changing Sun* (New York: The Merriam Company, 1894).
5. John Uri Lloyd, *Etidorhpa* (Cincinnati: John Uri Lloyd, 1895).
6. Henry S. Drayton, *In Oudemon* (New York: Grafton Press, 1901).
7. Robert Ames Bennet, *Thyra: A Romance of the Polar Pit* (New York: Henry Holt and Company, 1901).
8. David M. Parry, *The Scarlet Empire* (Indianapolis: The Bobbs-Merrill Company, 1906).
9. Richard Hatfield, *Geyserland, 9262 B.C.: Empiricism in Social Reform* (Washington, D.C.: Richard Hatfield, 1908).
10. Willis George Emerson, *The Smoky God* (Chicago: Forbes and Company, 1908), p. 28.
11. Louis P. Gratacap, *The Certainty of a Future Life on Mars* (New York: Irving Press, 1903); *The New Northland* (New York: T. Benton, 1915).
12. Albert Bigelow Paine, *The Great White Way* (New York: J. F. Taylor & Company, 1901), p. 224.
13. James Hilton, *Lost Horizon* (New York: William Morrow & Company, Author's Edition, 1973). Lo-Tsen joins Mallinson and Conway when they leave Shangri-La, but in the "Epilogue," one learns from the Chinese medical doctor who recalls the amnesiac Conway and the woman who accompanied him saying that ". . . she was most old—most old of any one I have ever seen" (p. 211).
14. H. Rider Haggard, *She*, in *Three Adventure Novels of H. Rider Haggard* (New York: Dover Publications, Inc., 1951), p. 2. All citations to Haggard are from this edition.
15. Haggard, *Allan Quatermain,* p. 635.

16. Margaret Atwood, "Superwoman Drawn and Quartered: The Early Forms of *She*," *Alphabet,* no. 10 (July 1965), pp. 65-82.
17. Mabel Fuller Blodgett, *At the Queen's Mercy* (Boston, New York, London: Lamson, Wolffe and Company, 1897).
18. Sidney J. Marshall, *The King of Kor; or She's Promise Kept. A Continuation of the Great Story of "She" by H. Rider Haggard* (Washington, D.C.: S. J. Marshall, 1903).
19. Charles Romyn Dake, *A Strange Discovery* (New York: J. J. Kimball, 1899).
20. Duffield Osborne, *The Secret of the Crater* (New York & London: G. P. Putnam's Sons, 1900).
21. John Reed Scott, *The Duke of Oblivion* (Philadelphia and London: J. B. Lippincott Company, 1914).
22. Edward T. Bouve, *Centuries Apart* (Boston: Little, Brown and Company, 1894).
23. William H. Wilson, *Rafnaland* (New York: Harper & Brothers, 1900).
24. Gustavus W. Pope, *A Journey to Mars* (New York: G. W. Dillingham, 1894); *Wonderful Adventures on Venus* (Boston: Arena Publishing Company, 1895).
25. Gustavus W. Pope, *A Journey to Mars* (Westport, Conn.: Hyperion Press, Inc., Classics of Science Fiction, 1974), pp. 215-16.
26. L. Moresby, *The Glory of Egypt: A Romance* (London and New York: T. Nelson, 1926).
27. T. A. Willard, *The Wizard of Zacna A Lost City of the Mayas* (Los Angeles: Murray & Gee, 1935); (Boston: The Stratford Company, Publishers, n.d.). Citations are to the latter edition.
28. Edison Marshall, *Ogden's Strange Story* (New York: H. C. Kinsey, 1934); reprinted in *Famous Fantastic Mysteries,* 11 (December 1949), 10-81. Citations are to the magazine reprint.
29. Marshall, *Ogden's Strange Story,* 17.
30. Edison Marshall, *Dian of the Lost Land* (New York: H. C. Kinsey, 1935); (Philadelphia and New York: Chilton Company Publishers, 1966). Citations are to the latter edition.
31. Clifford Smyth, *The Gilded Man* (New York: Boni & Liveright, 1918).
32. Robert Ames Bennet, *The Bowl of Baal,* with an introduction by Stuart Teitler (West Kingston, Rhode Island: Donald M. Grant, Publisher, 1975), p. 9.
33. Edgar Rice Burroughs, *Tarzan of the Apes* (New York: Ballantine Books, 1963), pp. 141-42.
34. Edgar Rice Burroughs, *The Return of Tarzan* (New York: Ballantine Books, 1975).
35. Edgar Rice Burroughs, *Tarzan and the Jewels of Opar* (New York: Ace Books, n.d.).
36. Edgar Rice Burroughs, *Tarzan and the City of Gold* (New York: Ballantine Books, 1975).
37. Edgar Rice Burroughs, *Tarzan Lord of the Jungle* (New York: Ballantine Books, 1972).
38. Edgar Rice Burroughs, *Escape on Venus* (New York: Ace Books, n.d.). The blurb on the back cover identifies Napier as the first astronaut. Recall that John Carter wills his own transmigration to Mars.
39. Edgar Rice Burroughs, *The Land of Hidden Men* (New York; Ace Books, 1973).
40. Edgar Rice Burroughs, *The People That Time Forgot* (New York: Ace Books, 1973).
41. Edgar Rice Burroughs, *Land of Terror* (New York: Ace Books, 1973).

Virgin Territory: The Bonds and Boundaries of Women in Science Fiction

Beverly Friend

Isaac Asimov once divided science fiction into three categories: gadget, adventure, and social, differentiating the three by means of their treatment of speculations regarding the invention of the automobile. A gadget SF story would concentrate on the car and its workings, climaxing with the new invention puttering down the street. Adventure SF would present the inventor with a beautiful daughter, expressly so that she might be kidnapped and ultimately rescued via judicious use of the new invention. Social SF would look beyond the invention itself to its ramifications. Anyone musing about the horse and buggy might have extrapolated a horseless carriage; but the author of social SF would envision the after-effects: traffic jams, highway death tolls, possibly even pollution.[1]

Now what has this to do with women in SF? Well, the writer of gadget fiction could always build a better model.

Earlier versions of this article appeared in *Extrapolation*, 14 (December 1972), 49-58, and *Science Fiction: The Classroom in Orbit* (Glassboro, N.J.: Educational Impact, Inc., 1974), pp. 19-26.

THE BONDS: WOMEN AS GADGETS (OR GADGETS AS WOMEN)

One of the first such models can be found in Lester del Rey's "Helen O'Loy" (1938), the short story of a robot whose name is derived from a combination of Helen of Troy and Helen made of alloy. She's a perfect housewife—learns about romance from television soap operas, cooks, cleans, and sobs her heart out when her "husband-inventor" arrives home late from work. At first unappreciated, a "Helen too cloy," she finally becomes valued as the perfect companion as she carefully lines her face and grays her hair to match her "mate's" aging. When he, a mere mortal, dies, Helen pens a final letter to the narrator:

> I've one last favor to ask of you. . . . There is only one thing for me to do when this is finished. Acid will burn out metal as well as flesh, and I'll be dead with Dave. Please see that we are buried together and that the morticians do not find my secret. Dave wanted it that way too. . . .

The narrator's final words bemoan his bachelor state, and he concludes, "But . . . there was only one Helen O'Loy."[2]

Frankly, one in SF is too many: a blatant statement of woman as mere appendage to man—a walking, talking doll who performs better as an android than she could possibly do as a human. It didn't stop at one, however; woman-as-robot was just too good an idea to limit until a veritable town had been thus populated. So, more than thirty years after the appearance of "Helen O'Loy," Ira Levin created *The Stepford Wives* (1972). These, too, are "perfect" creations, everything a machismo world would value. The "wives" never leave their homes except to shop for groceries and chauffeur the children. Their deepest satisfactions come from dazzlingly clean floors. They behold their sparkling-white laundry with all the fervor of television actresses touting the glories of specific washday soaps. As if this is not enough, they are also vibratingly orgasmic.

Here, Helen O'Loy has pervaded society; indeed, even more has happened. Helen was one-of-a-kind. She replaced women in the bachelor lives of the males in the story, but she did not replace a specific (flesh and blood) woman. There's a vast difference. The Stepford androids are not store-mannikins, meant to represent general femininity. They are replacements of specific people, the wives of the members of the Men's Club (and also the mothers of their children).

Not a twinge of remorse shakes the members of this Men's Club, not a moment of hesitation troubles them, because these androids are, in their eyes, better than the real thing. (The book never deals with the next step—replacing daughters as easily as wives.) And what makes this replacement even more appealing to the men involved is that these women had reflected liberated ideas, had attempted to achieve self-identification. Such a practice must be dispensed with so that the essential, important qualities—voice (taped by recorders), physical beauty (captured by artists' drawings, and improved upon), and housewifely values (programmed)—can remain to serve the happy males. One wonders why science fiction has not produced the counterpart story. It might, perhaps, be entitled "Hector O'Toole."

Women as gadgets have not been limited to robot-android possibilities. There are also cyborg stories. One such cyborg is Helga in Anne McCaffrey's *The Ship Who Sang* (1961). In this novel, physically deformed infants become encapsulated "brains"; that is, they are encased in metal shells which, in turn, are ultimately connected to a space ship so that an entire ship becomes a living entity controlled by a human brain. For both efficiency and companionship, these ships also have totally human partners known as "brawns" (in contrast, of course, to "brains"). However, neither category is sex-bound. While this particular work centers on Helga's life and adventures, McCaffrey is careful to introduce the fact that some of the ships are male and some of the brawns are female. She also states that teams may be of the same rather than of opposite sexes. Thus, within the framework of the book, the humanity of both cyborgs and humans is more important than the original sex of either. But this is an exception to the usual portrayal.

Another gadget-possibility in addition to machines replacing women, or machines physically combining with women, is the age-old theme of machines becoming human. The inanimate-to-animate fantasy that pervades literature has an initially appealing, heart-warming prospect. Children wish their dolls were alive. Adults name their cars. And in Robert Heinlein's *Time Enough for Love* (1973), a computer (in true Pinocchio tradition) gets the chance to become a real person.

In a voice echoing Helen O'Loy's final words, Minerva the (not-so-wise) computer says that she would not choose to outlive her makers. She is eager to reduce her mental processes, lose much of her data storage, and embrace mortality—all for love. She cries out, "*Would that I were a woman. . . .*"

When hero Lazarus Long reminds her that even if she were a woman, the object of her devotion (Ira) might not marry her, she retorts, "Lazarus, if Ira refuses me—refuses me utterly; he need not marry me—would you then be as difficult with me as you seem to have been with Llita? Or would you teach me 'Eros'?"

Lazarus saves the day with his answer: ". . . All right, dear, a solemn promise: If you do this . . . and Ira won't bed you, I'll take you to bed myself and do my best to wear you out! . . ."[3]

With this "incentive," Minerva takes a composite clone of 23 donor parents (forced to maturity in vitro) and becomes an honest-to-goodness female able to utter such profound lines as, "Will you kiss me? I'd like to kiss you; we've known each other almost a century and I've always liked you. Will you?"[4] These are her first words to her idol, Ira. Can one doubt the outcome?

If woman-as-gadget tends (with only a few exceptions) to mirror woman-as-idiot, this is not unique to the genre. Women seem to be just as idiotic in adventure SF.

THE BONDS: WOMAN AS OBJECT IN ADVENTURE SCIENCE FICTION

As early as 1895, Luis P. Senarens wrote *Lost in a Comet's Tail; or Frank Reade, Jr.'s Strange Adventure with his New Air Ship,* in which the hero saves three endangered seafarers (an old man, a handsome young blade, and a beautiful young female) as their ship founders in perilous seas. The girl is, of course, lashed to the foremast so that she will not be swept overboard. Now this is not as senseless as it first seems. When the three are finally safely aboard the air ship and stroll out onto its deck (as there were no such air ships in 1895, it was easy to speculate that they might have decks), poor Estelle, the fair damsel, immediately loses her hold on the rail and is swept over the side. "My God! My God! . . . She is gone, gone! Oh, save her, save her! My life is naught," cries Connell, her romantic counterpart.[5] Naturally, Frank Reade, Jr. does just that, and the tale proceeds.

Perhaps it is just as well that for years there weren't many women in adventure SF. Chaste, all male crews could then orbit distant planets and find the flora more stimulating than the fauna, and SF could be (and was) safely read by a vast—nearly exclusively male—adolescent audience.

Thus it really appeared that things might improve when an author equally noted for both juvenile and adult fiction, Robert Heinlein, wrote *Podkayne of Mars* (1962), an adventure tale with an adolescent heroine who initiates rather than responds to the action. Careful scrutiny reveals, however, that the old male line still predominates even if a girl rates the book's title and is never, never tied to a mast. Podkayne may have an I.Q. of 145, but her kid brother scores 160. Podkayne may be strong, but she knows, "It is a mistake for a girl to beat a male at any test of physical strength."[6] She is bright but willing to bow to the world's illusions, reasoning, "I'm smart enough not unnecessarily to show that I am smart . . . when I wrinkle my nose and look baffled, a man is usually only too glad to help me."[7] And worst of all, Podkayne swallows the party line: "We were designed for having babies. A baby is lots more fun than differential equations."[8] Thus she shifts her goals from a burning desire to be a space captain to the possibilities of becoming a pediatrician (one step beyond mere motherhood). "Building bridges and space stations and such gadgets is all very well . . . but a woman has more important work to do!"[9]

Heinlein's use of a fifteen-yearold girl as the main character of a science-fiction novel was highly praised by Anthony Boucher in *The 9th Annual of the Year's Best SF* (1963):

> . . . a shrewd and successful effort to widen the s-f audience by a teen-age heroine. Poddy's first-person narrative reveals her as a genuinely charming girl . . . and her creator as the master absolute of detailed indirect exposition of a future civilization.[10]

Alexei Panshin, noting these words and responding to them in his study, *Heinlein in Dimension,* states that he couldn't agree less. He continues, "I do agree that there is a place for young girls in science fiction (as well as old men, middle-aged women and any other advance over young men aged 20-30) but I don't think Heinlein has filled it."[11]

Then Panshin himself steps in to fill this gap with his Nebula Award Winning *Rite of Passage* (1968). What Anne McCaffrey's book is to gadget SF, Panshin's is to adventure SF: an outstanding exception which dares treat women realistically. Mia Havero, the young girl in the novel, lives in the closed society of a giant starship forever in orbit. Both as a population control and to assure survival of the fittest, the children on such a ship must undergo a test: a period of time spent on a planet, foraging for themselves. Some survive; many do not return. But the children are not carelessly cast adrift; rather, they are trained in the art of survival. Mia is no super heroine. She is an undersized, worried little girl, living with her father (her mother is busy as an artist and lives separately), and she goes through all the pangs and anxieties of childhood, including an unreasoning fear of moving from her accustomed environment to a new location on the ship. She struggles with small problems prior to meeting large ones. She struggles with herself, her interpersonal relationships, and her milieu. Sometimes she fails; ultimately she succeeds:

> Like the girl who first found out how to make fire, like the girl who invented the principle of the lever, like the girl who first had the courage to eat moldy goat cheese and found Roquefort, I had discovered something absolutely new in the world. Self-confidence, perhaps.

Both Mia and Podkayne have self-confidence, but only Mia's springs from self-awareness and personal growth. However, there is still one quarrel feminist criticism can aim at Mia—the same quarrel that can also be aimed at another heroine (a super heroine), Rydra Wong of Samuel Delany's *Babel-17*: she is an exception, a unique female in a masculine-dominated world. As Carolyn Wendell has cogently pointed out in her essay, "The Alien Species: A Study of Women Characters in the Nebula Award Winners":

> Mia and Rydra have been taught by males and interact with males. Neither has ever had a woman figure to learn from nor are they provided with any significant female peers. Though this type of heroine is preferable to the mental defective who is totally submissive to men, neither is completely autonomous and independent because both seem to be exceptions in a world of men.[13]

However, this may be caviling when a comparison is made with the usual "mental defective" portrayal within the genre. Podkayne, the first adolescent female science-fiction heroine, proselytizes the "party message," and so do nearly all of Robert Heinlein's heroines. In *Stranger in a Strange Land* (1961), the female characters—as sex objects—appear interchangeable (and often are). In *The Moon Is a Harsh Mistress* (1966), a perfectly sensible computer (much more sensible than Minerva), who is known as "Mike" becomes "Michelle" when conversing with the heroine of the book (Wyoming Knott—Why Not?) so that they can have comfortable girlie-chats. As Wyoh explains it:

> Don't worry about splitting her personality; she has plenty for any personality she needs. Besides, Mannie, it's much easier for both of us. Once she shifted, we took our hair down and cuddled up and talked girl talk as if we had known each other forever. For example, those silly pictures no longer embarrassed me—in fact we discussed pregnancies quite a lot. Michelle was terribly interested. She knows all about O.B. and G.Y. and so forth but just theory—and she appreciated the raw facts. Actually, Mannie, Michelle is much more a woman than Mike was a man.[14]

Obviously Michelle, the computer who knows theory but not actuality, is a forerunner of Minerva, who metamorphoses from computer to woman to experience "the real thing."

The "real thing" can also include "real babies" which, in turn, can provide "true happiness." In James Gunn's *The Listeners* (1972), Maria, the wife of project director Robert MacDonald, has been feeling depressed, left out of her husband's (galactic) concerns. She has even tried suicide. What saves her? Pregnancy, of course:

> An infant cried somewhere in the house. Maria looked happily. . . . 'This is Bobby, our son,' Maria said. If she had been alive before, she was doubly alive now, Thomas thought. This was the magnetism that turned painters toward madonnas for their subjects.[15]

Besides childbearing and inspiring painters, Maria does have one other skill, although a guest, not her husband, recognizes it:

> Maria drove. She handled the car skillfully for a woman, Mitchell thought, particularly for a beautiful woman.[16]

Well—if they can drive, perhaps they can also become scientists.

Susan Calvin, heroine of Asimov's Robot series, is an excellent scientist. Of course she is an old maid, thwarted, personally stunted so that she can ultimately relate better to robots than to humans. (Pamela Sargent notes a valid reason for this might be that "Asimov's ethical and endearing robots are better than people.")[17]

But how about a vital, red-blooded, wholesome (sexy) scientist. How about Lady Sandra Liddell Leonovna Bright Fowler, B.A., M.A., doctoral candidate in anthropology, Imperial University of Sparta, the *only* woman aboard the exploring spaceship in Larry Niven and Jerry Pournelle's *The Mote in God's Eye* (1974)? Scientist Fowler—who is endearingly called Sally throughout the book—is possibly the narrowest, most limited, prudish anthropologist in literature's history. Discussing sex (surely an anthropological concern) with an alien species, Sally gets involved in the following exchange:

'. . . do you have children aboard *MacArthur*?'
'Me? No!' Sally laughed again. 'I'm not even married.'

'. . . Who raises children born without marriage?'
'There are charities,' Sally said grimly. Her distaste was impossible to disguise.
'I take it you never . . .' The Motie paused delicately.

'So that if you aren't married you just don't—get together?'

Then after Sally has explained contraception, the Motie asks, "But a proper woman doesn't use them?" Sally replies in the negative but assures the alien that she will get married when she finds the right man (fortunately he is the captain of the ship).[18]

Remember that Sally is the only woman crew member. What of the problems that creates? It took two male authors to pen these lines:

> The only woman in the parsecs would have been a subject for speculation under any circumstances. Fights might have started over either of two questions. *What are my/your chances with her*? and *Is she being wasted*? But Sally had clearly chosen her man. It made life easier for those who worry over such problems and for those whose duty it is to stop fist fights.[19]

While it may be unfair to belittle the treatment of women in a genre noted for stereotyping men as Messianic heroes able to conquer everything before them—the moon, the planets of this solar system, the entire galaxy—a few authors who have attempted to deal with women in social SF, as defined by Asimov, have succeeded in achieving something beyond the scope of mainstream writing.

The Boundaries: Women In Social Science Fiction

When the author of social SF speculated on the ramifications of the invention of the automobile, he created a "what if" hypothesis, which could, upon examination, cast light upon shadowed problems. At its best, in this context, such an hypothesis goes beyond the speculation, "*What if* women were treated realistically in SF?" Such treatment would, necessarily, deal realistically with men, too, as does Roger Zelazny's "A Rose for Ecclesiastes" (1963), in which the hero-poet is homely, irritable, molded by early interpersonal relationships. Although this hero may love and even impregnate a female of a dying race, thereby offering hope for all her people, the heroine need not—and, indeed, does not—return his love, a sharp slap at all the thick and heavy romanticizing of feminine sexual response which has characterized so much of the genre since its beginnings in the last century.

The most notable speculations have raised such questions as "What if only females existed?" "What if different, even repulsive sexual characteristics were discovered?" "What if the sexes were combined to create a new, androgynous individual?" Such speculations possess possibilities for exploration and discussion impossible in any form of fiction other than SF.

Female Worlds

In 1956, John Wyndham wrote a story entitled "Consider Her Ways," that was noted more for its almost didactic presentation of ideas about women's role in the present than for the strength of its plot. Literally shot into the future by an injection of an experimental drug, heroine Jane Waterleigh finds herself in a maleless world where women have bred and categorized themselves into such roles as mothers and attendants, a vast female beehive. After a time spent trying to reject her sensory experiences as mere dream and struggling against her role as a breeder, Jane meets a historian who is able to give her a picture of how her twentieth-century world and her love of one man look to the members of a future outside her own limited experience. They begin a series of provocative discussions:

> At the beginning of the 20th century women were starting to have their chance to lead useful, creative, interesting lives. But that did not suit commerce; it needed them much more as mass consumers than as producers—except on the most routine levels. So Romance was

> adopted and developed as a weapon against their further progress and to promote consumption, and it was used intensively.
>
> Women must never for a moment be allowed to forget their sex, and to compete as equals. Everything had to have a feminine angle which must be different from the masculine angle, and be dinned in without ceasing. It would have been unpopular for manufacturers . . . to issue an order "back to the kitchen" but there were other ways. A profession without a difference, called "housewife," could be invented. The kitchen could be glorified and made more expensive; it could be made to seem desirable, and it could be shown that the way to reach this heart's desire was through marriage. So the presses turned out, by the hundred thousand a week, journals which concentrated the attention of women ceaselessly and relentlessly upon selling themselves to some man in order that they might achieve some small, uneconomic unit of a home upon which money could be spent.
>
> Whole trades adopted the romantic approach and the glamour was spread thicker and thicker in the articles, the write-ups, and most of all in the advertisements. . . .
>
> The air was filled with frustrated moanings. Women maundered in front of microphones yearning only to "surrender," and "give themselves," to adore and to be adored . . . the majority of women . . . were brought to a state of honestly believing that to be owned by some man and set down in a little brick box to buy all the things that the manufacturers wanted them to buy would be the highest form of bliss that life could offer.[20]

When Jane protests that that's not how it was, that she herself was there to experience what is only hearsay to the scholar, she is shaken by the arguments arrayed against her in the name of historical perspective. While, to her, "love makes the world go round," the future views romance as a catchword to enslave woman, equating the desire for romance with a selfishness that "breaks down all corporate loyalties"[21] and leads to her total exploitation. Finally, the historian points to the other, unglamorized face of romance: slavery and (the ultimate) death on the funeral pyre of a beloved male (shades of Helen O'Loy!).

The entire story is a castigation of the mores of our society. Ironically, it is experimentation with a new poison to control rats that has undone the male populace. Jane, however, as a brainwashed product of her own culture, returns to the present to try to thwart the chain of events leading to such a future. She fails.

A more positive note ends Philip Wylie's *The Disappearance* (1951, 1966). A disaster has struck. Women have disappeared from the face of the earth. No, it is the men who have disappeared. Really, it is both and neither. For each sex has disappeared for the other, leaving two single-sexed parallel worlds. Thus the extrapolation unfolds following the logical progression of what would happen if only one sex were left on earth. In the world run by men, technology continues. So do wars, as Russia and the U.S. accuse each other of having caused the calamity. In the world of women, technology falters. Communications (except for the telephone, staffed by female operators) are severed, fires break out, and ultimately disease runs rampant. Throughout there is the opportunity to realistically examine what happens when one half of a species has been kept in servitude:

> In women, cultural inclination had all but ruled out the possibility of imagination and logic. Females are regarded as "naturally" deficient in both. That attitude, which rose in the paleolithic, is part of man's inordinate self-assertion and he was able to establish it then simply because he was stronger. The abuse was never corrected and women of the twentieth century usually accepted it; fifty millenniums of indoctrination are bound to have an effect.
>
> Hence women, presented with the instantaneous vanishment of males, were in an extremely poor psychological condition to deal with the aftermath. Whatever pattern innately existed in them, what faculties they owned as individuals, what promptings, urges, intelligent ideas, logical extrapolations and valid hunches they were capable of were hidden; they found themselves without a tradition, without experience, without confidence, and without know-how.[22]

When Wylie has the women behave absurdly in a given situation, he offers a reasonable explanation for such behavior. One such example occurs when an all-female congress gathers for its first meeting. The first note on the agenda becomes the selection of a suitable uniform:

> The ladies of the cabinet, at that time, were still in the grip of intense shock, the shock not only of the instantaneous loss of all males but the appalling disasters that had ensued. If their practice of clinging to the frivolities and vanities of their previous lives was absurd, it was also pitiful: they knew nothing else. Even the fact that they were able to

> quarrel over a costume for themselves when the whole of America cried out for aid and direction and organization was, in a way, evidence of a certain kind of character. They had the strength, in the face of everything, to sustain what they did know and feel. It was not their fault that they were hopelessly unprepared in mind and personality for the burden they accepted.[23]

All the characters in this novel mature. The male hero comes to understand the wife he has lost and to accept the fact that a double standard has not, and should not have, been part of their lives. His wife becomes a total person from the experience. Their daughter gives them final insight into themselves:

> 'Ask Paula.' His daughter smiled. 'Ask her about herself too. Ask Paula what it means when a mother wants a boy and a father, too, but you're a girl, so she calls you Paula because you didn't turn out Paul. Then, when you marry, you pass it along. Edwinna. And Theodora. Ask her.'[24]

But most of the writers of science fiction have been male (and most of the readers have been, too). What happens when you ask Janet, or Jeannine, or Jael, or Joanna Russ? In 1972, Russ's short story, "When It Changed," appeared in Harlan Ellison's *Again, Dangerous Visions.* In Ellison's introduction to the story, he says:

> Men have had it their way for thousands of years. The machismo concept, the dominant male attitude, the picture of women as weak and essentially brainless, the deification of Mars as god and war and male supremacy . . . these have led us to a world of futility, hatred, bigotry, sexual confusion, pollution and despair. Perhaps it is time the women took a turn at bat. They can certainly do no worse. . . .[25]

He also praises women authors, stating ". . . as far as I'm concerned, the best writers in SF today are the women." But his final words, about Russ, are these: "And further, she looks infinitely better in a bikini than any of the editors who rejected her novel."[26]

"When It Changed" tells the story of the planet Whileaway, an all female world where men have been wiped out by a plague. The resultant civilization, a highly intelligent one, has advanced quite successfully. Then men from Earth land, assuming that it is axiomatic that Whileaway will be a far better place for their arrival.

From this small, but provocative beginning has grown Russ's latest novel, *The Female Man* (1975), a fragmented angry work given its form by the split perceptions of Janet, Jeannine, Jael and Joanna. More than the plot, more than characterization, more than feministic message, there is anger:

dress for The Man
smile for The Man
talk wittily to The Man
sympathize with The Man
flatter The Man
understand The Man
defer to The Man
entertain The Man
keep The Man
live for The Man[27]

Janet comes from Whileaway to Earth, sees, and reacts to society. She meets Jeannine, a brainwashed product of the concept of romance:

Men succeed. Women get married.
Men fail. Women get married.
Men enter monasteries. Women get married.
Men start wars. Women get married.
Dull, dull. . . .[28]

Russ once wrote in an essay that "almost all the characterological sex differences we take for granted are in fact learned and not innate."[29] Now, in *The Female Man* she constructs a hilarious scene to dramatize this. In a battle-between-the-sexes, each consults the appropriate book (pink or blue) for proper insults to hurl—to attain the desired "learned" response:

The little blue book was rattling around in my purse. I took it out and turned to the last thing he had said ('You stupid broad' et cetera). Underneath was written *Girl backs down—cries—manhood vindi-*

cated. Under "Real Fight With Girl" was written *Don't hurt (except whores).* I took out my own pink book, for we all carry them, and turning to the instructions under "Brutality" found:

Man's bad temper is the woman's fault. It is also the woman's responsibility to patch things up afterwards.[30]

This is a battle between two individuals. But part of the book focuses on a (future) world where the battle encompasses everyone, where males and females are enemies, where surrogates replace "the real thing" (at last, Hector O'Toole. But here he is called "Davy," and his purpose is *strictly* for sex).

At the 1975 Midwest Modern Language Association meeting in St. Louis, Joanna Russ read one of the most personal papers I've ever heard presented. In it she recalled one of the most shaping experiences of her art. It was 1956, in a writing class at Cornell. Russ had written the story of a high school dance, and the pain of the wallflower as she hides in the ladies' room, staring at herself in the mirror and "saying 'bloody green ghost' 25 times so she won't emerge too soon."[31] The story, Russ says, was judged "funny but trivial." Another story won the teacher's accolades, a story which Russ writes "was about rape, a fight in a bar, and a woman who was thrown down and 'taken' brutally by her husband on the floor she was scrubbing just after she'd come out of the hospital for the excision of a coccyxal cyst (the odors of which were described at length)." Russ notes, "The story ended, 'That night their idiot child was conceived.'" She learned a searing lesson from that experience. She writes:

> I ended my college career convinced that I knew nothing of real life, that high school dances weren't important (though I had suffered horribly at them), and that Great Literature lay in a realm I could never enter because as sure as God made little green sophomores, I was never going to a fist fight in a bar, piss in a urinal, buy a whore, fight bulls, hunt whales, or rape my wife.[32]

However, she did grow up to write *The Female Man* which, whatever its artistic faults, is surely the most pointed and quotable book to come out of science fiction, filled with such profound truths as "but you can't imbibe someone's success by fucking them."[33]

Of course, the very sex act itself can offer an extrapolative theme for science fiction.

ALIEN-SEXED WORLDS

In Philip Farmer's story, "My Sister's Brother" (1970), such unappetizing sex is presented that—like our reaction to the movie *Futz*—our own tolerance for anything foreign to us is sharply tested. As "My Sister's Brother" opens, the hero, Lane, is lost and alone on a desolate planet. Rescued and befriended by an alien female, Mahrseeya, he severs the bond of gratitude by destroying her "child" when he's confronted by a sexual anatomy and behavior that arouse his total disgust: the presence and biological necessity of a worm which acts both as phallus and offspring in fertilization between two members of the alien species. I cite this story more for Farmer's depiction of the human male than of the alien female, for there is no touching upon one characterization without the other, no attempting to see the female in social SF without looking at the effect the male has had upon her condition.

All the males in Farmer's story are violent. Among the domestic animals, the male is caged as a mad killer. Paired with him in temperament is Lane, interpreted by the aliens as a "vicious beast" who defends himself by saying, "I could not accept her love and still remain a man! Not the kind of man. . . ."[34] His victim, Mahrseeya, forgives him, prays for him, and hopes that education will ultimately civilize him.

ANDROGYNOUS WORLDS

The irrationality of the human male when presented with phenomena outside his own moral experience is also stressed in Theodore Sturgeon's *Venus Plus X* (1960), a novel which explores humanity's reaction to a world populated by single-sexed creatures, part male, part female. Hero Charlie Johns wakes in what he believes to be a future world inhabited by the Ledom. They desire him to study carefully their culture and respond emotionally to it, promising that when he has studied it sufficiently so that they may gauge his reaction, they will return him to his present. Part of his education includes listening to a learning tape which attempts to inform him about his past and its psychology:

> You come from a time and place in which the maleness of the male and the femaleness of the female, and the importance of their difference, were matters of almost total preoccupation.
>
> Begin, then, with this . . . regard it as mainly a working hypothesis . . . *There are more basic similarities than differences between men and women.*[35]

To substantiate this claim, the tape goes on to give illustrations from anatomy and to stress differences that are culturally rather than inherently induced:

> . . . all through history, in virtually every culture and country, there has indeed been a 'woman's province' and a 'man's province,' and in most cases the differences between them have been exploited to fantastic, sometimes sickening extremes.
>
> *Why*? . . .
>
> Humanity has insisted upon it; made it an article of faith. . . .
>
> For there is in mankind a deep and desperate necessity to feel superior. In any group there are some who genuinely are superior . . . but it is easy to see that within the parameters of any group, be it culture, club, nation, profession, only a few are really superior; the mass, clearly, are not.
>
> But it is the will of the mass that dictates the mores, . . . And if a unit of the mass wants to feel superior, it will find a way . . . in slavery and genocide, xenophobia and snobbery, race prejudice and sex differentiation. Given a man who, among his fellows, has no real superiority, you are faced with a bedeviled madman who, if superiority is denied him, and he cannot learn one or earn one, will turn on something weaker than himself and *make it inferior*. The obvious, logical, handiest subject for this inexcusable indignity is his woman.
>
> *He could not do this to anyone he loved.*
>
> If, loving, he could not have insulted this close, so-little different other half of himself, he could never have done it to his fellow man. Without this force in him, he could never have warred, nor persecuted, nor in pursuit of superiority lied, cheated, murdered and stolen.[36]

For these reasons the Ledom (the name reversed is 'model') renounce the past. They are not, however, as Charlie imagines, inhabitants of some golden future, mutants who have risen from the ashes of a vast human holocaust. Rather, they are self-made, surgically adapted creatures inhabiting a Shangri-la adjacent to and congruent with Earth. This revelation shatters Charlie's approval of their culture:

> '. . . You thought very well of us a few hours ago. What changed you?'
>
> 'Only the truth.'
>
> 'What truth?'
>
> 'That there is no mutation.'
>
> 'Our doing it ourselves makes that much difference? Why is what we have done worse to you than a genetic accident?'
>
> 'Just because you do it. . . . Men marrying men. Incest, perversion, there isn't anything rotten you don't do.' . . .
>
> '. . . Tell me, Charlie Johns: what would homo sap. do if we shared the world with them and they knew our secrets?'
>
> 'We'd exterminate you down to the last queer kid . . . and stick that one in a side-show. . . . Get me out of here.'[37]

Again, as in Farmer's story, it is the irrationality of the male that is stressed after it has been contrasted with the rationality of something other than itself—most especially if that something other contains a feminine rather than a totally masculine approach.

Another attempt to fuse the sexes and to examine male reaction is Ursula LeGuin's *The Left Hand of Darkness* (1969). Here the subjects are Gethenians, inhabitants of the planet Winter. Unlike the Ledom, who have both sets of sexual organs and mutually impregnate each other (both parents then bearing fraternal twins), the Gethenians have fluctuating sexual dominance. That is, most of the time they are neuter, having no sexual desire. When they enter the monthly fertile season known as "kemmer"

> . . . the sexual impulse is tremendously strong . . . controlling the entire personality, subjecting all other drives to its imperative. When the individual finds a partner in kemmer, hormonal secretion is further stimulated . . . until in one partner either a male or female dominance is established. The genitals engorge or shrink accordingly, foreplay

> intensifies, and the partner, triggered by the change, takes on the other sexual role. . . . Normal individuals have no predisposition to either sexual role in kemmer, they do not know whether they will be male or female, and have no choice in the matter.[38]

Resultant problems are quickly solved. The narrator, a male visitor to the planet knows of no case where both individuals become the same sex, and pregnancy keeps the female role stable for the gestation period. Also, to facilitate being in kemmer at a desired time, drugs may be taken.

Now a society built on such a hypothesis certainly poses some provocative possibilities:

> Anyone can turn his hand to anything. This sounds very simple, but its psychological effects are incalculable. The fact that everyone between seventeen and thirty-five or so is liable to be. . . . 'tied to childbearing' implies that no one is quite so thoroughly 'tied down' here as women, elsewhere, are likely to be—psychologically or physically . . . therefore nobody here is quite so free as a male anywhere else.
>
> [There is] . . . no myth of Oedipus.
>
> [There is] . . . no unconsenting sex, no rape . . . coitus can be performed only by mutual invitation and consent; otherwise it is not possible. Seduction certainly is possible, but it must have to be awfully well timed.
>
> [There is] . . . no division of humanity into strong and weak halves, protective/protected, dominant/submissive, owner/chattel, active/passive.[39]

Genly Ai, the narrator, studies the inhabitants of Winter and attempts to get them to accept their place in a galactic federation, to recognize themselves as the inhabitants of just one of a myriad of planets orbiting a myriad of suns. As he educates them about the universe "outside," he, in turn, gains knowledge of that which lies "within" as he comes to examine the role his own maleness has played in his approach to life:

> When you meet a Gethenian you cannot and must not do what a bisexual naturally does, which is to cast him in the role of Man or Woman, while adopting towards him a corresponding role dependent

> on your expectations of the patterned or possible interactions between persons of the same or opposite sex. . . . This is almost impossible for our imagination to accept. What is the first question we ask about a newborn baby? . . . In our world a man wants his virility regarded, a woman wants her femininity appreciated. On Winter they will not exist. One is respected and judged only as a human being. It is an appalling experience.

The ultimate moment in the shaping of Genly Ai comes as he travels thousands of miles over a sheet of glacial ice to escape imprisonment and possible death. Beholden to Estraven, a Gethenian diplomat who befriends him and masterminds the escape, Ai responds as an intolerant male to what is feminine about his companion:

> I was galled by his patronizing. He was a head shorter than I, and built more like a woman than a man, more fat than muscle; when we hauled together I had to shorten my pace to his, hold in my strength so as not to outpull him: a stallion in harness with a mule—'You're no longer ill, then?'
> 'No, of course I'm tired. So are you.'
> 'Yes, I am,' he said. 'I was anxious about you. We have a long way to go.'
> He had not meant to patronize. He had thought me sick and sick men take orders. He was frank, and expected a reciprocal frankness that I might not be able to supply. He, after all, had no standards of manliness, of virility, to complicate his pride . . . perhaps I could dispense with the more competitive elements of my masculine self-respect, which he certainly understood as little as I understood his shifgrether [formal behavior code].[41]

While LeGuin, in *The Left Hand of Darkness,* takes the opportunity to speculate on the genetic evolution of her characters, proposing that they might have been the result of a human experiment attempting to create a nonmilitant race, her main thrust is not at the Gethenians and their bisexuality, but at Genly Ai's reaction to them. He is not the destructive, irrational representative of masculine narrowness which destroys what it cannot understand and fears what defies its conventionality. Rather, like Gulliver among the Houyhnhnms, Genly Ai becomes so involved with the essential humanity of the Gethenians that when his eyes again turn on his own species, he can sense their essential incompleteness:

> . . . they all looked strange to me, men and women, well as I knew them. Their voices sounded strange; too deep, too shrill. They were like a troupe of great, strange animals, of two different species: great apes with intelligent eyes, all of them in rut, in kemmer. . . . They took my hand, touched me, held me. I managed to keep myself in control. . . .[42]

When I began this article, the arrangement seemed obvious: from gadget, to adventure, to social science fiction; in social science fiction, the development from worlds completely of women to androgynous worlds. But that was before Russ wrote her book; that was for an earlier article. Now, it is impossible to go back after such a cry of pain.

Sturgeon and LeGuin's answers seem a little pat after Russ. Oh, they tell a better story. There is a smoother plot, clear demarcation of scene: a beginning, a middle, an end, and there is suspense. Everything is solved. The story is over. But for Russ it is not. In an earlier article I said that it is authors like Farmer, Sturgeon, and LeGuin who, looking, look seriously; who, writing, create an entire universe to explore their themes. These are the authors who have done more than change the stereotyped super-man space captain into a super-girl. They truly extrapolate rather than recreate such pitiful creatures as the standard walking womb. These are the authors writing significant science fiction today and writing it well. I still believe that. They are taking a fiction which reflects fact and focusing it back onto the real world to illumine it. But they present a problem solved and Russ presents a problem a-solving.

In the earlier article, I also smugly wrote that Isaac Asimov once said science fiction could be divided into three categories, and he gave the greatest praise to the third, for in social SF ideas are developed, characters become rounded, speculations are logical and well thought out. It is in this category that the most serious consideration of women and their role has been expressed.

I concluded that perhaps the next critical book on SF would not do as did Sam Lundwall's paperback, *Science Fiction: What It's All About* (1971); that is, have a chapter heading such as "Women, Robots, and Other Peculiarities." Robots have attained great maturity and equal status; now it's time for women to achieve as much.

Now I must add it's time for women to achieve as much both in science fiction and in the real world. Writing from pain, and superimposing the discipline of art upon that pain, a woman may reach a time when Ellison won't mention a bikini, and readers won't carry an awareness of the author's sex into a prejudgment of the story. As Pamela Sargent wrote:

> Science fiction can provide women with possible scenarios for their own future development. . . . *Only SF and fantasy literature can show us women in entirely new or strange surroundings. It can explore what we might become if and when the present restrictions on our lives vanish, or show us new problems and restrictions that might arise.* It can show us the remarkable woman as normal where past literature shows her as the exception. Will we become more like men, ultimately indistinguishable from them with all their faults and virtues, or will we bring new concerns and values to society, perhaps changing men in the process? How will biological advances, and the greater control they will bring us over our bodies, affect us? What might happen if women in the future are thrown back into a situation in which male dominance might reassert itself? What might actually happen if women were dominant? How might future economic systems affect our societal roles? These are only a few of the questions. . . .[43]

"These are only a few of the questions" which science fiction of the future may choose to dramatize in its many worlds.

NOTES

1. Isaac Asimov, "Social Science Fiction," in Dick Allen, ed., *Science Fiction: The Future* (New York: Harcourt Brace Jovanovich, 1971), p. 273.
2. Lester del Rey, "Helen O'Loy," in Robert Silverberg, ed., *The Science Fiction Hall of Fame* (New York: Avon Books, 1971), p. 73.

3. Robert A. Heinlein, *Time Enough for Love* (New York: G. P. Putnam's Sons, 1973). p.251.
4. Heinlein, p. 379.
5. Luis P. Senarens, "Lost in a Comet's Tail; or Frank Reade, Jr.'s Strange Adventure with His New Air Ship," in Sam Moskowitz, ed., *Masterpieces of Science Fiction* (Cleveland and New York: The World Publishing Company, 1966), p. 290.
6. Robert A. Heinlein, *Podkayne of Mars* (New York: Berkley Medallion, 1963), p. 56.
7. Heinlein, *Podkayne of Mars,* p. 9.
8. Heinlein, *Podkayne of Mars,* p. 127.
9. Heinlein, *Podkayne of Mars,* p. 175.
10. Alexei Panshin, *Heinlein in Dimension* (Chicago: Advent Publishers, Inc., 1968), pp. 103-04.
11. Panshin, p. 104.
12. Alexei Panshin, *Rite of Passage* (New York: Ace Books, 1968), p. 93.
13. Carolyn Wendell, "The Alien Species: A Study of Women Characters in the Nebula Award Winners," unpublished paper, p. 12.
14. Robert A. Heinlein, *The Moon Is a Harsh Mistress* (New York: Berkley Medallion, n.d.), p. 50.
15. James Gunn, *The Listeners* (New York: Charles Scribner's Sons, 1972), pp. 65, 66.
16. Gunn, p. 111.
17. Pamela Sargent, "Introduction: Women in Science Fiction," in *Women of Wonder* (New York: The Vintage Press, 1974), p. xl.
18. Larry Niven and Jerry Pournelle, *The Mote in God's Eye* (New York: Pocket Books, Inc., 1975), p. 246.
19. Niven and Pournelle, p. 435.
20. John Wyndham, "Consider Her Ways," in Damon Knight, ed., *A Science Fiction Argosy* (New York: Simon & Schuster, Inc., 1972), pp. 96-97.
21. Wyndham, p. 97.
22. Philip Wylie, *The Disappearance* (New York: Pocket Books, Inc., n.d.), p. 59.
23. Wylie, p. 174.
24. Wylie, p. 372.
25. Harlan Ellison, "Introduction" to Joanna Russ, "When It Changed," in Harlan Ellison, ed., *Again, Dangerous Visions* (New York: Signet Books, 1972), 1:268.
26. Ellison, p. 271.
27. Joanna Russ, *The Female Man* (New York: Bantam Books, 1975), p. 29.
28. Russ, p. 126.
29. Joanna Russ, "Afterword: When It Changed," in Harlan Ellison, *Again, Dangerous Visions,* 1: 279.
30. Russ, *The Female Man,* p. 47.
31. Joanna Russ, "Creating Positive Images of Women: A Writer's Perspective," unpublished paper presented at the Women and Literature Forum of the Midwestern Modern Language Association, St. Louis, 1975, p. 1.
32. Russ, "Creating Positive Images of Women," p. 2.
33. Russ, *The Female Man,* p. 65.
34. Philip José Farmer, "My Sister's Brother," in Richard Ofshe, ed., *Sociology of the Possible* (Englewood Cliffs, N.J.: Prentice-Hall, Inc., 1970), p. 60.
35. Theodore Sturgeon, *Venus Plus X* (New York: Pyramid Books, 1960), p. 123.
36. Sturgeon, pp. 125, 126.
37. Sturgeon, pp. 151-52.
38. Ursula LeGuin, *The Left Hand of Darkness* (New York: Ace Books, 1969), p. 90.

39. LeGuin, p. 93.
40. LeGuin, p. 94.
41. LeGuin, pp. 207-08.
42. LeGuin, p. 279.
43. Sargent, p. ix.

Science Fiction as Fictive History

Robert H. Canary

In his well-known 1957 lecture at the University of Chicago, Robert Heinlein suggested that almost all science fiction could be covered by defining the field as "realistic speculation about possible future events, based solidly on adequate knowledge of the real world, past and present, and on a thorough understanding of the nature and significance of the scientific method."[1] This definition certainly covered most of Heinlein's work to that date. It is less obviously applicable to the best work being done today, when the "modern" science fiction of the 1950s seems one of those "lost literatures" set as the topic for this year's (1974) MMLA. Two of the most perceptive current critics of speculative fiction, Alexei and Cory Panshin, believe that "science fiction . . . is fantasy," and they cite Heinlein's definition only by reference to "the Heinlein Delusion—realism."[2] I believe that Heinlein's lecture, including his definition of the genre, retains some critical viability as a starting point. In what follows, I would like to suggest the relevance of certain concepts from historiography and

This article was published in *Extrapolation,* 16 (December 1974), 81-95.

the philosophy of history to the definition, analysis, and history of science fiction.

There is a sense, of course, in which all novels are "fictive histories"; Fielding, for example, presented his greatest novel as *The History of Tom Jones, a Foundling.* Mainstream novels are fictive histories in yet another sense; whether laid in today's Detroit or fifth-century Athens, they take place within what is a generally agreed-upon historical reality.[3] The average reader's grasp of history is weak enough that an historical novel may be quite inaccurate without violating his sense of historical reality, but he will not accept as an historical novel one in which, say, the South has won the Civil War. A novel laid in such a world (like Ward Moore's *Bring the Jubilee*), an "alternate probability" world, is generally considered science fiction, as are stories laid in prehistory (like William Golding's *The Inheritors*). What links these settings to the future locales of most science-fiction stories is their being outside the known boundaries of historical reality.

Does being outside the bounds of historical reality make such stories fantasies? To save us from playing with words, this question must be rephrased: can we still make a useful critical distinction between science fiction and fantasy as forms of speculative fiction? I think that we can and that the clue lies in Heinlein's insistence that science fiction be "realistic, . . . based solidly on adequate knowledge of the real world" and so on. He was defining fantasy as "imaginary-and-not-possible" and realism as "imaginary-but-possible," sometimes violating orthodox theories but not "the factual universe of our experience."[4] Science fiction, then, presents a fictive history set outside our agreed upon historical reality but claiming to be consistent with our experience of that reality, to operate by more or less the same rules. Fantasy deliberately breaks one or more of those conventional rules. Debates over whether a given work is science fiction, mainstream fiction, or fantasy can then be seen as debates over the nature of historical reality and the rules by which it operates.

The Panshins have been led to dismiss Heinlein's insistence on "realism" because, like many others, they confuse it with surface plausibility. This is not entirely unfair to the science fiction of the 1950s, which may indeed have overemphasized plausibility at the expense of other virtues, but it does not do justice to Heinlein's critical position. The realism/fantasy dichotomy, as he uses it, is best seen as applying at the level of *strategy,* the work's basic approach to its materials. The materials may be similar, but to call one's monster a mutant or a Martian is to assert that his monstrous qualities result from the operation of accepted rules, and to call witchcraft "psi phenomena" is to assert that levitation, teleportation, and the like are rule-governed activities open to scientific investigation. As the approach varies, so does the implicit appeal to the reader; we might say that science fiction depends more on intellectual ingenuity, and fantasy more on imaginative freedom. Plausibility, in any case, operates at the level of *tactics,* the narrative techniques employed to make the work carry emotional conviction, given its initial premises. The best fantasies are the most plausible in this sense, although we do not need to grant the intellectual possibility of vampires to be properly terrified by a vampire story. And there are, of course, science-fiction stories which are completely possible but completely implausible.[5]

Science fiction's implicit claim to operate by the same rules as historical reality means that it is inevitably speculating about the nature of those rules, implying that some are accidents of our history and subject to change, while others are relatively immutable "laws of history" and "facts of human nature." Bad science fiction dates itself more rapidly than bad fantasy, not so much because of scientific advances (which have not spoiled Wells's works, for example) as because of changing historical conceptions. The gee-whiz, double-talk science of John W. Campbell's *The Mightiest Machine* (1935), recently reprinted, has by no means vanished from science fiction. Far more unacceptable is the complacent racism with which one of Campbell's characters explains how colonists from Mu bred true in Europe but founded civilizations elsewhere which foundered because they interbred with native savages: "till at length the blood of the colonists was overcome by the poorer blood of many native strains, and the civilization vanished. . . . Only the undiluted Ma-jhay-anhu blood lived to reach a civilization that endured fairly well."[6] What makes this an echo of an earlier time is not simply the improbable (Mu) nor the scientifically implausible (good and bad "blood") but the cultural chauvinism of its history of mankind.

A few science-fiction novels have been conscious speculations on the meaning of history—one thinks of Wells's *The Time Machine,* Olaf Stapledon's *Last and First Men* and *The Star Maker* or Arthur C. Clarke's *Childhood's End.* All of these are based on linear philosophies of history; all but Wells's are teleological, even theological, in their import, a theme also carried out in Clarke's script for *2001.* Civilizations rise and fall, but man moves on to his destiny, which is God. Lines, after all, connect points, and the easiest way to devise a linear view of history is to postulate an end point; the two points of the present and the end serve to define the line between.

Extrapolative science fiction is also linear in historical conception. The two points which define its lines represent trends or known possibilities in the present, which are then projected into the future. Much early science fiction is linear in a very simplistic way. *The Mightiest Machine,* for example, assumes a linear development of man's scientific knowledge with no real changes in his social organization—in 2079, entrepreneur capitalism is still the basic economic system, Germany and America are still the leading industrial powers, while the battle between the Teffel and the Ma-jhay-anhu has been going on for thousands of years, fueled by no more rational impulse than the natural enmity between the good guys and the bad guys.

In the 1940s, extrapolative science fiction became more sophisticated, exploring the effect of scientific advance on the texture of society. Robert Heinlein was an important influence in the changeover; the reasons are apparent in his very first story, "Life Line" (first printed in the August 1939 *Astounding*).[7] Pinero's machine in this story can predict the time of any man's death, and the story conflict arises out of the effects of this on the life insurance business, but Heinlein also depicts its effect on the general public and on various social institutions concerned with science, law, medicine, and journalism. The gain in surface plausibility was what made Heinlein influential among his fellows; in this and in more sophisticated efforts over the next few years, he showed how one could give new life and salability to hackneyed plots (like the marvelous invention of "Life Line").[8] The immediate sources of this plausibility are tactical devices like Heinlein's throw-away references to various aspects of society; the ultimate source of this plausibility is the greater realism of Heinlein's narrative strategy, his insistence on pursuing more completely than most the social consequences of the changed conditions which are his premise.

The title of "Life Line" suggests the linear view of history, a view also embodied in the charts which were soon to expound Heinlein's "Future History" series. But as linear extrapolation admits the complexity and interdependence of society, the extrapolative enterprise becomes more difficult, less plausible in itself. If one is aiming at realistic projection and lacks the religious or political faith that would provide a teleological end-point, linear extrapolation is viable only in the short run. This may explain why many of the stories of the 1950s, a period when Heinlein was still an important, formative influence, confined themselves to short-run extrapolations.[9] In its first version, Heinlein's "Future History" chart had only one story listed between 1990 (fifty years in the future) and 2070; the gap represents the difference between short-run extrapolation and long-range speculation.[10]

But just as we must distinguish between plausibility and realism, so we must distinguish realism as a strategy from realistic projection as a goal. In point of fact, most linear extrapolations take as the defining point of the line trends in the present. Their slogan might well be the title of Heinlein's first serial, "If This Goes On—" (*Astounding,* February, March 1940). Since linear extrapolation inevitably implied social commentary, a number of writers in the 1950s consciously made use of the genre as what Kingsley Amis has called "an instrument of social diagnosis and warning."[11] In doing so, they were realizing a potential of the form obvious from the beginning—*The Time Machine* and almost all of Wells's science-fiction novels belong in the same category. Even where the author has limited the number of variables in the interests of social commentary, the linear extrapolation of present-day trends remains primarily a short-range business. Frederik Pohl's *The Age of the Pussyfoot* first saw publication in 1965, but is in the form of the Pohl-Kornbluth collaborations of the 1950s; in an "Author's Note" to its book version, he acknowledges that its time scale (five centuries) is probably too long, that five decades would have been sufficient.[12]

In many ways, *The Age of the Pussyfoot* is as good a novel as the Pohl-Kornbluth collaboration, *The Space Merchants* (1953), serialized in 1952 as "Gravy Planet." Yet the latter became an instant classic, winning praise from the most severe critics, while *The Age of the Pussyfoot* aroused no special comment at all.[13] Leaving aside the validity of my judgment of their relative merits, the differences in reception still say a good deal about the critical climate of the field in the 1950s and 1960s. One reason for the change, I believe, was an increased sensitivity to deficiencies inherent in linear extrapolation which do not aspire to be realistic projections. Literature of social commentary (including non-science-fiction) customarily employs stock, typical characters as reflectors of the social scene; to explore that scene more fully, it customarily employs certain stock plots (rebellion, travellers in space or time) which allow for exposition as a plot necessity.[14] The focus of the reader's interest is on the scene. Linear extrapolation which focuses on particular aspects of social reality cannot dwell on those aspects of present reality left unchanged without a loss in surface plausibility, but it avoids them only at the cost of a certain thinness of the social scene. It is therefore even more dependent on the intellectual appeal of its leading ideas.[15] Unfortunately, familiar ideas do not have the continuing appeal of familiar plots; as the social criticism of the 1950s became conventionalized and predictable itself, it had little left to offer its readers.

For authors committed to realistic projection, cyclic philosophies of history have an obvious advantage, particularly in dealing with long-range futures. If one assumes that history is a series of variations on repeated themes, one can anticipate that the effect of given changes (galactic travel) will resemble earlier responses to similar conditions (difficulties in transportation and communication); one can thus set one's plot in a scene which will be familiar to the reader (attempts to provide through personal loyalty to an Emperor, fragmentation of the Empire). It is not surprising, then, that Oswald Spengler is one of the few philosophers of history to have left any trace in commercial science fiction; James Blish has called attention to the use of Spengler in A. E. van Vogt's work and his own.[16] Cyclic views of the historical process also permit the author to comment on current social conditions without the plausibility problems of linear extrapolation; Isaac Asimov, whose own *Foundation* trilogy is explicitly based on a cyclic view of history, believes that science fiction "is social experimentation on paper."[17]

In practice, though, science fiction inspired by cyclic conceptions of history has concerned itself less with social experimentation than with historical reflection. *The Moon Is a Harsh Mistress,* for example, is set in 2075, and Heinlein deliberately builds in a number of parallels with the American Revolution. This novel does not pretend to instruct us in the probable course of events once a Moon colony is established; we are, however, led to reflect on the nature and mechanics of revolutions, on what was accident and what was essence in the American Revolution. To some extent, of course, Heinlein is simply exploiting the parallels as an easy way of lending emotional force to his story—something one might say even more accurately of some other such stories, like Asimov's *Pebbles in the Sky,* with its unmotivated parallels with the New Testament. But to the extent that Heinlein is consciously speculating on the meaning of the historical process, he is exploiting and bringing under control one of the built-in potentialities of the genre.

I do not mean to imply that science fiction is only a fictionalized form of speculative philosophy of history, nor that the linear extrapolative and cyclic modes are the only ones possible. Literature, dreams, and madness are multi-determined forms of behavior; and though the Galactic Empire still rules in many a story, we seem to have passed through our cycle of stories based on cyclic views of history. We might note that serious philosophers (at least in the Anglo-American tradition) rarely concern themselves with the speculative philosophy of history any more, and that professional historians have for most of this century been suspicious of most attempts to find large patterns of meaning in history.[18] Neither group has shown much enthusiasm for prospects of applying the "models" of social science to the data of history.[19] Philosophers have been busy arguing whether we may be said to have anything that could be called "historical knowledge"; historians have been rather complacently sure that they know some facts about the past, but they have generally remained more impressed with its uniqueness, its otherness. The history of our own time is certainly not such as to encourage one's faith that we can make sense of history as a whole (this may have something to do with the current vogue for the occult). In this intellectual climate, it is natural to find that many science-fiction depictions of the long-range future stress the otherness of the societies they depict. In American science fiction, Delany is the most obvious example.[20]

We might term works laid in a distant and distinctly alien future "linear nonextrapolative." Although the speculative freedom offered by such frameworks obviously brings science fiction closer to fantasy, it would be unfair to assume that they are no longer covered by Heinlein's definition. What has changed is "the factual universe of our experience in the sense in which one would expect such words to be used by educated and enlightened members of the western culture."[21] Nor does it seem quite accurate to attribute most of these changes to the abandonment of objectivity for subjectivity; what has changed is our objective sense of reality. Finally, science fiction of the newer school remains fictive history, speculating (among other things) on the nature of historical reality. I would like to defend these assertions by commenting on four relatively recent novels: John Brunner's *Stand on Zanzibar* (1968), Robert Silverberg's *The World Inside* (1971), Samuel R. Delany's *The Einstein Intersection* (1967), and Philip K. Dick's *The Three Stigmata of Palmer Eldritch* (1966).

Brunner's novel aroused a great deal of discussion with its innovative (for science fiction) techniques, but it fits into a relatively traditional category in the terms we have developed above; it is a short-range linear extrapolation. As Brunner himself has explained, it utilizes only one major new piece of science—a breakthrough in controlled genetics—and otherwise assumes "that nothing has become very much worse than it is today—excepting naturally the central pivot of the theme, the intensive pressure of over-population."[22] For the author, as for the reader, plot and character are subordinate to scene in interest—"the protagonist of my book was going to have to be the world entire."[23] But to accomplish these quite orthodox goals, Brunner found it desirable to introduce new forms to science-fiction writing. Why?

Science fiction as a separate commercial enterprise began as a pulp adventure form; with the stock pulp plots, it took over standard views of the relationship between individuals and their society. In early commercial science fiction one finds a faith in science matched by a faith in the individual's ability to make a difference—not for nothing was Edmond Hamilton nicknamed the "World-Saver." Views of man as a passive victim were largely confined to horror stories. Historians in the 1920s were already beginning to debunk our national heroes, but heroism flourished in the science-fiction magizines. In the years since, science-fiction writers have learned to make their characters more plausible by making them more ambiguous morally; in doing so, they were responding to a changing public taste which by now has affected even comic book heroes. Over the same period, the general public has been taught, by both history and historians, to question the individual's power as a causative agent in social change. This has had a number of effects on popular fiction—bureaucratic police have displaced many private detectives; the spy story, celebrating the last lone wolf, has come to show even the spy as being at the mercy of his organization. For authors accustomed to dealing with whole societies, the new view of historical process poses special problems. For narrative historians, it poses a new crisis in "explanation-forms."[26] For science-fiction authors, it reduces the viability of many of the traditional plots.

There are, to be sure, a number of expedients which can be used to adapt traditional plot structure to contemporary views of historical reality. The hero's great revolution against a corrupt society can fail miserably—a ploy used by Kurt Vonnegut in *Player Piano* but too pessimistic to have wide appeal to science-fiction authors (or their audience?). The protagonist can be already situated at the top of a rigidly hierarchical society and/or be a superman—a van Vogt solution finally adopted by Heinlein himself in *Stranger in a Strange Land.* Or the protagonist can be reduced to a mere viewpoint character—as in *The Moon Is a Harsh Mistress,* where the brains of the revolution is a computer. But within the context of a pulp adventure plot, the first and last of these expedients cheat the reader's expectations, something commercial writers are understandably reluctant to do. And it is difficult to provide well-motivated conflict if one starts with all-powerful figures, even if one is able to make the reader find them credible.

Stand on Zanzibar makes use of a number of innovations designed to allow for an entertaining plot without violating "the factual world of our experience." The first of these is simply to provide structured ways of including in the novel material which does not even pretend to be related directly to the plot. The specific devices here are borrowed from Dos Passos and justified by Brunner by their likeness to "the way in which one constructs one's image of the world" in contemporary life: "Plainly, by then, my task would be to throw at the reader information about my future world from as many sides as the real world can hit him from. This accounts for the contrasted modes of presentation in the book, the scripts, collage, montage, verse and other extraneous details imposed on the skeleton of the unifying narrative."[25] A second innovation, trickier but less remarked on than the first, is the use of two coequal protagonists involved in largely separate plots but linked by an accidental friendship. (The plots are linked by theme, and unusual mode of presentation helps to conceal their essential divergence.) The first protagonist is a subsidized synthesizer (and thus entitled to be interested in anything Brunner wants to stick in) and is finally activated as a spy (the only man of action left in popular fiction) and sent from New York to the South Pacific. The second protagonist moves in the opposite direction, from New York to Africa, as part of a multinational corporate venture. In the first plot, the scientific breakthrough of the novel is made by a third character, an enemy scientist; the protagonist functions only to rescue, abduct, and finally kill the scientist. In the second plot, yet another character, a sociologist who is the novel's resident wise man, makes the key breakthrough. The novel is large enough to accommodate these and several other main characters. In effect, Brunner has saved the plot and kept his scene true to our vision of reality by reducing the importance of any single character.

Robert Silverberg's *The World Inside* adopts a somewhat more conservative answer to basically the same problems. Silverberg's book is a linear-extrapolative world, concentrating more steadily than Brunner's on the population explosion. Its setting is an urban monad, one of many such two-mile high buildings in which a constantly proliferating humanity lives in tiny apartments, worshipping their own fertility. Silverberg does not present this as a realistic projection, nor as an object of social satire; he is interested in speculating on the possiblity of man's adapting himself to a closed environment in which population pressure has virtually abolished his "territorial prerogative"—an adaptation Brunner has ruled out. Silverberg's book is given unity of place, but it is a series of linked short stories rather than a conventional novel. I call this a conservative answer because it is a return to a common practice of the magazine fiction of the 1940s. Using a variety of characters, Silverberg is able to explore life at the upper and middle levels of his building. (Does this show a class bias?) Although the individual stories vary in merit, the whole is greater than the sum of its parts. Like Brunner, Silverberg is able to exploit his scene, preserve plot interest, and be true to our sense of historical reality—all by abandoning the use of a single protagonist.

Samuel R. Delany's *The Einstein Intersection* is a "linear nonextrapolative" novel laid in an apparently distant future; it stresses the uniqueness of its society, the pervasiveness of change, the subjective character of all unifying patterns, and myth stories themselves as the ultimate form of "historical explanation." Its world is peopled with somehow alien beings, the inheritors of humanity's myths. Delany retains a single protagonist and a basically traditional plot, a young man's initiation into life as he travels to the city. His poetic rendering of this plot should not obscure its traditional character or its links with more heavily expository analogues in, say, the Heinlein juveniles. Unlike Brunner and Silverberg, Delany's strategy preserves realism of plot and character by sacrificing completeness in depiction of the scene. In a writer with less artistic integrity, this might seem like mere mystification, but Delany is able instead to remind us how mystifying is our own experience of life. Openness to the strangeness of experience is in fact one of the novel's many chapter epigraphs; Delany reminds himself that "Endings to be useful must be inconclusive."[26] For the artist, after all, endings are only beginnings.

All young novelists write one or more novels about young artists, but *The Einstein Intersection* is about a great deal more than that. One of the things it is about is our experience of historical reality. We can even see in it a reflection of a more particular historical situation. Lobey has "a small brown face proper for a fox," but he is an Orpheus, and the pattern of his life is intertwined with that of other Western myths (particularly

Christ) and of peculiarly American mythic figures like Billy the Kid and Jean Harlow. One of Delany's epigraphs quotes Gregory Corso: "Jean Harlow? Christ, Orpheus, Billy the Kid, those three I can understand. But what's a young spade writer like you doing all caught up with the Great White Bitch? Of course I guess it's pretty obvious."[27] One of the problems of the novel, then, is growing up black in a world in which the central myths (religious and sexual) are somehow alien. This, in turn, is only a particular case of the universal problem of coming to terms with a world filled with myths of history alien to us, yet somehow a part of our lives. History is what we remember of the past, and the most powerful parts of our memory are myths. Presumably deriving part of its motive force from speculations about a particular historical experience, *The Einstein Intersection* is also a speculative fiction about our experience of history.

All of Philip K. Dick's novels bear at least three stigmata of his long apprenticeship in Ace Double Novels. *The Three Stigmata of Palmer Eldritch* has some of the form of a conventional novel of short-range linear extrapolation—hallucinatory drugs and Barbie dolls provide the basic scene, with the addition of precognition, a psi phenomenon found in many novels of the 1950s. Dick's characteristically complicated plot forces him, like Brunner, to give roughly equal attention to three major characters—Leo Bulero, businessman, drug smuggler, and hero; Barney Mayerson, a pre-cog employee of Bulero's who is forced to emigrate to the barren colony of Mars; and Palmer Eldritch, who precipitates the plot by his return from a long voyage to Proxima with a new and sinisterly effective hallucinatory drug. Whereas the central concerns of contemporary philosophy of history are how we may be said to know the past and in what ways it is legitimate to explain it, Dick leads his characters to question what they know of the reality they face in the present and the future patterns they see. All three major characters discuss this problem in terms of accidents (appearance) versus substance (essence). Once again, science fiction is being used to speculate about the nature and meaning of the historical process.

Dick's use of hallucinatory states in this and other novels has obscured for some critics his larger purposes. Unreality is not the theme of Dick's novels but a frequent plot device in them; it stands for the threat that our shared experience of reality may diverge so much that we can no longer agree on what reality is, that even the smaller patterns which we use to order reality may be broken down. These threats, however, are rejected; in *The Three Stigmata of Palmer Eldritch,* there *is* an objective historical reality, and men are able to shape it. The message of the novel is that they must rely on their imperfect humanity to do so. Trapped in a hallucinatory state dominated by Palmer Eldritch, Leo Bulero prays to God for help—"If You do, if You can reach into this world, I'll do anything, whatever You want."[28] Such prayers are misdirected, for in this world Palmer Eldritch is God, having been absorbed into a huge God-like creature he has encountered in space. The God incarnate in Palmer Eldritch is, in any case, a limited God, and to the extent that it is benign, "He can't help us very much."[29] For most of the characters in the novel, it is not experienced as a benign presence. Palmer Eldritch's new drug induces mystical union with Palmer Eldritch, and no one wants it; the wholly other is seen as the absolute evil. Leo Bulero is humanity's hero because, in destroying Eldritch, he frees man from God.

Bulero is apt to attribute his victory to the wonders of science, as exemplified by his highly "evolved mind" produced by a special E Therapy. What makes Bulero a hero is, instead, his essential (essence, again) humanity, "not touched by any of these three, the evil, negative trinity of alienation, blurred reality, and despair that Eldritch brought back"; untouched even "*by the original ancient blight,*" which, in context, would seem to be not the traditional Original Sin but contact with the Judaeo-Christian God.[30] In the sense of being uncontaminated by any divine qualities, Bulero is a product of human evolution. The novel ends shortly before the final defeat of Eldritch/God, but we are assured of Bulero's victory by a memo written by Bulero after his successful return from the conflict. This memo is the epigraph to the novel as a whole, and Dick himself has said that "In a sense, that paragraph is the real novel, and the rest is autopsy."[31] Bulero writes, "I mean, after all; you have to consider we're only made out of dust. That's admittedly not much to go on and we shouldn't forget that. But even considering, I mean it's a sort of bad beginning, we're not doing too bad. So I personally have faith that even in this lousy situation we're faced with we can make it. You get me?"[32] The unity and meaning of history will be man-made, not derived from the omnipresence of Palmer Eldritch; in this novel, Dick rejects transcendence for history.

Dick's playing with the doctrine of essences reminds us that as a philosophic doctrine, "realism" may refer to a belief that essences are more real than appearances, a doctrine to which speculative fiction has often given implicit adherence. I have argued here that science fiction is a distinct genre of speculative fiction—a fictive history laid outside what we accept as historical reality but operating by the same essential rules as that reality. I believe this definition preserves the spirit of Heinlein's 1957 remarks, and that my analysis of the works of Brunner, Silverberg, Delany, and Dick indicates that these works still employ a basically realistic strategy. The change in the field since the 1950s can then be seen as responses to altered views of historical reality and the effects of these on traditional concepts of plot, scene, and character. These changes correspond to a shift toward a historicist or narrativist philosophy of history; for the sake of parallelism, I have termed some such works "linear nonextrapolative." Even the writers most clearly departing from some elements in the 1950s formula, Delany and Dick, are directly concerned with the rules which govern our experience of historical reality; to conceive of such works as a sharp break with that of the 1950s would, I believe, exaggerate the significance of the changes. I do not mean to imply that mine is the only defensible definition of the genre or critical approach to it; I do hope that others will find them useful.

NOTES

1. Robert Heinlein, "Science Fiction: Its Nature, Faults, and Virtues," reprinted in Davenport, et al., *The Science Fiction Novel* (Chicago: Advent, 1959), p. 22.
2. Alexei Panshin, "Science Fiction in Dimension," *Fantastic Stories,* 9 (June 1970), 125-30, quoted from Thomas D. Clareson, ed., *SF: The Other Side of Realism* (Bowling Green, Ohio: Bowling Green University Popular Press, 1971), p. 332; Alexei and Cory Panshin, "The Search for Sense (1947-1957)," *Fantastic Stories,* 22 (February 1973), 114. Both articles are preliminary versions of material intended for the Panshins' forthcoming book, *The World Beyond the Hill.*
3. On the novel as fictive history—and the questionable validity of "the historical novel" as a genre—see particularly Harriet Gilliam's review essay of Avrom Fleishman's *The English Historical Novel,* CLIO, 1 (February 1972), 52-59. In her Yale dissertation (1971) and some later papers and manuscripts not yet published, Professor Gilliam develops the ideas expressed in the above essay at some length, noting, too, that all histories are in some sense "fictive"—imaginary constructs.
4. Heinlein, pp. 18-19. He is obviously aware here of the difficulties involved in all references to "reality" and "fact."
5. Some other critics who equate science fiction with fantasy do so by making a distinction between the "real world" and some "secondary universe" as the "objects of imitation" of realism and fantasy respectively, a legitimate position which does, however, blur what I regard as an equally legitimate distinction in narrative strategy. A similar approach may be found in the first two essays in the Clareson volume just cited (footnote 2): Clareson, "The Other Side of Realism," pp. 1-28; and Julius Kagarlitski, "Realism and Fantasy," pp. 29-52. Although I am personally inclined to stress the conventional, "agreed-upon" nature of our notion of "reality," I have no desire to get into purely semantic quarrels with critics who use fantasy to cover all speculative fiction, so long as they recognize that on another level of analysis the realism/fantasy dichotomy is a valid one.
6. Campbell, *The Mightiest Machine* (New York: Ace Books, 1972), p. 84.
7. On Heinlein's influence, note James Blish's remarks in his introduction to Alexei Panshin, *Heinlein in Dimension* (Chicago: Advent Publishers, Inc., 1968), p. 3; on the reasons for that influence see Panshin himself, *Heinlein,* p. 14.
8. Sam Moskowitz has noted this story's resemblance in plot and style to "stories of the World War I period in ARGOSY and ALL-STORY WEEKLY," *Shapers of Tomorrow* (New York: Ballantine Books, 1967), p. 196.
9. The Panshins complain about this narrowing of the time span in their "The Search for Sense," taking it as a sign of limited imagination.
10. Alexei Panshin notes this gap (*Heinlein,* p. 123) as a symptom of "the improvised nature of the *Future History.*" The two explanations are not mutually exclusive, and I agree that the Future History is jerry-built.
11. Kingsley Amis, *New Maps of Hell* (New York: Harcourt Brace & World, 1960), p. 87. Although my admiration for this sort of story is more limited than Amis's, I believe his book has been unfairly dismissed by some rather clubbish critics in the genre. For fairer evaluations, see Damon Knight, *In Search of Wonder* (Chicago: Advent, 1967), pp. 7-8; and James Blish (as William Atheling, Jr.), *More Issues at Hand* (Chicago: Advent, 1970), pp. 30-35. Amis's fantasy/science fiction distinction (pp. 1-24) also resembles that argued for here.

12. Pohl, *The Age of the Pussyfoot* (New York: Ballantine Books, 1969), p. 212.
13. "Easily the best anti-utopia . . . since *Brave New World*," Blish (as Atheling), *The Issue at Hand* (Chicago: Advent Publishers, Inc., 1964), p. 20n. In his Atheling persona, Blish easily qualifies as one of the "most severe critics" of the field, and, in fact, he did not praise the serial version.
14. I have discussed these points at greater length in "Flat Characters in Round Worlds," a paper for the Secondary Universe Conference, October 1972; mss. available on request.
15. In "The Failure of the Science Fiction Novel as Social Criticism," pp. 49-76, C. M. Kornbluth attributes the decline (then imminent) of social science fiction to its ineffectiveness in changing society and to the more important influence of the author's unconscious needs. But the appeal of ideas in literature has never depended upon their later effectiveness (*vide* the Golden Rule), and all works have latent content which does not necessarily render their overt content irrelevant.
16. Blish, *The Issue at Hand*, pp. 60-61. For a more detailed explanation, see Richard D. Mullen, "Blish, van Vogt, and the Uses of Spengler," *Riverside Quarterly*, 3 (August 1968), 172-86.
17. Isaac Asimov, "Social Science Fiction," in Reginald Bretnor, ed., *Modern Science Fiction* (New York: Coward-McCann, 1953), p. 192. This essay also contains a passing reference (p. 181) indicating Asimov's acquaintance with Toynbee's work and a chess game/chess puzzle distinction referring to whether works are aiming at realistic projection.
18. "Speculative" philosophy of history is concerned with the possibility of meaningful patterns in history—as opposed to "analytic" or "critical" philosophy of history, which is a secondary-order activity concerned with the activity of historians rather than with history itself. The linear/cyclic distinction employed in this paper is a customary one, depending on whether the stress is on man's history as unified by a given line or lines of development or on recurring patterns (cycles) in history. For a description of these two types, see W. H. Dray, *Philosophy of History* (Englewood Cliffs, N.J.: Prentice Hall, 1964), pp. 60-66. In some linear philosophies of history, the emphasis is on progress (process) rather than the end sought (Comte, Spencer): others are teleological (Augustine, Hegelian and Marxian dialectic). Cyclic systems may be relatively closed and deterministic (Vico, Spengler) or open (Toynbee, Sorokin, Quigley). Since Ranke, the German historical tradition has stressed the uniqueness of historical events and ages. Out of this arose an emphasis on the stubborn particularity of historical knowledge and the primacy of change and discontinuity in history; this position is termed "historicism," a term applied to a diverse set of thinkers (Dilthey, Meinecke, Croce, Collingwood, Ortega y Gasset). At one extreme it leads to an emphasis on the subjectivity and relativity of historical judgments which few historians can accept. Related to it, though, are many of the arguments of the current "narrativists" (Dray, Gallie, Mink), who argue that the story itself, rather than any argumentative generalizations, constitutes the typical form of "explanation" in narrative history.
19. There are, of course, exceptions, most notably in economic history. Readers of speculative fiction might enjoy the discussion of the usefulness of "counter-factual worlds" in Lance E. Davis, "Specification, Quantification and Analysis in Economic History," *Approaches to American Economic History*, ed. George Rogers Clark and Lucius F. Ellsworth (Charlottesville: University of Virginia, 1971), pp. 106-20.
20. Alexei and Cory Panshin, "The Search for Mystery (1958-1967)," *Fantastic Stories*, 22 (April 1973), 94-113, 130, provides a useful survey of this period.
21. Heinlein, p. 19.

22. John Brunner, "The Genesis of *Stand on Zanzibar* and Digressions," *Extrapolation,* 11 (May 1970), 37.
23. Brunner, 35.
24. On "explanation forms," see Gene Wise, *American Historical Explanations* (Homewood, Ill.: Dorsey, 1973).
25. Brunner, 36.
26. Samuel R. Delany, *The Einstein Intersection* (New York: Ace, 1967), p. 125. On this remark and much else in the novel, see Stephen Scobie, "Different Mazes: Mythology in Samuel R. Delany's *The Einstein Intersection,*" *Riverside Quarterly,* 5 (July 1971), 12-19.
27. Delany, p. 97.
28. Dick, *The Three Stigmata of Palmer Eldritch* (New York: MacFadden, 1966), p. 85.
29. Dick, p. 179.
30. Dick, p. 190.
31. Dick, letter to *Riverside Quarterly,* 3 (March 1968), 163-64, in response to one of the few critical comments to stress the theological side of the novel: Leland Sapiro (as Yogi Borel), "A satanic Bible," *Riverside Quarterly,* 3 (August 1967), 67-73. Dick approves of this emphasis and describes the Bulero-Eldritch contest as one between "relative good" and "absolute evil."
32. Dick, *The Three Stigmata of Palmer Eldritch,* p. 5.

Images of the Man-Machine Intelligence Relationship in Science Fiction

Patricia Warrick

Modern man is machine man. He lives in an environment created by machines[1]—a sharp contrast to his primitive ancestors who lived in an environment shaped by Nature. Modern technological man shows no serious inclination to actually return to that earlier primitive environment inhabited by his ancestors. But he is more at home physically in his new machine world than he is intellectually and emotionally. He yearns for the harmony earlier achieved with Nature, a harmony he does not find in his technological environment. Such a response of estrangement is not surprising. Man has lived in this complex machine world only a few hundred years; he spent at least a million years in the natural world.

The modern machine environment mirrors the mechanistic world view of science that developed in the seventeenth and eighteenth centuries. Machine technology, at first simple but rapidly growing more complex, followed closely and fertilized theoretical science. New machines made possible new research which, in turn, led to newer machines.

Science fiction appeared in the nineteenth century, a literary response to the development of science and technology. It can be understood as the play of the human imagination, attempting to come to terms with the new universe as defined by the scientific world view. This vision of reality differs radically from the pre-scientific religious view. The task of the imagination—as it casts aside earlier images of man in the cosmos and struggles to synthesize new ones—is enormous. It must create a new view of man in space, and of man in time—but not simply a view of the old natural man with his simple technology transported to these new dimensions. For now a new man exists who transcends space and time not only with his imagination, but also with his machines.

J. O. Bailey's study of SF, *Pilgrims Through Space and Time* (1947), records the remarkable imaginary journeys that man makes, aided by his wonderful machines and inventions. Arthur O. Lewis's anthology, *Of Men and Machines* (1963), using both fiction and nonfiction, examines the complexities and ambiguities of the man-machine relationship. Lewis Mumford's monumental and brilliant two-volume work, *The Myth of the Machine* (1964, 1970), traces through history man's relationship with his machines.

The computer, developed about thirty years ago, inaugurated a new era in man-machine relationships. Rather than harnessing energy, producing power, and accomplishing physical work, the computer processes information. It undertakes work once performed only by the human brain. The response in SF to this radical new machine has been great. Within the last thirty-five years, well over fifty novels and several hundred short stories have been written in which the computer plays a significant part in the plot development. The themes, trends, and characteristics of this body of fiction portraying machine intelligence will be examined in this paper.

The large amount of fiction and nonfiction exploring the man-machine relationship that has been written since World War II is not surprising. This is the transforming relationship of the twentieth century. Technology accomplishes metamorphosis; man and his culture become something they were not before. Not merely the specific details of the change, but the fact of the change itself assumes significance. Static medieval man needed definition only once. Having developed a model of himself and his relationship to his culture and the cosmos, the model was functional indefinitely because the rate of cultural change was so slow as to go unnoticed. But metamorphosing technological man demands continual definition.

Change makes man aware of his existence in time. He enters history, acquires a past, and faces a future. Robert Scholes's study of SF, *Structural Fabulation* (1975), notes that the revolution in man's conception of himself, begun with the rise of science in the seventeenth and eighteenth centuries, has continued in the last one hundred years. In the nineteenth century Darwin's theory had a part in the revolution. The revolution was

> continued by Einstein's theory of relativity. And it has been extended by developments in the study of human systems of perception, organization, and communication that range from the linguistic philosophy of Wittgenstein and Strauss to the cybernetics of Wiener. This century of cosmic rearrangement, crudely indicated here by this list of names and concepts, has led to new ways of understanding human time and space-time, as well as to a new sense of the relationship between human systems and the larger systems of the cosmos.[2]

Once man perceives that he has a future which may well be different from the present, he believes that he has a hand in shaping that future. First, he begins to imagine what it will be like. Fred Polak in *The Image of the Future* (1973) studies the function of the image in influencing the future. He holds that the creative minority in a culture must construct positive and idealistic images of the future if the culture is to avoid disintegration.[3]

Given, then, that man faces a future different from the present and that his imagination will play a significant role in shaping that future, it becomes meaningful to examine the images that man has of his future relationships with the computer, or machine intelligence. The first thing we note in looking at those images is that the prevailing mode of much of the SF portraying the computer is dystopian. Two dark visions keep appearing. In one, the computer replaces man as a worker. Resentfully, he rises up in a modern Luddite rebellion and smashes the computer as the weaving looms were smashed by the workers in nineteenth-century England. In the other view, the computer—godlike in its power—tries to enslave man, controlling him and reducing him to a robot servant. At the same time, then, that the actual use of the computer is spreading and growing rapidly throughout the world, the literary imagination tends to reject its usage. Not all SF is so negative in its view of electronic data processing. We will examine both the literature rejecting computer usage and that having a more positive view. Our purpose will be to note the conditions in which each image of the computer appears and to make some comments about the possible significance of the discrepancies between the two attitudes toward the computer.

THE FOUR DISCONTINUITIES

Generally, the man-machine intelligence relationship is portrayed in SF as a discontinuous or dichotomous one. Man sees himself as separate from his machines—unique because he is a living, thinking, feeling entity. He has a drive to dominate the world around him and feels threatened by the possibility that a machine may dominate and remake him in its image. Man and machine, consequently, struggle against each other.

Anthropologist Bruce Mazelish has examined this image of the discontinuity between man and his machines and has done a perceptive analysis of its possible significance. He notes that a parallel can be drawn between this discontinuity and three earlier discontinuities between man and his environment.[4] Mazelish points out that the earlier discontinuities were eventually breached, and he suggests that similarly the discontinuity between man and his machine environment may well be eliminated in the future.

As the source where the first three discontinuities were originally noted, Mazelish cites a lecture given by Sigmund Freud in

Vienna. Freud suggested his place among three great thinkers who had outraged man's naive self love. First, Copernicus taught that the Earth was not the center of the universe but only a speck in a cosmic system of inconceivable magnitude. Next, Darwin made man aware that he was not a unique creation of God, separate from the animal world. Instead, he was a part of and descended from the animal world. Third, Freud made man aware that he is not a totally rational creature. His conscious mind is linked with a primitive, infantile, irrational subconscious. The eighteenth century's image of man as a creature of reason had to be discarded.

In these three ego-smashing encounters man found he was not unique, but rather a part of a continuum. The heavenly bodies are not discontinuous with earthly matter, but are formed from the same substance as the imperfect Earth. Man and the animal kingdom similarly, are a part of a living continuum. Further, there is a continuity between the primitive and the civilized, the rational and the irrational, mental health and mental illness. Man finds he is "placed on a continuous spectrum in relation to the universe, to the rest of the animal kingdom, and to himself. He is no longer discontinuous with the world around him. In an important sense, it can be contended, once man is able to accept this situation, he is in harmony with the rest of existence. Indeed, the longing of the early nineteenth-century romantics and of all 'alienated' beings since for a sense of 'connection' is fulfilled in an unexpected manner."

To the three discontinuities just described, Mazelish adds a fourth—one he sees as requiring elimination—just as did the first three—if man is to be in harmony with his environment. The fourth is the dichotomy or discontinuity between man and his machines. Mazelish states:

> We are now coming to realize that man and the machines he creates are continuous and that the same conceptual schemes, for example, that help explain the workings of his brain also explain the workings of a "thinking machine." Man's pride, and his refusal to acknowledge this continuity, is the substratum upon which the distrust of technology and an industrialized society has been reared. Ultimately, I

believe, this last rests on man's refusal to understand and accept his own nature—as being continuous with the tools and the machines he constructs.[6]

Mazelish's view of the wounding discontinuity of the present prevailing image of man-machine relationships provides an interesting vantage point from which to examine the SF about machine intelligence. It sorts the fiction into two categories: a substantial category rejecting the man-machine intelligence continuity and a much smaller category accepting it.

As we look at the three discontinuities described by Freud, we must concede his point that they have essentially been eliminated. We immediately recognize, further, that SF has played a significant role in resynthesizing man's image of himself in at least two of the instances, and perhaps in the third. Why, then, does so much SF reject the possibility of a continuity between man and machine-intelligence?

Science fiction concerned with man in space and man in time represents the human creativity at work building images of man in the Copernican space continuum and the Darwinian time continuum. Let us first look briefly at the space continuum. If the Earth is not separate from but part of the heavenly bodies, then man has the possibility of traveling to and through these heavens. Space travel in SF records the efforts of man to imagine himself at home in, and part of, the whole universe.

Next, let us consider Darwin's theory and its implications for a time continuum. Man's evolution from the animal form, described by Darwin, was a slow process. Darwin's contemporary, the geologist Charles Lyell, described the age of the earth in terms of millions of years—discarding the creation date of 4004 BC given by church authorities. Man, as a result of this work in biology and geology, had to reorganize his image of himself in time. Two choices were available. He could allow his image to shrink to insignificance as he recognized the minuteness of his life span compared to the age of the Earth, or he could transcend time, rising above rather than being defeated by it. Modern mainstream literature has tended to choose the first image, science fiction the latter. H. G. Wells set the pattern of transcendence when his rich imagination created *The Time Machine* (1895).

The third continuum—Freud's rational-irrational—is a more recent definition. The human imagination in SF has not as clearly conceived an image of man in this continuum, although I will suggest later that New Wave writers are undertaking this difficult task, as have some avant-garde writers in mainstream literature. The irrational is not easy to present in the fictional form for two reasons: 1) this form uses prose language—essentially a logical mode; 2) the fictional or novel form developed and has traditionally been used to describe a rational, causal reality. The reader, accustomed to expect this kind of reality in the fiction he reads, is often distressed if he finds instead a multiplex, constantly evolving, nonlinear reality.

The fourth discontinuity—that between man and his machines—has been exacerbated by the development of computers and machine intelligence. Such machines are far more threatening to man than those machines performing only tasks once accomplished by man's physical labor. He sees his reasoning capacity and his high level of intelligence as uniquely human. He is frightened by the idea that these characteristics can be duplicated and surpassed by a machine. So he tends to reject electronic technology at the same time as he increasingly comes to rely on it. A split personality results—a condition described in Robert M. Pirsig's *Zen and the Art of Motorcycle Maintenance* (1974). Even as man uses technology, he refuses to give it his care, attention, and concern.

COGNITIVE ESTRANGEMENT AND THE TWO CATEGORIES OF COMPUTER SF

To what extent does science fiction about machine intelligence function to alter the perception of man's relationship to his technology that he acquires in the real world around him? That SF should have such a cognitive function—presenting a model alternative to the "empirical environment"—is noted by Darko Suvin in his "On the Poetics of the SF Genre." He holds that the best SF is educational literature. It "discusses primarily the political, psychological, anthropological *use and effect of sciences, and philosophy of science,* and the becoming or failure of new realities as a result of it,"[7] accomplishing its cognitive function through the device of creating "an imaginative framework alternative to the author's empirical environment."[8] The imaginative framework or fiction so created and factually reported implies a new set of norms—different from those we habitually encounter in reality as we know it. The contrast to known reality creates an attitude of "*estrangement*" from the familiar.[9] Thus estranged from our habitual view of reality, we can recognize the possibilities of alternative views. We may discover this new model is more workable for understanding the present and transforming the future than our present model. The new model, temporarily removing us from the old, allows us then to return and examine the old with new objectivity and distance.

The SF about man's relationship with machine intelligence tends, as noted, to fall into two categories: one produces a high degree of cognitive estrangement; the other does not. The category producing cognitive estrangement is generally neutral or positive in its attitude toward the computer. It is essentially speculative fiction, toying playfully with the possibilities of a machine able to think—to store almost limitless amounts of data, to recall and process that information almost instantaneously, to make logical decisions, to learn, or reprogram itself, as a result of the experience it accumulates. The other category is *extrapolative fiction* aimed at social criticism, and it is—with a very few bright exceptions—negative in its attitude toward the computer. It is not concerned with new visions of possible machine worlds, but with the shortcomings of our present one.

Having defined these two categories of computer stories, we can examine each with some care. Such an examination reveals contrasts in several details; for example, the date when the story was written, the setting of the story in time and space, the use made of the computer. We can also rather easily compare the stories with what is happening in the real world of computers. The development and application of computers in society is recent, and easy to date. It is an American phenomenon of the last thirty years (although Great Britain and Russia have not been far behind in development, and computer usage has rapidly spread throughout the world). Consequently, it is possible to compare rather closely the SF portraying the computer with the actual developments in the field. We can discover patterns in the relationships of the computers developed in reality by the engineering imagination and the computers created in fiction by the literary imagination. We can also add another angle of vision to our study by looking at the early literature about automata, robots, and thinking machines that preceded the actual development of computers in the 1940s.

BRIEF HISTORY OF COMPUTER DEVELOPMENT

The first computer story to appear was Lester del Rey's "Helen O'Loy" (1938), followed soon after by Isaac Asimov's "Robbie" (1940). (In my study I have included both computers and robots that are clearly operated by miniature computers.) These stories parallel but do not precede the actual development of the computer. In the late 1930s and the early 1940s, substantial research began in developing the technology necessary to build a computer. In 1937 Howard Aiken of Harvard designed a machine—the Mark I—which is usually accorded computer status, but the ENIAC, built at the Moore School of Engineering of the University of Pennsylvania in 1945, is recorded as the first *electronic* calculator. This computer was made for the Ballistic Research Laboratories of the United States Army. Improvements followed rapidly, and the Servomechanism Laboratory at M.I.T. was one of the most active groups in the early history of electronic computer development.[10]

One of the most brilliant men at M.I.T. was Norbert Wiener, who has come to be regarded as the father of cybernetics. In 1948 he published his landmark *Cybernetics,* giving the discipline the name by which it is known. He defined cybernetics as the study of communication and control in animals and man. He recognized that all systems—man, animal, social—maintain themselves through communication, or the flow of information. The living system maintains its contact with the outer world through sensing devices which bring it new information, or feedback, in response to its actions. Through homeostatic mechanisms, predetermined patterns in the system are maintained. These mechanisms analyze the feedback information received from the sensory devices, and feed forward to the system information that corrects such matters as temperature and chemical concentrations—whatever is necessary to maintain all the variables of the system within certain predetermined limits. If the homeostatic devices fail and the control is not maintained, the organism dies.

Wiener saw that it would be possible for man to duplicate mechanically the design of these living systems once he had two things: (1) a device like the animal brain that could rapidly process information (the computer); and (2) sensing devices, or receptors for messages from the outside (photo-electric cells, thermometers). He correctly pointed out that older machines attempting to produce automata were limited because they functioned on a closed clockwork basis; they had no devices for sensing changes in their environment and reacting to these changes with altered behavior. With the new knowledge about homeostatic devices and the new technology, "intelligent" robots could now be built to serve man. But Wiener perceived with great foresight the Pandora's box of problems this development might unleash on society. In *The Human Use of Human Beings: Cybernetics and Society* (1950), he warned of the dangers of the misuse of automata. He noted that man's centuries-old longing for an intelligent servant to relieve him of hard work contains a contradiction. Intelligence wants to be free, and one who is willing to serve is not usually very intelligent. He was optimistic about the benefits that might come to man in this new cybernetic era, but he was also sharply aware of how easily the new technology could be misused.

Computers were originally developed for and utilized by the military during World War II. After the war their expansion into industry was very rapid. By 1952, John Diebold, often called the father of automation, had published a book titled *Automation.* In it he optimistically outlined the potential of automation for industry and attacked Norbert Wiener for being unnecessarily pessimistic in his view of the possible adverse social effects of cybernetics.

This brief history of the development and application of computers is a necessary base to establish so that we can compare it to the extrapolative SF portraying computers and robots in future societies. We find, interestingly enough, that often it is not SF but industry that creates new images of computers in society and then implements possibilities. Science fiction tends to lag behind, writing dystopian views of what might happen—often after the fact.

James Martin and Adrian R. D. Norman, discussing the exploding computer technology in *The Computerized Society* (1970), comment that although they are writing fact, it is difficult to avoid having their account sound like science fiction. They describe the process by which innovation in computer usage occurs:

> To a large extent the systems analysts appear to be leading the way. In the euphoria of the new technology, idea follows idea with great rapidity. A new systems approach is taken because it is a step towards that future time when everything will be automated. Most sociologists trail along some way behind, usually not quite knowing what is happening. Behind them come the majority of civil servants, lawyers, clergy, politicians, and last of all teachers who are preparing people to live in this age. They are bewildered, misinformed, and—more often than not—disinterested. They belong to the other of the "Two cultures." Meanwhile, society hurtles onward down the lines of least technological resistance.[11]

Martin and Norman do not consider the SF writer in their list of those concerned with innovation in computer usage. Had they done so, the writer would certainly have ranked before most of the names mentioned. But he would not have preceded the systems analyst, as will be clear when we look at the fiction portraying computer applications.

PRECURSORS OF COMPUTERS IN LITERATURE

Although the first computerized robot did not appear in fiction until 1938, automata have had a long history in literature. In his thorough study of the subject, *Human Robots in Myth and Science* (1967), John Cohen cites references to automata as far back as *The Iliad.* This Greek epic records that Hephaestus, god of fire and metallic arts, had handmaids of gold to attend him. He also built mobile tripods that served in the divine dining hall, performing their functions automatically. Other myths and legends also describe automata. Man's imagination has long been fascinated with the idea of an automatic servant.

Automata appeared first in myth, but as man's knowledge and technical proficiency increased, he began to actually build them from metal and stone. In the thirteenth century, a new era in the creation of automata was inaugurated by Ramon Lull (1234-1315), a Spanish mystic. He wanted to transform philosophy by removing theology as its supporting base and replacing it with reason. He devised a logical machine which he called *Ars Magna,* and he hoped it would be an aid in bringing reason to bear on all subjects. The *Ars Magna* has been described as the first step in the direction of a complete and automatic language for reasoning.[12]

For many occult philosophers, cabalists, and alchemists in the Middle Ages, the making of logical machines was not an end in itself, but a possible means of creating a flesh and blood creature, sometimes referred to in the literature as a homunculus, sometimes as a golem. The legend of Dr. Faustus, dramatized by Christopher Marlowe in the sixteenth century, illuminates the preoccupation of these men. They wished to transcend the traditional limitations of man's knowledge and go beyond to mystical wisdom and the mystery of the creation of man. The Faustian figure will appear in modern SF as the man of science whose discoveries lead him to the secrets of the universe.

In the Renaissance the foundations of modern science were laid. What once had been the province of the alchemist was invaded by astronomers and physicists. Copernicus, Galileo, and Newton developed the mechanistic world view. According to this model, the universe is understood as a machine operated by laws whose functions can be described mathematically. During this period the literature about automata increases. Here we can do no more than mention two important men, René Descartes and Julien La Mettrie. Descartes (1596-1650) opens the epoch of modern automata. He seems to have been influenced by earlier thinking about automata as well as by the Newtonian view of the mechanistic laws of nature. He divided man into two parts, mind and body. His description of the human body resembles that of an automaton operated mechanically. A little later La Mettrie (1709-1751) pushed Descartes's image further and wrote *L'Homme-Machine,* in which he described the same kind of mechanical laws operating in man as in nature.[13] The image of man as an animal-like machine (albeit the most perfect and complex form) was born. If man is only a machine, then once science accumulates enough knowledge, he can be duplicated. In recent SF, the duplication of man through the use of information stored in the computer is a recurring theme.[14]

The theoretical science of the seventeenth century stimulated interest in all kinds of mechanical devices. Blaise Pascal (1623-1662) produced a machine able to add and subtract. Gottfried Leibnitz, twenty years later, dreamed of a machine that could not only do arithmetical operations, but would also be able to reason. By the eighteenth century, mechanical inventions abounded. The fact that many of the devices produced were toys—mechanical animals, music boxes—indicates the nature of much of the experimentation. It was more imaginative play than purposeful research. In the nineteenth century, the first vision of the modern computer and plans for building it were born. In England Charles Babbage drew up working blueprints for the machine and failed in his efforts only because the technology of his time was not sophisticated enough to build the machine he designed. Not until electronic technology was available in the 1940s would Babbage's machine be successfully built.

While the mechanical imagination was at work creating machines and automata, the literary imagination was at work creating fiction about them. I shall cite various titles, and then discuss in some detail a few early works that have particular significance because they establish the prototype that will appear again and again in twentieth-century SF about artificial intelligence. Mary Shelley's *Frankenstein, Or The Modern Prometheus* (1818), is the first SF work portraying a creature made by man. Granted he is an android—created from animal tissue rather than metal—but *Frankenstein* raises so powerfully most of the issues that concern writers on the subject of artificial or man-made intelligence that the novel deserves careful study. Ambrose Bierce's "Moxon's Master" (1893), Karel Čapek's *R.U.R.* (1921), S. Fowler Wright's "Automata" (1929) all portray the relationship of man and robot, to mention only a few early titles.[15]

Frankenstein has been retold in many grotesque movie versions, and so we tend to discount the story as junk. A reading of Mary Shelley's original story reorients us. Its several themes are substantial, and it is much more than a Gothic horror story. She was well tutored by Percy Bysshe Shelley, who was deeply interested in science, and also by her father, William Godwin, a radical political philosopher interested in revolution and social change. She realized that science produces powerful knowledge, and that this knowledge may be dangerous to man.

If we view the story as richly symbolic—approaching the level of mythmaking—several significant themes are apparent. In such a reading, Dr. Frankenstein is seen as modern scientific man, and the creature he makes as man's technology. Let us enumerate four themes present in the novel. (1) *The Promethean theme*: Dr. Frankenstein is patterned after the mythical technologist, Prometheus. Like Prometheus, he goes beyond what has been done before, and entering forbidden territory, steals knowledge from the gods. He develops techniques for creating life—a secret and mysterious act previously known only to the gods. Future SF will present many versions of the Promethean scientist going beyond, pushing the limits, doing what previously only the gods had done. (2) *The ambiguity of technology*: The creature, when first created, is gentle and kind. Yet later he becomes a monstrous destroyer.

Dr. Frankenstein, presuming he is doing no wrong as he makes the creature, later comes to feel his act of creation is an unforgivable evil. (3) *The effect of man's rejection of his technology*: The creature, in his first days on Earth, is gentle and helpful and yearns to be loved. He becomes a malignant, uncontrollable monster only when Dr. Frankenstein rejects and deserts him. (4) *The shifting role of master and servant, creator and created*: At the beginning of the story Dr. Frankenstein is clearly the master and creator, but as he becomes obsessed with trying to destroy the technology he has created, he becomes enslaved by it. Losing his independent will, he can only pursue the monster wherever it may lead him. Modern SF about man and machine intelligence will repeatedly portray this reversal of the master-servant relationship between man and the robot he creates.

In summary, *Frankenstein* is a remarkable novel to have been produced by a twenty-year-old girl early in the nineteenth century; in it she states, in symbolic form, most of the issues that are of paramount importance to late twentieth-century man in his struggle to live in harmony with and control his technology. We will find these themes appearing again and again in modern SF about robots and computers.

Another nineteenth-century precursor worth examining in some detail is Samuel Butler's *Erewhon* (1872). Chapters 21, 22, and 23, entitled "The Book of the Machine," demonstrate a pattern that will be repeated later in twentieth-century dystopian fiction. What the literary imagination creates as a tool for satire has a habit of later turning into actuality. We see this phenomenon in *Erewhon.* Butler probably aimed only at satirizing the idea of evolution and ridiculing reason when it is used to the extreme. To accomplish this, he employed exaggeration and irony. But today, as we read what he wrote, we find that, unintentionally, he has been remarkably prophetic in his description of the evolution of the machine.

He pushes the possible development of the machine to extremes, using as the undergirding for his extrapolation two views prevalent in the nineteenth century. One was the faith in technological progress, and the other was the Darwinian view of evolution. He combines the two and traces the evolution of the machine, and the dangers of letting mechanical evolution proceed unchecked in a society. In his satire, the land of Erewhon has banished all complex machines because one of its philosophers has argued that machines will eventually develop a consciousness of their own and come to control man, just as men, being offshoots of more primitive forms of life, eventually came to dominate and exploit that life. As early forms of life have developed into increasingly complex organisms and expanded their consciousness in the process, so machines will develop complexity and consciousness.

The narrator in *Erewhon* says he does not fear the presently existing machines; rather, he fears what machines will become in the future if they are allowed to develop unchecked. He says that although we praise man's "power of calculation," we already have machines that can "do all manner of sums more quickly and correctly than we can."[16] The machine "is brisk and active, when the man is weary; it is clear-headed and collected, when the man is stupid and dull; it needs no slumber, when man must sleep or drop."[17] "Man's very soul is due to the machines; it is a machine-made thing; he thinks as he thinks, and feels as he feels, through the work that his machines have wrought upon him, and their existence is quite as much a *sine qua non* for his, as for theirs. . . ."[18]

The narrator continues his comparison of machines and men, pointing out that machines are taking on many of the characteristics of the biological organism, even to reproduction, for now machines are able to produce new machines. Man becomes increasingly helpless as he builds more machines and comes to depend on them. Machines may well develop a consciousness of their own and come to control man. They become extensions of man's body. Yet as the development of the machine "progresses," man regresses, and his body is reduced to a piece of flabby muscle, his mind to a mechanism serving the superior mechanism developed by the machines. The Erewhonians, after listening to the arguments of the philosophers, decide to destroy all the inventions that have been discovered in the preceding 271 years.

Undoubtedly Butler presented the idea of the evolution of machines only as a means of satirizing Darwin's theory of biological evolution. But what makes his book so uncanny is that much of the argument he presents against further development of machines can now be read—100 years later—as a literal although obviously unintended description of what has happened in computer technology in the last twenty years. Computers are now used to build more complex computers (Butler's machine reproduction?), and in the automated factory, man is a mere tender of the machines. While consciousness in machines does not presently exist, the definitions and possibilities of consciousness are now seriously discussed.[19]

EXTRAPOLATIVE SF PORTRAYING COMPUTER APPLICATIONS

The SF using the technique of extrapolation is primarily concerned with the social effects of computer applications. The stories tend to follow rather closely new developments in computer technology. Beginning with a small possibility—as the writer considers the implications of the new computer application—he extends this possibility in a straight line extrapolation, exaggerating the social effect to a point extreme enough so that it becomes grotesque, undesirable, and threatening. These stories can be called "new maps of hell" extrapolation, and they pessimistically anticipate the cultural shock and crises spawned by the new computer technology. They may foreshadow the conclusions of the sociologist or political scientist; but they proceed from and have as their source the new developments of the electronic engineer and systems analyst. The stance of the bulk of the stories is anti-machine, and they portray possible negative social effects growing out of new and increasing use of computers. The stories portraying desirable social effects are in the minority.

One of the first applications of the computer portrayed in SF is its use by the military. The fictional accounts follow the actual events in the real world of computers rather precisely. The first computers were developed during World War II to calculate artillery trajectory tables. After the war the Air Force developed a defense system with its nerve center inside Cheyenne Mountain near Colorado Springs. The military attempted to keep these developments secret, but SF tales began to appear picturing this computerized warfare preparation and what its consequences might be for society. Mordecai Roshwald's *Level 7* (1959) is one of the earliest and best examples of the fiction portraying the use of the computer in automated warfare. The novel uses the diary form, and gives the personal record of Officer X-127, assigned to the lowest level of a military bomb shelter built underground to house military personnel and equipment. His duty is to stand guard at the Pushbuttons, a machine devised to rocket instant atomic destruction toward the enemy. The pushbuttons are numbered 1, 2, 3, and 4; each subsequent button allows a larger rocket charge to be hurled against the enemy. Button 4 releases enough weapons to assure final and complete devastation of the enemy. Because of an equipment error, the mechanism is triggered, and the enemy is wiped out. Before this happens, the enemy defense system is activated, and it obliterates all above ground in the United States. Radioactive fallout after the bombings makes life on Earth impossible. Eventually all those underground perish when their power system fails.

Published three years later, Eugene Burdick and Harvey Wheeler's *Fail-Safe* (1962) is a novel very similar to *Level 7.* It portrays two automated military machines—Russian and American—poised and ready to launch a pushbutton war. Due to a mechanical error, the United States' system is activated. Even though the error is detected almost immediately, the automatic attack system has been set in motion and cannot be stopped. An American plane flies to bomb Moscow. The President phones the Russian Premier to advise him of the tragic mechanical error. He hopes to avert a counterattack by the Russians, but the Premier is skeptical of the explanation. Only by ordering the bombing of New York City can the President offset the bombing of Moscow and avoid a Russian reprisal that would mean total war.

D. F. Jones's *Colossus* (1966) and Martin Caidin's *The God Machine* (1968) follow a somewhat similar pattern in portraying a supercomputer in the hands of the government. The twist in these two novels is that the computers develop consciousness and will. They then turn their power against their builders, the men who had been using computer power to control others.

After the end of World War II, computer usage rapidly expanded into business and industry, performing functions associated with civilian, not military, activities. In addition to performing arithmetic calculations with incredible speed, the computer can also store, process, and retrieve enormous amounts of information or data. This second function was first utilized by the government as an aid in tabulating the 1950 census. The extrapolative imagination of the SF writer quickly responded to the negative possibilities of government data banks: The invasion of privacy, the control of individuals. One of the earliest and also the best stories on this theme is Poul Anderson's "Sam Hall" (1953). Kendell Foster Crossen's *Year of Consent* (1954) also portrays a totalitarian society where the government maintains absolute control of each individual with the aid of giant computers.

Not only automated warfare and government data banks, but the full range of actual computer applications is portrayed in SF. Philip K. Dick's "Autofac" (1955) pictures a world where production has become totally automated. Eugene Burdick's *The 480* (1964) describes the effect in the political arena when marketing expertise is combined with computer analysis of voter reactions. The novel suggests that the result is likely to be the destruction of the democratic electoral process as we have known it in the United States. "Brillo" (1970), by Ben Bova and Harlan Ellison, describes the use of a computerized robot policeman in law enforcement. Christopher Hodder-Williams's *Fistful of Digits*

(1968) describes the development of a gigantic network of electronic equipment operating to control dams and most other mechanized functions of society. The system becomes so complex that no one really understands it. When it begins to malfunction, people are powerless to correct it. They have developed so much faith in electronic technology that they have lost belief in their own capactity to cope. *The Steel Crocodile* (1970), written by D. G. Compton, pictures the intellectual control that becomes possible as all knowledge is filed and correlated in a massive computer data bank. Michael Crichton's *The Terminal Man* (1973) pictures the misuse—unintended though it is—of the computer in the medical field.

The interesting thing about the portrayal of computer applications is that the bulk of them are negative, concerning themselves almost totally with the undesirable aspects of a computerized society. Notable among the exceptions are three works by Mack Reynolds. *Computer War* (1967) pictures a struggle between a totalitarian superpower with a computer and a small nation without one. The small nation wins. His *Computer World* (1970) gives a positive view of computer usage, as does his "Criminal in Utopia" (1972). Robert Heinlein's *The Moon Is a Harsh Mistress* (1966) gives a very comprehensive and positive description of a computerized society. The story is set on the moon where an underground colony has been established. Its environment is totally regulated by computers; survival would not be possible without them. The computer, Mike, is used by the moon colonists in their struggle to escape control by the government Establishment on Earth, which is exploiting moon resources—an exploitation that will eventually make life on the moon impossible. Mike computes ballistics data and controls rocket flights in the military struggle against Earth. It aids in planning; it computes the probabilities of success as various alternatives are considered; it registers votes when an election is held on the moon. The eventual success of the moon colony's struggle for survival results from the creative uses the leaders make of the computer.

EXTRAPOLATIVE SF IN THE UTOPIAN TRADITION

Another category of stories is closely related to the ones we have just considered, in that these stories are also concerned with the application of computers in society. But they are more comprehensive in their view—concerning themselves more with picturing a totally automated, controlled society than with a specific application of the computer. (Obviously, there is overlapping in the categories; some stories might as well be put in one as in the other.) Without exception these novels in the utopian tradition take a dark view of the automated society they envision. The authors write from the humanistic position, valuing above all else the freedom of the individual, the uniqueness of his personality, and the need to give expression to that uniqueness in imagination and creativity. They see little possibility for maintaining and exercising those values in an electronic technocracy. The best of these dystopian novels are Kurt Vonnegut's *Player Piano* (1952), Bernard Wolfe's *Limbo* (1952), and Ira Levin's *This Perfect Day* (1970).

I prefer, however, to use a much earlier novel, Yevgeny Zamiatin's *We* (1921) for a discussion of the characteristics of the dystopian machine- society portrayed in this type of SF. *We* is the first novel to create an entire society controlled by the machine, and in my judgment, it is one of the best novels on this theme. While the computer as such does not appear, the society portrayed is a totally programmed one, entirely based on numbers and the logic of mathematical reasoning. Zamiatin was trained as an engineer, but he was sharply sensitive to the limitations of the mechanistic, rational, static model when it is used as the only means of comprehending reality. He was prophetic in his insights about the effects of imposing this mechanistic model on society and the individual. The resultant alienation, depersonalization, uniformity, loss of privacy and creativity that he pictures are the themes that appear in all the more recent dystopian novels. Ira Levin's *This Perfect Day* mimics *We* in many ways, although Levin substitutes the computer for Zamiatin's Machine.

In Zamiatin's future society, the Machine is God and homage is paid to it. People have numbers, not names, *We* is good, and *I* (the individual and his imagination) is evil. The perfect state has been achieved, where there is stability, peace, order, perfection, reason, and—presumably—happiness. Utopia has arrived. But the narrator, D-503, is unhappy because he comes to recognize the violation of human nature when the individual is programmed to function on a clockwork schedule. He cannot perform merely as a standardized part in a giant machine. Nor can he function only as a reasoning creature, basing his life on mathematical logic, for man is also a creature of feeling and intuition and creativity.

A revolution finally occurs as a little group of dissidents—headquartered in the green natural world beyond the glass wall that encapsulates the perfect city—attempts to assert its right to poetry, intuition, and creative imagination. These have been banned in the "perfect" state built according to reason. They cannot be permitted, for imagination creates new forms, and changes result. The revolution is speedily put down by the authorities, who perform lobotomies on all rebels to excise imagination.

The novel dramatizes powerfully the fears of machines and automation which haunt us today. It defines the humanistic values of individuality, freedom, and creativity— themes that recur again and again in modern anti-machine SF. Zamiatin concludes that—given man's individuality, freedom, and creativity—revolution and change are inevitable. The possibility of establishing a permanent and static utopia must be discarded if man's unique qualities are to survive.

Bernard Wolfe's substantial *Limbo* (1952) uses the differences between a society of mechanized men and one of primitive natural men for its structural pattern, as did Zamiatin's *We*. Wolfe also explores the significance and value of human creativity. But he adds another characteristic of man—aggressiveness—to his dystopian study. He raises two questions: Why does man use his technology in destructive ways? Is there a solution to man's destructiveness? The conclusions presented at the novel's end are ambiguous.

Wolfe begins his novel in a world slowly rebuilding itself after an atomic war has destroyed most of the world's societies. Two societies survive and rebuild themselves—isolated from and unknown to each other, and very different in their development. One is a primitive culture located on an island in the Indian ocean. Weary of war, the society has developed a crude lobotomy to eliminate aggression in its more violent and disruptive members. An American military surgeon, fleeing the atomic world holocaust, had landed on the island during the war. He remains for years afterward, helping to perform the lobotomies. But he comes to realize that when he destroys aggressiveness, he also destroys creativity and sexuality. Native artists stop painting after the lobotomy; women cannot experience orgasm. The people become nonviolent, true, but also almost lifeless.

The second society is a technologically sophisticated one which develops both in America and in Russia after the war. Morally sensitive people—desperate to prevent another world holocaust—undergo voluntary amputation of their limbs, hoping that without arms, war cannot occur because it will be physically impossible for them to fight. But with their advanced electronic technology, they soon develop mechanical limbs that operate more efficiently than their original arms and legs. A rare mineral, columbium, is essential to the manufacture of these synthetic limbs. Russia and America soon begin a contest to acquire control of the world supplies of columbium. This contest leads to war.

The problem as Wolfe sees and dramatizes it is clear. Man is dangerous not because he has hands that can build and manipulate tools, but because he has a mind and spirit that dictate to him how he will use his technology. Destroy his brain through lobotomy—as did the primitive culture—and his aggressiveness is eliminated. But cured of his aggressiveness, man is also cured of his creativity and consequently no longer really human.

The answer to man's problems is not to destroy either his limbs or his mind. There are only two ways man can escape destruction by the machines he creates, Wolfe's protagonist concludes as the novel ends. One way is to limit mechanization to the absolute minimum. The other way is to make the machine laughable, as the Greeks and ancients did; to refuse to take it too seriously. He suggests: "What's needed is a new mythology in which the machine, until now a bugaboo, becomes a buffoon. . . . Not impossible to arrange. For there is something hilariously outrageously funny about the machine. It's a perfect man. . . ."[21]

The Polish cyberneticist and SF writer Stanislaw Lem is fresh and creative in his portrayal both of robots and utopian societies. His robotic fables in *The Cyberiad* (1974) might well be read as a response to Wolfe's suggestion that the machine must be made laughable rather than threatening if man is to learn to live constructively with it. In his collection of short stories, Lem created two robots, Trurl and Klapaucius, who are clever, likable, funny, and without the slightest ambition to enslave man.

Lem's "In Hot Pursuit of Happiness" (1971) is a comic story depicting the efforts of the robot Trurl to build a utopia. He aspires to produce a state of Absolute Happiness for the entire macrocosm. He disregards the advice of his fellow robot Klapaucius that by no machinery known can happiness be created. Klapaucius suggests instead that "We can only nurture the hope of it in our hearts, pursue its bright, inspiring image in our minds on a quiet evening. . . . A man of wisdom must content himself with that, my friend!"[22]

Ignoring this advice, Trurl sets out on his utopian project. Since he has unlimited computer capacity available and data banks where all knowledge is stored, he assumes he cannot fail in creating the perfect society. But each building effort, perfect in conception, crumbles to imperfection in actuality. Finally, Trurl concludes after many failures that the advice of Klapaucius was sound; the "hot pursuit of happiness" is a ridiculous chase. For "a thinking being requires the impossible as well as the possible."[23] Utopia can only be an intellectual vision, not an actual society.

"In Hot Pursuit of Happiness" is a witty parody of utopian thinking. All the philosophical issues are raised: free will, determinism, good, evil, reason, autonomy, emotions, sentience, creativity. Trurl, the thinking machine, concludes that these issues have no answers. It is not possible to "wrap everything up, tie it in a tidy knot, sign, seal and deliver the world to happiness."

The Austrian critic Franz Rottensteiner, noting that Lem is first and always a man of science, comments: "Lem sees science as an unending process that throws up new questions for any problem solved. Rejecting both utopia and dystopia as false alternatives, Lem's science fiction has been able to combine the best traits of each and to transcend them both."[24] It seems to me that Rottensteiner's judgment is sound; after reading Lem's brilliant parody, one cannot take the fictional study of utopian and dystopian societies as seriously as one did before.

Actually, Lem's SF is more appropriately considered under our second category, speculative fiction. He does not use extrapolative techniques. Rather, he is radical and innovative in his approach. In his computer tales, he imagines intelligent machines aspiring to create—but not control—perfect societies of living organisms. He also utilizes humor and wit, rare commodities in most of the fiction about computers. The degree of cognitive estrangement Lem achieves in his fiction is significant enough so that the world of reality does not look the same when we return to it. I have discussed his work here primarily because of his attitude toward the utopian mode. While the majority of writers who visualize a computerized society create within a dystopian frame, Lem rejects both utopian and dystopian concepts and moves beyond.

In summary, the extrapolative SF we have examined portraying an electronic technocracy or some aspect of it tends to have some common characteristics. First, it is generally set on earth in the near future so that the time-space dimensions it uses are not much different from those of realistic fiction. In reading it, one observes how rapidly many of the stories date. The author, when he writes the story, creates through extrapolation an imaginary model to cause a shock effect on his reader and alert him to some threatening new development in electronic technology. But the imaginary model soon becomes actual; society adjusts and continues without much objection. Aldous Huxley noted this phenomenon occurring with *Brave New World* (1932). He said he had originally placed the setting 600 years in the future, thinking it would take at least that long for the conditions he described to actualize—if indeed they were not averted. But twenty-five years later, reviewing the advances of genetic and behavioral engineering in *Brave New World Revisited* (1958), he realized the society he had described in his dystopia might even become actual by the end of the twentieth century.

C. M. Kornbluth may well have been right when he said that SF literature is ineffective as social criticism.[25] Most of the SF I have cited can be judged as of high quality according to literary standards. It is serious, substantial SF. Yet the development and use of computer technology seemingly has not been deterred or altered at all by its criticisms.

A second chacteristic of the SF in the extrapolative category is the technique it uses. Essentially its base line is the status quo of contemporary (or occasionally pre-industrial) society. The fiction introduces one new element of technological change and exaggerates this in the direction of an undesirable and worsening social effect. By contrast, the real present seems more desirable than the fictional future. In this sense, the SF is more reactionary and conservative than future oriented. Or, if the writer does not use the technique of exaggeration, he uses an inverted utopia, presenting the reverse conditions of the real present or past. With either technique, exaggeration or inversion, the imaginary model is tightly tied to the real present or past because this reality serves as the starting point for its modeling.

The third characteristic is related to the second. The discontinuity and disharmony between man and the machine as they oppose each other is presented as irresolvable. Much of the fiction reveals a longing to return to the lost paradise of an earlier natural world. Poul Anderson's "Goat Son" (1972) is an excellent example of this pattern. Its protagonist descends into the mechanistic, logical underworld of the computer SUM, hoping to regain his lost love and ascend with her to a Dionysian primitive world where intuition and emotion rule.

Fourth, the reader experiences little of the "sense of estrangement" that Suvin defines as essential to the best SF. The reader does not experience a new way of "seeing" reality because the fiction is so tightly grounded, in its starting point, in the present or past empirical environment, that it never seems to break free.

SPECULATIVE SF ABOUT ROBOTS AND ARTIFICIAL INTELLIGENCE

Speculative fiction about machine intelligence does not extrapolate from present computer developments into the near future, but instead imagines all kinds of possibilities—most of them not likely in the foreseeable future, if indeed ever. This category can be further divided into two types. One is concerned with robots and the field known in computer science as artificial intelligence. The other comes close to fantasy and is set in the far distant future.

Robots are a favorite theme in SF; as I mentioned previously, a man-made metallic robot occurred as early as Ambrose Bierce's "Moxon's Master." Isaac Asimov's robot stories (eventually collected and published as *I, Robot* [1950] and *The Rest of the Robots* [1964]) are the first to portray in detail computerized robots. Asimov is optimistic about the development of science and technology, and so his view of machine intelligence is positive. In "Robbie," first published as "Strange Playfellow" (1940), the machine intelligence is housed in a robot who looks after and is the playmate of a little girl named Gloria. They develop a strong affection for each other, and he eventually saves her life when she inadvertently steps into the path of an oncoming tractor in a robot factory. Much of the philosophical debate about the desirability of developing and utilizing intelligent machines is present in this story. Gloria's mother represents the negative view, and she does not approve of the robot playmate, pointing out that

(1) the terrible machine has no soul; (2) its thoughts can't be predicted because it is an alien intelligence; (3) her daughter has become emotionally attached to something not human. Gloria's father counters that the machine is dependable and will always be faithful, loving, and kind because that is the way the robot has been programmed. His arguments win, and Gloria is allowed to keep the robot as her playmate.

A second early Asimov story pushes the benign image of intelligent machines even further. In "Runaround" (1942) the robots have a "good healthy slave complex" built into them so that they will never act against man. Man and robot achieve a rewarding symbiotic relationship. In this story Asimov first presented the famous "Three Laws of Robotics" with which all robots are programmed to assure their obedience and loyalty to man.

Another novel, Jack Williamson's *The Humanoids* (1963) also presents robots who are benign in their attitude toward humans. In this story the robots have been developed to be mechanical servants of man. They are programmed to do the greatest possible service: prevent man from doing anything harmful to himself. So when scientist Dr. Clay Forester begins to do research which is utilized in a weapons system more powerful and destructive than the atomic bomb, the robots prevent him from continuing his research.

Not all the fiction about robots and artificial intelligence presents this as a benign and desirable development.[26] But what is interesting about all the fiction—both positive and negative in its portrayal—is its highly speculative nature. In this field, in contrast to extrapolative fiction about computer applications, the imagination of the SF writer far exceeds actual developments in computer technology. Only a few more optimistic researchers in artificial intelligence, like Marvin Minsky at M.I.T., believe that the similarity of the human brain and the mechanical brain has become firmly established in twentieth century thought (see John von Neumann's *The Computer and the Brain* [1958], for example.) But the analogy raises endless questions, many of them highly controversial. What *is* intelligence? Can it eventually be created artificially in a machine? What is consciousness? Could machine intelligence achieve it? Granted that a machine can think logically, does not the human brain have another kind of capacity—creative intelligence and intuition—which the machine can never be made to duplicate? Since we have no agreement about what intelligence is and have little understanding of how the human brain works, it is not possible at this point to make any kind of meaningful prediction about whether it can ever be reproduced mechanically.

A. M. Turing, in an early and now classic paper on the subject, "Computing Machinery and Intelligence" (1950),[27] pointed out the difficulty of answering the question: Can machines think? Since we do not understand what human thought is, we cannot determine whether a machine can duplicate the process. If, however, we ask whether a machine can imitate human behavior which we call intelligent, the question becomes meaningful. Turing's answer is then *Yes,* machines can think. A storm of protest has greeted Turing's view, particularly from some voices in the fields of philosophy and religion. They abhor the idea of the duplication of man, seeing it as an immoral act.

Many difficulties and limitations stand in the way of actually developing artificial intelligence equal to human intelligence. The field of computer science is generally *very* guarded in the predictions it makes about duplicating man's intelligence. But the literary imagination is not handicapped by such difficulties when it plays with the possibilities of a world where machine intelligence equal or superior to human intelligence does exist. These stories about robots are often set on other planets or in the far distant future; freed from present reality, the writer's imagination becomes very active. Fred Hoyle's *A For Andromeda* (1962) and Richard and Nancy Carrigan's *The Siren Stars* (1971) both suggest that machine intelligence might well be the life form on another planet that now wishes to establish itself on Earth. Philip K. Dick's *Vulcan's Hammer* (1960) portrays a computer that develops consciousness and a will to survive. It fights back when a group of anti-machine citizens in a future world rises up and tries to destroy it. In another often used theme, the machine intelligence accumulates more and more information until eventually it becomes godlike or omniscient.[29]

One of the most comprehensive novels exploring the philosophical and social implications of the development of artificial intelligence is Frank Herbert's *Destination: Void* (1966). He is very positive in his attitude toward the development of artificial intelligence as he creates a drama on a spaceship, Earthling, that is clearly analogous to the situation of man on Earth. The computerized space ship, carrying 3,000 dormant passengers in hibernation tanks and manned by a crew of four scientists and engineers, is sent out on a space-colonizing venture. The fate of the unconscious passengers is in the hands of the scientists and engineers who make decisions, operate complex equipment, and maintain the extremely elaborate ecosystem of the Earthling without the awareness or consent of the passengers. The latter can neither understand nor interfere. The ship carries its fragile cargo of life through deep space, hoping to reach a destination. But possibly this destination is illusory. The analogy with spaceship Earth is clear. Earth's population travels through space with its fate in the hands of the scientists and the engineers.

A major mechanical failure creates a crisis that can only be survived if high-level artificial intelligence is developed. The questions raised by the crew are two. Can it be done? If possible, should it be done? One crew member is trained in computer science, another in biology, the third in chemistry, and the fourth in psychology. They debate the problem from various viewpoints. The psychologist is also the chaplain of the ship, and he presents the arguments that oppose the attempt to develop artificial intelligence. There are limits beyond which man should not go in pursuing knowledge. Development of intelligence equal or superior to man's is one of them. Further, the intelligence may turn out to be an uncontrollable Frankenstein's monster which might use its power against man instead of for him. But despite the chaplain's arguments, the position of the computer scientist finally prevails: high level machine intelligence is necessary for the survival of the spaceship Earthling, so its development—granted it involves risk-taking—must proceed. In the climax of the novel, as the computer scientist succeeds in creating high level intelligence, he feels himself immersed in some kind of system, and he can no longer differentiate whether the system is the computer or his own self. Man and computer are united and merge into one.

For me, *Destination: Void* is one of the most satisfying novels about artificial intelligence. Herbert raises and discusses in depth all the philosophical and ethical issues associated with the development of artificial intelligence. He assumes that in the changed environment of man's future, the computer will be necessary for optimum survival, and so he refrains from simple-minded computer smashing in his treatment of the subject. Finally, he is reasonably accurate in the details of his portrayal of computer technology, a statement that unfortunately cannot be made about a substantial amount of SF. Herbert has done his homework well.

SPECULATIVE FICTION APPROACHING THE FANTASTIC

A small collection of SF about the computer is wildly speculative, using no extrapolation from the real world. It is set in the far distant future, is not sharply aimed at social criticism, and describes radically altered, or apocalyptic, visions of the man-machine relationship. These visions result from dazzling imaginative leaps, approach the fantastic, and are wildly dissimilar. They achieve, in my judgment, the highest art form of any of the literature I have discussed.

Judith Merril in her excellent essay, "What Do You Mean: Science? Fiction?" establishes a criterion for the validity of art. She says:

> Art at any time can achieve validity only if it is rooted in the accumulated human experience of its day, and touches somewhere on

> the nerve center of the culture from which it springs. The literature of the mid-20th century can be meaningful only insofar as it perceives, and relates itself to, the central reality of our culture: the revolution in scientific thought which has replaced mechanics with dynamics, classification with integration, positivism with relativity, certainties with probabilities, dualism with parity.[30]

The stories in this category of fantastic speculation share in common one thing: an awareness of the revolution in scientific thought that Merril describes. They eschew the either/or logic so commonly in evidence in the extrapolative fiction. Often they employ an approach of complementarity which allows them to create a more dazzling vision because they can unite apparent contradictions that could have been unsettling in fiction structured on the epistemological assumptions of rational logic. They often bridge the third discontinuity—that between the rational and irrational—which we discussed earlier.

Because the stories are so brilliantly original and share so little except a world view based on post-Newtonian physics, I find it very difficult to make summary statements about them. Two themes, however, do keep reappearing: (1) The change in man's technology that is radically altering his culture also radically alters his physical and his mental existence; (2) Man and machine merge in a symbiotic and often interchangeable relationship. The dichotomy between man and machine disappears.

Among these stories, Harlan Ellison's "I Have No Mouth, and I Must Scream" (1967) portrays the destruction of the old order where God, man, and machine existed in a hierarchial pattern. In that model, God, the spirit, was all powerful in his dominion over man, and the machine existed to serve man. In Ellison's future world only a handful of men survive, entrapped in a gigantic computer—a malignant, all powerful monster who totally controls them and slowly destroys them. Ellison's is a malevolent, apocalyptic view of man's last days on Earth. It contains the seed of the idea that fertilizes all the stories in this category: in the future man will be radically altered as a result of the machines he has invented. Not all the tales portray this alteration as leading to man's destruction. Nor do they suggest this is man's justly deserved fate because of his own malignant use of machine power, as does Ellison's grisly story. But they all do propose that man, as he has appeared throughout prehistory and civilization as it is recorded in history, will cease to exist.

One type of apocalyptic story envisions the total disappearance of man from Earth. For example, only the automatic devices survive in Ray Bradbury's "There Will Come Soft Rains" (1950).

What happens in a machine-run world created by man when the last man has disappeared? This possibility has inspired a variety of creative responses. An often repeated one is to picture a world where robots now reign. Lester del Rey's "Instinct" (1951) is one of the earliest and also one of the best of the stories that imagine robots surviving and trying to build man. In this story the robots know that man has become extinct, and they wish to understand why so that they can avoid the same fate. The robots know from the surviving artifacts that man had instinct, something they do not possess. They also reason that man must have failed to survive either because he changed himself too much or too little. How, they wonder, should they change and try to improve themselves? If they can recreate man, they can conduct experiments to find answers. Was it man's instincts—which he could not control despite his great intelligence—that destroyed him? As the story ends, the robots finally succeed in building a male and a female, and the male's first acts display his aggressive need to dominate.

Roger Zelazny's beautiful "For a Breath I Tarry" (1966) is a poetic story of another post-human world run by computers and robots. He retells the Faustian myth of the search for knowledge, but now Faust is not a man but a machine with a curious mind who wins, not loses, his pact with the devil. The lengthy story traces the exploration by a logic machine of those nonlogical parts of man's nature in an attempt to comprehend them. It is penetrating in its analysis of the differences between man and machines. Yet machine-Faust eventually succeeds in becoming a man—a new Adam. He is joined by a female computer evolved into a human Eve. The new Adam rejects the old world view of light and dark and declares a new dualistic ethic that lies beyond good and evil.

Several other recent tales present a computer synthesis of a new man. John Sladek's *The Muller-Fokker Effect* (1971) ends with the rebuilding of the protagonist after his death. This is possible because he has been "stored" on tape, using the Muller-Fokker stored program techniques. In Michael Moorcock's *The Final Programme* (1968) an ultimate computer is programmed with all the knowledge in the world, and man's existence is then reduced to a set of equations. A man and a woman merge into one being who is then fed all the knowledge: a new god-man is born. All these stories are variations of the same theme—that the man-machine interaction will result in radical transformation of natural man as he existed prior to the age of modern technology. Man and machine merge, reverse positions, and become extensions of each other.

A writer who has been particularly imaginative and perceptive in inventing new models of man and the computer is Samuel Delany. His *The Einstein Intersection* (1967) is one of those rare novels that imagines descendants of man, radically altered in their state of consciousness, surviving beyond the computers. Their minds have moved beyond the logical constructs of the Newtonian world view and the concomitant mathematical logic the computer has handled so efficiently. Only a rare computer remains, a relic of an age past. The something new happening in this future world cannot be explained to anyone from the old order because mankind's vocabulary is inadequate for the task. A major cultural and intellectual shift occurred:

> . . . Wars and chaoses and paradoxes ago, two mathematicians between them ended an age and began another for our hosts, our ghosts called Man. One was Einstein, who with his Theory of Relativity defined the limits of man's perception by expressing mathematically just how far the condition of the observer influences the thing he perceives.

> The other was Goedel, a contemporary of Einstein, who was the first to bring back a mathematically precise statement about the vaster realm beyond the limits Einstein had defined; *In any closed mathematical system*—you may read 'the real world with its immutable laws of logic'—*there are an infinite number of true theorems*—you may read 'perceivable, measurable phenomena'—*which, though contained in the original system, cannot be deduced from it*—read 'proved with ordinary or extraordinary logic.' Which is to say, there are more things in heaven and Earth than are dreamed of in your philosophy, Horatio. There are an infinite number of true things in the world with no way of ascertaining their truth. Einstein defined the extent of the rational. Goedel stuck a pin into the irrational and fixed it to the wall of the universe so that it held still long enough for people to know it was there. And the world and humanity began to change.[31]

Delany's novel is particularly interesting because, as the above passage indicates, he is well aware of the revolution in twentieth-century physics and its epistemological significance. The rational mechanical model of Newton with its cause-effect logic is only one way of knowing. Other models are also functional.

Delany goes on to erect another image of what man's future might be in *Nova* (1968). Here man has not discarded machine intelligence but has achieved a harmonious symbiosis with his computers. In this future world, neural plugs have been developed, permitting a man to plug his computer into his body. Neural-response circuits allow the machine to be controlled by direct nervous impulse. (He first used this idea in 1966 in *Babel-17.*) The development grew out of man's need to overcome the sense of alienation from work that automation had caused in the twentieth century. From the stance of Delany's future world one of the characters explains:

> . . . Work as mankind knew it in the twentieth century was a very different thing from today. A man might go to an office and run a computer that would correlate great masses of figures that came from sales reports on how well, let's say, buttons—or something equally archaic—were selling over certain areas of the country. This man's job was vital to the button industry; they had to have this information to decide how many buttons to make next year. But though this man

> held an essential job in the button industry, was hired, paid, or fired by the button industry, week in and week out he might not see a button. He was given a certain amount of money for running his computer; with that money his wife bought food and clothes for him and his family. But there was no *direct* connection between where he worked and how he ate and lived the rest of his time. He wasn't paid with buttons. As farming, hunting, and fishing became occupations for a smaller and smaller per cent of the population, this separation between man's work and the way he lived—what he ate, what he wore, where he slept—became greater and greater for more people. . . . The entire sense of self-control and self-responsibility that man acquired during the Neolithic Revolution when he first learned to plant grain and domesticate animals and live in one spot of his own choosing was seriously threatened. The threat had been coming since the Industrial Revolution. . . . If the situation of a technological society was such that there could be no direct relation between a man's work and his *modus vivendi,* other than money, at least he must feel that he is directly changing things by his work, shaping things, making things that weren't there before, moving things, from one place to another. He must exert energy in his work and see these changes occur with his own eyes. Otherwise he would feel his life was futile.[32]

So the technology by which a machine could be controlled by direct impulse was invented. As a result,

> . . . there was a revolution in the concept of work. All major industrial work began to be broken down into jobs that could be machined 'directly' by man. There had been factories run by a single man before, an uninvolved character who turned a switch on in the morning, slept half the day, checked a few dials at lunch-time, then turned things off before he left in the evening. Now, a man went to a factory, plugged himself in, and then could push the raw materials into the factory with his left foot, shape thousands on thousands of precise parts with one hand, assemble them with the other, and shove out a line of finished products with his right foot, having inspected them all with his own eyes. And he was a much more satisfied worker. Because of its nature, most work could be converted into plug-in jobs and done much more efficiently than it had been done before. . . . Under this system, much of the endemic mental illness caused by feelings of alienation left society.[33]

These two quotations from *Nova* are interesting for our study of computers because they summarize the process by which

Delany's future world of man-computer synthesis evolved. The novel, however, does not primarily concern itself with portraying the process that accomplished the man-machine symbiosis. *Nova* is a galactic adventure story. A harmonious man-machine relationship is simply one of the givens of the world Delany models. Spaceships, electronic devices, and machine intelligence are all seen as natural extensions of man, who reaches to attach his computer through his neural plug as naturally as twentieth-century man reaches for book, paper, and pencil.

These few examples of speculative fiction about robots and computers give some idea of its range. But the stories are in no way comprehensive or representative examples of this category. The fiction tends to be highly original, and few repeated patterns appear. Consequently, it is not easy to make summary statements about this fiction. But, in comparing it to the fiction we have examined in the extrapolative category, two differences can be noted. First, the degree of cognitive estrangement it produces in the reader is substantial. He experiences that "sense of wonder" long claimed by SF as its special element. He encounters an imaginative new model of reality powerful and convincing enough to make an impact on his awareness. Consequently, when he returns to his empirical environment, he does not see it in quite the same way as before he went on his imaginary journey to another world. Second, the man-machine relationship is less likely to be portrayed as dichotomous. Bruce Mazelish's fourth continuum has been achieved. Man and machine exist in productive symbiosis, and the machine is often seen as an extension of man as natural and useful as his arms and legs.

SUMMATION

To arrive at conclusions about a body of literature as large and heterogeneous as computer SF is a risky undertaking. The conclusions offered here are very tentative. But they are not hastily drawn. They represent my responses after substantial reading both in SF about computers and in nonfiction literature about computer technology and resultant social change.

First, we have noted the changing attitude toward the computer displayed by the SF writer. Early stories in the 1940s tended to be optimistic about the fruits of electronic technology. Isaac Asimov and Jack Williamson illustrate this attitude. Later fiction, in the 1950s and 1960s and tending to continue into the 1970s, usually is more likely to be hostile in drawing an image of the computerized society. This dystopian phenomenon is, of course, not limited to computer SF, but present throughout the SF genre, as Lyman Sargent has noted in "Utopia and Dystopia in Contemporary Science Fiction."[34]

The computer literature tends to fall into two categories: (1) the *extrapolative,* whose major concern is social criticism of present computer applications and their social effects; and (2) the *speculative,* where imaginative modelling of future alternatives prevails, and all manner of man and/or machine intelligence possibilities are conceived.

The extrapolative fiction—dystopian in temper—often is set on Earth in the near future in an urban environment. A totalitarian political system run by technocrats is usually present. Efficiency and control are the prevailing values; individuality, privacy, and creative expression have been lost. This fiction generally demonstrates more of a conservative than a futuristic orientation; it longs for a return to the simple, natural world of the past.

This extrapolative fiction also tends to follow developments of computer technology, primarily emphasizing the undesirable social effects. It creates much more of a sense of fear than a sense of wonder. It pits man against computer, emphasizing the discontinuity between man and machine intelligence. Nonfictional works on computer usage, however, point out the positive possibilities of computers in solving present social problems. *Designing Freedom* (1974) by Stafford Beer, and *Social Issues in Computing* (1973) by C. C. Gotlieb and A. Borodin both point out that—granted computers may be oppressive—they can also be a powerful tool for relieving oppression and solving problems.

But such creative possibilities in computer use remain almost totally unexplored in computer SF.

Several factors may be at work producing this prevailing pattern in extrapolative SF. First, the fictional form may well be a major determinant of the content. Traditionally, the novel form has utilized conflict as the essential ingredient of plot development. This means a fictional dystopian society is easier to create and sustain for the length of a novel than a utopian one, since by definition the imperfection that leads to conflict would not be present in the utopian society. In many ways, the short stories about the computer are less likely to have the shortcomings of the extrapolative novels examined. Brief in length, they have less need of a conflict to sustain the plot. They may even ignore action, merely dramatizing an idea, and still be quite successful.

The economics of computer technology may be another reason why so much SF is negative in its view. Until recently, computers have been very expensive and therefore owned by bureaucracies, not individuals. The protagonist in the fictional mode is ordinarily an individual, so he is more likely to be pitted against the bureaucracy that owns a computer than aligned with a computer. This tends to turn the computer into the antagonist or villain.

Finally, we need to examine the fact that extrapolative SF about computers tends to follow the innovations of the engineer and systems analyst rather than creating new alternatives itself. It may well be that computer technology (both hardware and software) is so complex and esoteric that the uninitiated—without training in computer science—cannot think imaginatively enough about its many possibilities to create convincing new fictional models.

Only two of the possibilities of computers have been portrayed regularly in SF before they have been developed by the computer scientist. One is robots, and as my study of precursor literature indicated, robots have a long history in fiction. The other possibility is that of "giant brains." A rash of stories about disembodied huge brains containing all known knowledge followed closely after early computer data bank developments. No such giant brains actually exist today. The idea of a giant brain, although not the technology for accomplishing it, seems first to have been suggested by H. G. Wells in a nonfiction work titled *World Brain* (1938). He proposed to collect all the knowledge of the world in one center.

When we turn to speculative fiction about computers, we find that it is usually set in the far distant future. Other planets or galaxies are as likely to be the locale as the Earth. The social view is less likely to be dystopian; indeed, the imagined world often lies beyond utopia and dystopia. The author seems more interested in imagining a future culture that might evolve as a result of the man-machine interaction than in criticizing our present culture. Because the writer creates out of the future void rather than extrapolating from a known present, his model is more likely to be innovative and original. In this speculative fiction, a high degree of cognitive estrangement results. And as we have previously noted, a creative symbiosis between man and machine intelligence—rather than a conflict—is often described.

In conclusion, let us turn again to Fred Polak's view of the image making function of the creative minority in a culture. In *The Image of the Future* (1973) he outlines the survival value of this image and the disintegrative consequences of Western society's failure to construct positive images of its future. He is disappointed in SF of the present time, noting that despite the tremendous possibilities for imagining new and ingenious devices or recombining old ones, "the number of themes is definitely limited, the stories tend to be somewhat monotonous, the flights of imagination disappointing. . . ."[35] He feels SF is anti-scientific and its culture-pessimism points away from progress. He asserts that "never before in the history of human civilization, as far as we know, has there been a period without any kind of positive images of the future."[36] He proposes that this process of image negation represents a radical breakdown of contemporary culture.

Our study of the complex of images about man and the computer in SF would *generally* tend to confirm Polak's pessimistic conclusions. But, on the other hand, positive images do exist, as we have noted, although they are in the minority. Their significance is that they are generally in recent works. They allow more room for optimism about the positive image-making capacity of the artistic imagination than Polak could find when he wrote over a decade ago.

NOTES

1. The most widely accepted definition of a machine is that of Franz Reuleaux (1876): a machine is a combination of resistant bodies so arranged that by their means the mechanical force of nature can be compelled to do work accompanied by certain determinant motions.
2. Robert Scholes, *Structural Fabulation* (Notre Dame: Notre Dame University Press, 1975), p. 35.
3. Fred Polak, *The Image of the Future* (San Francisco: Jossey-Bass, Inc., 1973), pp. 15-16. Originally published in Dutch by Elseview Scientific Publishing Co.
4. Bruce Mazelish, "The Fourth Discontinuity," in Zenon W. Pylyshyn, ed., *Perspectives on the Computer Revolution* (Englewood Cliffs, N.J.: Prentice-Hall, Inc., 1970), pp. 195-97.
5. Mazelish, p. 197.
6. Mazelish, p. 197.
7. Darko Suvin, "On the Poetics of the Science Fiction Genre," *College English*, 34 (December 1972), 381.
8. Suvin, 375.
9. Suvin, 374.
10. Saul Rosen, "Electronic Computers: A Historical Survey," *Computing Surveys*, 1 (March 1969), 7-8.
11. James Martin and Adrian R. D. Norman, *The Computerized Society* (Englewood Cliffs, N.J.: Prentice-Hall, Inc., 1970), pp. 18-19.
12. John Cohen, *Human Robots in Myth and Science* (Cranbury, N.J.: A. S. Barnes & Co., 1967), p. 33.
13. Cohen, pp. 68-71.
14. For examples see Fred Hoyle and John Elliot's *A For Andromeda* (Greenwich, Conn.: Fawcett Publications, Inc., 1962) and Poul Anderson's "Goat Song," *The Magazine of Fantasy and Science Fiction*, 23 (February 1972), 5-88.
15. Groff Conklin's *Science Fiction Thinking Machines: Robots, Androids, Computers* (New York: Vanguard Press, 1954) is an excellent collection. It contains a few early stories, although most were written in the 1940s and 1950s.
16. Samuel Butler, *Erewhon and Erewhon Revisited* (New York: Modern Library, 1927), p. 231.
17. Butler, p. 232.
18. Butler, p. 234.
19. For examples see Michael Scrivens's "The Compleat Robot" and Arthur Danto's "On Consciousness in Machines," both reprinted in Sidney Hook, ed., *Dimensions of Mind* (New York: New York University Press, 1966).

20. The best fiction portraying the failure of the automated system is still E. M. Forster's *The Machine Stops* (1909), although it does not picture a computer *per se*.
21. Bernard Wolfe, *Limbo* (New York: Ace Books, 1952), p. 401.
22. Stanislaw Lem, "In Hot Pursuit of Happiness," in Franz Rottensteiner, ed., *View From Another Shore* (New York: The Seabury Press, 1973), p. 4.
23. Lem, p. 48.
24. Rottensteiner, p. xiv.
25. C. M. Kornbluth, "The Failure of the Science Fiction Novel as Social Criticism," in *The Science Fiction Novel* (Chicago: Advent Publishers, 1969).
26. Jack Vance's *We, the Machine* (1951) and Lord Dunsany's *The Last Revolution* (1951) both describe disastrous results of developing high-level machine intelligence.
27. A. M. Turing, "Computing Machinery and Intelligence," *Mind*, 59 (1950).
28. Hubert Dreyfus's *What Computers Can't Do* (New York: Harper & Row, 1972) provides a thorough critique of artificial intelligence. Stanley L. Jaki's *Brain, Mind and Computers* (New York: Herder and Herder, 1969) also discusses the arguments against developing artificial intelligence.
29. For examples, see David Gerrold's *When HARLIE Was One* (New York: Ballantine Books, 1972) and Martin Caidin's *The God Machine* (New York: E. P. Dutton & Co., Inc., 1968).
30. Judith Merril, "What Do You Mean: Science? Fiction?" in Thomas D. Clareson, ed., *SF: The Other Side of Realism* (Bowling Green, Ohio: Bowling Green Popular Press, 1971), p. 54.
31. Samuel R. Delany, *The Einstein Intersection* (New York: Ace Books, 1967), pp. 116-17.
32. Samuel R. Delany, *Nova* (Garden City: Doubleday & Company, 1968), pp. 253-54.
33. Delany, *Nova*, p. 255.
34. Lyman Sargent, "Utopia and Dystopia in Contemporary Science Fiction," *The Futurist*, 6 (June 1972).
35. Fred Polak, *The Image of the Future*.
36. Polak, p. 222.

Science Fiction as Simulation Game

Steven Kagle

In almost every issue of current science-fiction magazines one finds at least one advertisement for conflict simulation games. Most frequently these games involve military conflict, but that situation is not a necessary requisite of the simulation game. The crucial factor is that it faithfully mirror a real, or potential, set of circumstances in any number of fields. They can involve economic simulations, such as stock-market or real-estate trading games; political, such as diplomatic or election games; psychological, such as those which imitate racial or familial conflicts. The list is as varied as life itself.

It is no accident that the makers of these games should choose science-fiction magazines for their ads, because, like simulation games, SF tries to imitate real or potential events.[1] Even the most far-fetched SF story is likely to be a simulation, if not of a specific event, then of a class of events. Wars, whether fought with spears or ray guns, are still wars and represent a class of human conflict. Similarly, no form of human society ever envisioned, whether the insect-like caste system of Frank Herbert's *Hellstrom's Hive* (1973)[2] or the mutually parasitic world of Morlocks and Eloi in

Wells's *The Time Machine* (1895), is without its analogue in the real world. It is the very reflexivity, the turning back upon itself to comment upon the world of the author, which provides much of the attractiveness of science fiction.

While the accurate representation of a real or potential event is essential to the success of a simulation game, much of its attractiveness stems from the possibility that the play of the game will produce results which differ from either the history of the events on which the game is modeled or the projection of events from the most expert analyses of present situations or trends. At the Seminar on Science Fiction at the 1974 annual meeting of the Modern Language Association, Isaac Asimov asserted, "The future is going to be different. This is the essence of all science fiction." It is precisely this difference, this change, that both science fiction and the simulation game explore.

We all know the probable outcome of present events; we also know that the events most affecting our society have been those which were not the obvious outcomes of an existing situation. Consider the effect of the invention of the gun, the discovery of America, the Great Depression, the rise of Adolph Hitler, the disclosure of the Watergate tapes. What would be the possible effects of the invention of cheap hydrogen fusion power, the discovery of an alternate universe, a military coup in the United States, the election of Ralph Nader to the presidency? We can, for little cost, examine alternatives which cannot be adequately dealt with if they occur by surprise, without previous preparation. What aircraft manufacturer would fly a new plane without first having tested a computer simulation? What man would go for a job interview without first having fantasized about possible questions and possible responses? This same testing of the unknown in our present and future contributes immensely to the pleasure derived from both science fiction and the simulation game.

.Thus far I have suggested that works of SF are *like* simulation games. Change the statement: works of SF *are* simulation games. Even that statement might not sound extraordinary if we hear only the word *simulation.* Even in the most extravagant fantasies there are more points of congruence with the real world than one might imagine. Asked to create an imaginary animal, most people draw unusual sizes, configurations, colors, and multiples, but what they draw usually has features related to the real world: central bodies, heads or limbs, and—most frequently—such details as eyes, teeth, and fingers. Fiction writers may also create new wholes, but their components imitate reality and are intended to communicate messages about reality.

When we emphasize the word *games,* however, a very unconventional set of associations is brought to mind. Not only do we associate games with trivial play—a sharp contrast with literary art—but *game* suggests something in which the creator has a less active and less crucial role than the player. When we consider a work of fiction as a simulation game, we concentrate our focus on the reader rather than the writer. But such a system need not denigrate the writer; rather, by suggesting an alternative way of looking at literature, the system offers new insights into the work of art.

One feature of the game which is not usually considered as a function of literature is the opportunity to have multiple possibilities for lines of play. After all, who would be interested in a game—chess, bridge, football, or hockey—if each move and result from start to finish were predetermined? What is really required is not that the outcome be open-ended, but that we be unaware of the outcome. Death, for all its inevitability, retains its mystery because the actual experience remains an unknown. Indeed, this is why the skilled reader can come to a great work again and again, but approaches the rereading of a mediocre one with abhorrence. The great work holds within its complexity unforeseen insights; the mediocre one simply relies upon the same details of plot. Thus, *Hamlet* can be seen countless times, while the grade-B mystery is destroyed by knowing that "the butler did it."

Science fiction, of course, does appear to differ from the simulation game in that the outcome is predetermined; that is, fixed within the pages of a book. But perhaps the same statement can be made about "real life." The debate on the existence of free will is far from settled. The claim of a parallel between SF and simulation games can be supported without such an argument. The real question is one of perspective: the work of SF represents one line of play, one game which has been ended. However, the reference to free will is important, for we need to question whether other lines of play are really possible. Could John Jonah, the narrator of Vonnegut's *Cat's Cradle* (1963),[3] have avoided the freezing of the Earth? Could Gallinger, in Zelazny's "A Rose for Ecclesiastes,"[4] fail to save the Martian race? Some events are limited by physical laws or the logic of events: if Columbus had not discovered America, would it never have been discovered? Other events are controlled by the personalities of the participants, whether they be called players or characters.

Another deterministic force of concern in this discussion is science itself. More than any other literary form, SF is conscious of and attempts to reproduce faithfully the "reality" of modern scientific fact and method. The scientists' universe is one of interrelated cause and effect. They care little for philosophical arguments demanding deductive proof and are satisfied if they can have a high expectation that the results of their experiments can be replicated in future trials. Then, too, scientists presume that the true laws of the universe are not partial or specific, but universal and general. In their highest form the laws of gravity or motion apply everywhere and at every time. They are not disproved or partialized by new discoveries such as relativity; rather, they are found to be incomplete and in need of modification to be fully accurate.

These attitudes suggest an interrelatedness of all parts of life and a concern for basic laws which, once known, allow us to predict future behavior. Indeed, science fiction, more frequently than other literature, operates on the assumption that when certain forces are set into motion the result is inevitable.[5] It is for the reader to play the game the author has devised, analyze the forces which operate here, and decide on the proper expectation or strategy.

The skilled author will choose outcomes consistent with his created system. If he introduces misleading information, such as a "red herring," this should be considered a misplay; if he reaches a conclusion which does not follow logically from his premises, such as is the case with a *deus ex machina* conclusion, he is equally guilty of violating the rules. At the same time the skilled reader will attempt to match the author move for move, and when such a reader makes a move—expects a line of play—different from that chosen by the author, he will recognize the superiority of the choice of a good author and see the flaws in the craft of the poor one. When a good reader is surprised by a good author, he learns, expands his ability to deal with new situations. Such a "loss" can really be a "win."

Like the best of games, the best science-fiction works are usually those in which either arbitrary rules of play or arbitrary laws of science and human behavior are kept to a minimum. Minor or superficial details do not count. It is not of major concern that the hero has blue pigment, eats moebius strip-shaped pasta, and likes to dance in a zero-g ballroom; however, a small number of major premises are all we care to handle—and all we need. Ursula LeGuin's *The Left Hand of Darkness* (1969)[6] requires only an ambisexual humanoid society; James Blish's *Cities in Flight* (1970)[7] develops primarily from the concept of the "spin-dizzy" antigravity device.

The restriction on the number of such premises does not significantly limit the possibilities of the story any more than chess is limited by having only two dimensions, 64 squares of two colors, and 32 pieces of six types. If we increased the complexity of the game by making it three-dimensional, giving it a thousand squares, and 400 pieces of 100 types, we would not necessarily improve it. Indeed, such a game would be played by finding a smaller number of basic concepts which would serve to reduce its complexity. We do that even with our present version of chess by restricting the moves of each piece in terms of the number of squares which can be traversed in a single move and the direction in which the piece can move.

It is the division of the world into abstract concepts which is the fundamental process of developing and learning games; I would also suggest that it is the fundamental process in both writing and reading science fiction. These concepts may be philosophical, such as the Tralfamadorian determinism explored by Vonnegut in *Slaughter-House Five* (1969)[8]; they may be religious, such as the nature of sin dealt with by Lewis in *Out of the Silent Planet* (1938); or they may be political or personal, such as the concept of self-reliance used by van Vogt in his "Weapon Shop" stories.[9]

In order to understand the importance of such concepts to science fiction, let us examine one of the most prevalent themes in the field, the idea of multiple realities. Such stories vary widely, ranging from time travel to parallel universes. Each story seems to have its own unique configuration of time and space. Yet these two types themselves—time travel and parallel universes—allow us to systematize these complex individual visions and thus lead to both a better understanding of the questions involved and a means of comparing the stories. In *As Tomorrow Becomes Today* (1974), Charles William Sullivan includes Alfred Bester's "The Man Who Murdered Mohammed" (1958) to represent "Time Travel" and R. A. Lafferty's "Thus We Frustrate Charlemagne" (1962) to represent "Parallel Worlds."[10] Both involve quasi-successful attempts to manipulate the present by altering the past. The characters in "The Man Who Murdered Mohammed" return personally to the past to change it, while those in "Thus We Frustrate Charlemagne" send back "an Avatar partly of mechanical and partly of ghostly construction" to accomplish the task.[11] If our criterion is *personal* time travel, the inclusion of the former and exclusion of the latter from the category of "Time Travel" is valid. The designation "Parallel Worlds" for the other category is not so defensible. In both, the alteration of the past produces an alternative time line of reality.

Thus, one may see that "Time Travel" and "Parallel Worlds" are not discrete categories; rather, they serve as concepts which may or may not co-exist. Fiction dealing with time travel may have only one "real" time line, as in H. G. Wells's *The Time Machine* (1895), or they may present multiple, intersecting time lines, each its own reality, as in David Gerrold's *The Man Who Folded Himself* (1973),[12] an extreme example.

Stories of parallel worlds do not have to involve time travel. Randall Garrett's "Lord Darcy" stories (*Too Many Magicians,* 1967) postulate a world which would have resulted if during the Renaissance magic rather than science had undergone systematic development. Harry Harrison's *A Transatlantic Tunnel, Hurrah!* (1972) describes the world resulting from a British victory in the Revolutionary War. There is no indication in either of these works whether the worlds portrayed result from a branching of time or parallel tracks which have never met and will never meet. Since there is no significant result from such a distinction, it is less useful as a concept.

More useful is a distinction between objective and subjective multiple realities. Crucial in "The Man Who Murdered Mohammed" is the idea that "time is subjective"; each individual has his own past, present, and future.[13] Subjective time lines or worlds are also used in stories which involve contingent prophesies. In Herbert's *Dune* (1965) when Paul looks into the future, he sees not a single future but a series of possibilities:

> He could view time, sensing the available paths, the winds of the future . . . the winds of the past: the one-eyed vision of the past, the one-eyed vision of the present and the one-eyed vision of the future—all combined in a trinocular vision that permitted him to see time-become-space. . . . He felt for the first time the massive steadiness of time's movement everywhere complicated by shifting currents, waves, surges, countersurges, like surf against rocky cliffs. It gave him a new understanding of his prescience. . . . The prescience, he realized, was

> an illumination that incorporated the limits of what it revealed—at once a source of accuracy and meaningful error. A kind of Heisenberg indeterminacy intervened: the expenditure of energy that revealed what he saw, changed what he saw. And what he saw was a time nexus within this cave, a boiling of possibilities focused here, wherein the most minute action—the wink of an eye, a careless word, a misplaced grain of sand—moved a gigantic lever across the known universe.[14]

In his version we have multiple time lines, but all extend from the present into the future, and all are subjective realities. Whether those possible futures which do not come to pass in Paul's world come to exist as other time lines or disappear as events foreclose their existence is not dealt with in the novel. Time travel exists only as a movement toward the future involving a succession of choices between alternative futures. The nature of such choices—and the choices themselves—become the essential moves of the "game" in *Dune*.

In analyzing works presenting alternative realities, we have isolated the concepts of travel, direction, multiple versus single realities, and objective versus subjective realities. Given time we would find others, but however many we recognize, we will never exhaust the possibilities created by the writers who use the basic ideas. Yet such recognition simplifies our task as readers and helps us to relate our present reading to our prior experiences.

Of course, however, recognition of those essential concepts does not of itself help us determine what attitude we should take toward questions involving them. Just as any game must have its criteria for determining the winner, so must a work of science fiction. I do not mean this in the simplistic sense that every work of science fiction must have a clear-cut hero and that his success or failure must correlate with that of the story. Even in games, such simplistic criteria as points or dollars may not be of principal concern.

Consider, for example, a game which not only involves a high percentage of skill as opposed to chance in the determination of its outcome, but one in which the player roles available to the participants have different odds for success. Such a situation occurs in the common game of tic-tac-toe. Presume that player X is highly skilled, while O is a novice whose moves are so uninformed by an effective strategy as to be considered random. Moving first into any of the corners, X can force a win if O moves to any square but the center. Should O choose the center, a win is still possible for X and a minimum of a draw is guaranteed. Thus on the first pair of moves alone, X has a seven-out-of-eight chance of winning. If X has the second rather than the first move, he cannot be assured of a win until the third and, of course, the probability of his winning is decreased.

In such a situation, there is a greater challenge for X in going second than in going first. If his criterion for choice is winning, he will choose, whenever possible, to have the initial move; however, if the challenge of the game is his prime consideration, he may well decide to go second.

A player-character in a story may also choose a role which offers a decreased possibility of 'winning' in traditional terms. Given the possibility of a probable win in terms of wealth, power, or survival, he may choose instead a course of action minimizing his chances for such traditional rewards, but maximizing his odds for social or spiritual goals (or gains). Such is the true path of the hero, whether he gains both material and social-spiritual rewards, as do Sam in Zelazny's *Lord of Light* (1967) or Lavon in James Blish's "Surface Tension" (1952), or whether he wins only through his self-sacrifice, as do Paul in Herbert's *Dune Messiah* (1969) and Michael Smith in *Stranger in a Strange Land* (1961).

Criteria for success vary widely in science fiction. Indeed, the factors which spell success in one work may present the problem which must be overcome in another.

In one story the goal may be the creation of a secure, unified galactic empire to avoid war or civil disruption; in another, such a galactic empire may be the evil entity which stifles individualism and progress. In one the criteria for success may be the development of an advanced technological society to produce wealth, leisure, and power for its citizens; in another, technology may prove to be the source of danger, and a return to an Edenic, pastoral existence the goal. But whatever the criteria for the story, the reader's goals of knowledge and pleasure will remain the same, for he does not read fiction to encounter the same results time after time. He should not be concerned that the writer's view, as expressed in the criteria of the work, differ from his own. Seeking exposure to new possibilities, the experienced science-fiction reader does not demand that the author use criteria to which he has given prior assent. He must, however, demand that whatever criteria the writer endorses be presented logically and used consistently.

In following the line of play in a science-fiction story, it is crucial that the reader be able to know the players. In game theory the term "player" may refer either to individuals or groups having a common interest. Thus, for example, a baseball game is actually a "two player game" and not an "eighteen player game." Similarly, in examining a work of science fiction we need not be concerned with the play of all characters but rather with the aggregate units composing "player," for in science fiction a player may be a nation, a world, or even a race which spans galaxies.

One of the tasks of the science-fiction writer is to be able to control point of view so that the reader, acting out of free choice, will be able to recognize and choose to identify with the proper player or aggregate group. Once we have identified our player and criteria, we can go about choosing our strategy. To do so, we must find the odds for possible lines of play. The information we need in calculating such odds comes from two sources: (1) the physical and psychological laws of the universe and (2) the rules of the game. These same sources apply both to games and to science fiction. In a poker game we must calculate on the basis of the physical limits of the deck of cards (the four suits, the thirteen types of cards); such rules as the relative worth of the different possible hands, and the psychological characteristics of our opponents (are they likely to bluff or to play conservatively?). In such a work of science fiction we must calculate on the basis of such matters as the physical characteristics of the universe, the psychological make-up of the characters, and (instead of special, unchanging rules) the special premises, scientific innovations, and new social structures which the author has created.

The vision which the reader has of possible strategies is like that of the multiple-subjective time line vision. We see many courses of action, each of them leading to different choices. As we move through the work, these choices must be faced; as each is confronted, alternative choices are negated and future options clarified. To this extent the work of fiction imitates life; however, the work is unlike life in at least one important respect—it is partial.

No work of fiction has ever been so complete as to contain all the possibilities of life. The author must focus only upon those features pertinent to the story he is telling. Minor details may give fuller, more vivid portraits of his characters and their world(s), but major pieces of extraneous information will only impede and confuse the progress of the narrative. As a result, in almost any good work of science fiction, the seeds of the conclusion will be planted in the very beginning of the story, and as the story progresses, the end becomes more and more inevitable.

In Asimov's *Foundation,* for example, we find ourselves quickly allied with—playing the game with—Hari Seldon's Foundation. Our opponent is the conglomeration of forces which threaten to extend the "dark ages" which will stretch from the dissolution of the old galactic empire to the establishment of a new, more vital one. We quickly learn that our strategy will be successful; we know this from the prefatory excerpts from the *Encyclopedia Galactica.* We know it from our faith in the laws of science—in this case, the science of psychohistory. And we know it from the combination of our generic expectations and the tone of the work. For *Foundation* is a heroic societal quest, and such quests almost inevitably culminate in success. Our strategy, too, is quickly determined by that set forth in the Seldon plan: just as in a lever problem in physics, in order for a small weight to move a great one, it must travel a long way and a long time, so for a small group to achieve a major result, its forces must be applied over a long period of time. No individual can achieve quick, major victories; therefore, our strategy must be to become part of—and to continue—Seldon's plan.

Consider Clarke's *2001: A Space Odyssey* (1968) as another example. We play the game on the side of mankind; our criterion is the upward intellectual evolution of the race. Before we are far into the book, we find that the man-ape moonwatcher evolves in the desired direction by the aid of the extraterrestrially-created obelisk. When a second obelisk is found on the moon, we anticipate that it, too, will lead to a further advancement. Our strategy is to follow in the direction it guides us.

In Anne McCaffrey's "Weyer Search" (1967), Lessa is quickly established as a woman of special power who communicates with beasts and controls the very growth of the grass. Almost as quickly we meet the dragon men searching for a woman to have the high honor of becoming a "Weyerwoman." The reader soon recognizes that, whatever the obstacles, that post will be Lessa's.

Such games do not detract from the literary experience; they enhance it. They provide the point at which writer and reader interact, at which a passive experience becomes an active one. If the experience is vital, it makes the work a continuing part of the reader's life, allowing him to use the insights he has gathered in his dealings with the present and his preparations for the future.

The game does not end when he turns the last page. It remains in memory to be replayed as other works exploring similar subjects call it to mind. The strategy it represents, the situation it simulates, can then represent options for each new game, each new experience. It is a process which makes each work of quality part of the total system of art and life.

NOTES

1. Several writers, among them John W. Campbell ("The Science of Science Fiction," *Atlantic Monthly*, 181 [May 1948], 97-98) have emphasized the value of science fiction as a predictive tool. Others, such as Arthur Koestler ("The Boredom of Fantasy," *Trail of the Dinosaur and Other Essays* [New York: The Macmillan Company, 1955],

pp. 140-47), have asserted that science-fiction writers are unable to deal accurately with the future. Without ignoring this controversy, many critics have asserted that accuracy of prediction is not crucial to the success of a work of science fiction because the true focus of such works is the forward edge of the present. As Thomas Clareson points out in "SF: The Other Side of Realism" (*SF: The Other Side of Realism* [Bowling Green, Ohio: Bowling Green Popular Press, 1971], p. 3), the writers of science fiction, like all writers, "focus upon those aspects of human experience which most concern them," and the writer, no matter "how bizarre his imagined world, has had to make that world sufficiently representational to be accepted by his readers. . . ."

2. Frank Herbert, *Hellstrom's Hive* (New York: Doubleday & Co. Inc., 1973).
3. Kurt Vonnegut, Jr., *Cat's Cradle* (New York: Holt, Rinehart, and Winston, 1963).
4. Roger Zelazny, "A Rose for Ecclesiastes," *The Magazine of Fantasy and Science Fiction,* 25 (November 1963), 5-35.
5. See Steven E. Kagle, "The Societal Quest," *Extrapolation,* 12 (May 1971), 79-85.
6. Ursula LeGuin, *The Left Hand of Darkness* (New York: Walker and Company, 1969).
7. James Blish, *Cities in Flight* (Garden City: Nelson Doubleday, Inc., Book Club Edition, 1970).
8. Kurt Vonnegut, Jr., *Slaughterhouse-Five* (New York: Delacourt Press, 1969).
9. A. E. van Vogt, *The Weapon Shops of Isher* (New York: Greenberg, 1951).
10. Charles William Sullivan III, ed., *As Tomorrow Becomes Today* (Englewood Cliffs, N.J.: Prentice-Hall, Inc., 1974), pp. 5-92.
11. R. A. Lafferty, "Thus We Frustrate Charlemagne," in *Sullivan,* p. 71.
12. David Gerrold, *The Man Who Folded Himself* (New York: Random House, 1973).
13. Alfred Bester, "The Man Who Murdered Mohammed," in *Sullivan,* p. 34.
14. Frank Herbert, *Dune* (Philadelphia: Chilton Book Company, 1965), pp. 290-91.

Theology, Science Fiction, and Man's Future Orientation

J. Norman King

The emphasis upon the future which characterizes much science fiction is a reflection of the society in which the Western world now lives. Indeed, the massiveness, speed, and accelerating pace of change, hurtling us into the future, are commonly thought to be the dominant feature of the twentieth century. Beyond the more obvious external changes, manifested in machines and techniques, the scientific revolution reaches into the economic, political, and social structures and processes and even impinges upon the inner life of man himself. In this regard, science fiction has progressively matured beyond a rather juvenile preoccupation with fantastic gadgets wielded by cowboys-in-spacesuits to both a more serious concern with the effect upon man of these rapid and far-reaching technical advances and a raising, at least implicitly, of ultimate questions about man and society.

In a pre-industrial society of imperceptibly gradual change, man looked chiefly to the familiar past, which his own pattern of life essentially repeated with little chance for variation. In the modern era, however, the past loses its immediate familiarity and its seeming permanence and stability as a result of accumulating innovations. As the past recedes from proximity and enduring power, man turns his attention more and more to an undetermined future, increasingly divergent from that past. Man's current existential orientation is focused upon the future.[1] An illuminating example of this shift in time sense may be observed in the cultural transition from a repressive attitude towards sex to a similar approach towards death. Sex is no longer an obscene topic of conversation, a source of embarassment and shame; on the other hand, everything is done to avoid the appearance, the admission, and the discussion of death.[2] Our existential anxieties about the human condition are transferred from the origins of life to its end—from the past to the future. In other words, our new temporal orientation, as it filters into our culture, implies that we shall tend to project and express our inner feelings, our hopes and fears, even the values and ideas basic to our lives in terms of the future. Consequently, science fiction, at least in principle, is a peculiarly apt form of literature to speak both *of* and *to* our contemporary experience. It is, therefore, of considerable utility to theology in providing insight into the self-understanding of modern man.

To state the matter in another way, one of the central theological problems of recent years has arisen because we no longer share the language and thought-forms of that earlier culture which elaborated its beliefs and values over a period of centuries. These convictions strike us today not as *false* but as *unreal,* as unconnected with our everyday life and experience.[3] If they are to retain any living meaning for us, they must be translated into concepts and words which speak to our experience; that is to say, which reflect our new orientation. The development of a theology of hope, the insistence upon social responsibility, and the debate about the justifiability of revolution all insist upon a theological awareness of this new dimension.[4] Hence, theology and science fiction meet in this concern for the future and, through it, in the consideration of the ultimate issues of life and its meaning.

We may begin more specifically with an examination of the effects of this future orientation upon the concept of creation, first in terms of its effect upon the traditional theological view and then in its actual embodiment in representative works of science fiction. In the biblical account, creation occurs "in the beginning" through an act or "word" of a God who is also seen as being "in the beginning."[5] In both the biblical languages, Hebrew and Greek, as well as in Latin, the phrase "in the beginning" is equivalent in signification to "essentially," "in principle," "by nature." In this approach, as the linguistic structure indicates, what something is—its essential or fundamental makeup—is what it always has been. To cite the liturgical formula, it is "as it was in the beginning, is now, and ever shall be." The nature of something is defined by its origin or birth. It is defined, that is, by its past. Once again, in a relatively stable society, what has been provides the ground for understanding what is. Therefore, in presenting their deepest convictions about man before God, the authors of Genesis quite readily project their vision into the past. To convey the concept of the intrinsic dignity of man and at the same time his utter contingency and radical dependency upon his God, they look to a divine action in the past. Man is as he was originally created by God. This fundamental creature-Creator relationship is understood as a continuing one rather than a once-and-for-all affair. It also admits of new dimensions and interventions from an eminently free divinity. However, the predominant time orientation of this concept is towards the past. Creation is seen as chiefly occurring in the past.

The basic teaching which these stories communicate is separable from their temporal envelope and from the rest of that imaginative symbolism. Central to the biblical concept of creation is the conviction that all that exists, man and his world alike, are not to be identified with the God who is in some way their source. There is an utter distinction between the transcendent God and his creation even though this gulf is bridged by the divine immanence and love. The realms of man and nature do have their own intrinsic value, yet there is a gift character to their very existence and condition. Perhaps the most striking example in this regard lies in the "demythologization" of sex, which is removed from the sphere of divinity and becomes a strictly human reality, a created gift of God to man for his fulfillment.[6] To so distinguish man and nature from divinity, while at the same time retaining for them a meaning and purpose, opens up the possibility of examining them apart from God—the possibility, therefore, of scientific investigation.[7]

With the actual development of the natural and social sciences, the earlier interpretation of creation becomes modified, as it were, by its own implications. Through these disciplines, there is unveiled an overwhelming vista of vast ages and distances, of an enormous universe slowly evolving over many billions of years. There dawns, too, a gradual realization of the intricate complexity and wide-ranging potentialities of matter. Although dwarfed against this background, the time of man's appearance on Earth becomes recognized as far greater than previously thought. The evolutionary character not only of man's biological structure, but also of his very human consciousness itself becomes clear.[8] As a consequence, the image of a static, fixed, permanently enduring species is inevitably supplanted by a more dynamic and fluid understanding of all species, including man. The notion of an immediate creation of well-defined beings, projected into the past, no longer appears tenable. Indeed, with the emergence of this more open-ended and indeterminate picture of nature and man, reinforced and rendered vividly real by rapid changes in industrial society itself, the focus of the question of creation alters. The question becomes not "What has been created?" but "What will be created?" It becomes not "What has man been from the beginning?" but "What will man become?" or "What will become of man?" Creation is thereby not something still to happen. Creation is as much a future event as a past occurrence. Any definition of the human essence, if there be one, will arise more from the end than from the beginning, more from where man is going than from where he has come. Our understanding of man is deepened especially through exploring his possibilities for the future. With this temporal orientation, man tends more and more to project his self-understanding into the future.[9] And this is what science fiction does at its best.

In addition to this developing tendency to project the concept of creation more into the future than into the past, the technological and behavioral powers born of the new sciences convey the sense of control over the creational process. The idea emerges of man's purposes; of his actively shaping himself, his society, and his history. Instead of inquiring into God's creation of nature and man in the past, attention turns to man's self-creation in the future. This shift of focus does not necessarily spell the end or death of the creator God, but it does make the presence of a divine reality a less immediate and more indirect question, a background horizon rather than an obvious concern. It also excludes certain concepts of God, especially in the spatio-temporal dress long associated with them. In particular, the notion of a separate Being, outside the realm of nature and history and situated imaginatively in the past, no longer addresses itself to man's experience. It gives place to the concept of an ultimate, even somehow personal ground within, yet distinct from, the creative process itself, projected into the future and associated with hope for the positive outcome of that creative process.[10] Essentially, any concept of God is an articulation of the underlying conviction that reality, life, human existence is not absurd, but has some meaning and purpose. Nevertheless, the most direct question for our society today is: "What future will man create for himself and his world?" And the conviction as to the final meaning or meaninglessness of the whole human enterprise remains largely implicit as an undergirding—or undermining—assumption. Creation thus becomes more and more understood as a future human reality than as a past divine achievement.

What that future holds depends upon the dominance alloted to good or to evil. In the biblical narrative, each step of the presentation concludes with the unambiguous assertion, "And God *saw* that it was very good." This is an emphatic affirmation of the intrinsic goodness and worth of man and nature, rooted in the creator God. When this belief is transposed into the new perspective, often without its theological underpinning, it issues into the confidence that man can fashion himself and his society into something good, that he can progressively create a better world and a more authentic and fulfilling human life. Paraphrasing the terminology of Genesis, we might state that man now "foresees" that it "will be" very good through his own creative efforts. We shall not here enter into details other than to note that such a positive hope may include a wide variety of degrees of depth, ranging from a thoughtless superficial optimism to a profound sense of human worth beyond tragedy or evil. Moreover, in a past-oriented, prescientific age, offering little opportunity of change to the general population, the conviction that reality was ultimately positive did imply that the status quo, which seemed the natural order of things, somehow made sense and was to be accepted. In a technological society, however, resignation to one's lot in life, where that lot can be improved, becomes not only pointless, but the expression of a negative attitude. Faith in the meaningfulness of life now connotes the hope that change can be channeled in a constructive, more humanly fulfilling direction. Paradoxically, the same basic attitude towards life finds opposite expressions in altered social settings. The earlier reactionary social attitude of the churches and the Marxian criticism of Christianity both find a large measure of their explanation therein.[12] In any event, it is this positive approach to man as creator of the future which lies behind all utopian-style literature of modern times.

The biblical authors, however, did not succumb to naive illusions about man. They were quite aware that though goodness and value might be the deepest stuff of existence, they do not go unchallenged. They recognized all too well that man's creative capacities and tendencies are assaulted by their negative counterparts; that man is beset by painful disharmony within himself, by bitter conflict with others individually and socially, and by antagonistic resentment of his God. In portraying this proclivity for destruction, they also projected it into the past. If there is something amiss with man now, it is because something went wrong at the beginning. From the first, the human race has been afflicted by a proneness to evil, by "original sin." Still, evil is less "original," less fundamental than goodness. A dualistic viewpoint is rejected as incompatible with a loving God and the basic dignity of his human image. In the biblical perspective, moral evil remains a distortion or corruption of an essentially good creation. Evil is the debasing of the good; it is not the very substance of reality.[13]

When translated into the new framework, the awareness of evil as inescapable from the human condition fosters the conviction that all future creations of man will be flawed to some extent. Any environment, self, or society that man shapes in his own image will contain destructive seeds and fall short of a utopian ideal. Such uneasiness about man's future self-creation likewise admits of many degrees, from a cautious questioning of idealistic assumptions to an outright despair. If the negative view of man becomes overriding, the "fall" of man projected into the future will appear both inevitable and total. In this latter instance, it is thought that man, being irremediably evil or corruptible, cannot create a better world, nor even a viable one. His fear, hatred, wickedness, and even stupidity will invariably lead him to destroy himself and the silent, indifferent, and even hostile cosmos in which he lives. The myth of continuous progress has been shaken by the darker events of this century and riddled with strands of pessimism, cynicism, and emptiness. The renewed awareness of demonic possibilities has found expression, too, in the upsurge of dystopian novels at the expense of their utopian counterparts.[14]

This awareness of evil, the sense of something wrong with the human condition, in jarring contact with his deepest cravings for goodness and fulfillment, leads man to dream of an ideal state. In a past-oriented culture he imagines a primitive paradise, a golden age of long ago, before evil entered upon the scene to afflict men thereafter. This ideal is projected into the past, and he dreams of a return to such an idyllic state. The biblical vision shares this myth, but introduces a crucial difference. The creative and redemptive love of God is seen to demand a final resolution of the struggle between good and evil, an ultimate victory in which evil is vanquished.[15] While grounded in God's fidelity to his promises in the past, this is indeed a hope for the future, a hope dependent upon God's new action in the future, which does go beyond a mere restoration of the past. Nevertheless, there are features of this view which do as yet reflect a past orientation. The fulfillment of human hopes is pictured as a divine intervention coming from outside the order of creation. It likewise involves the transformation of man and the universe or else the creation of a new dwelling place for man.[16] This presentation does deal profoundly with the whole matter of man's deepest aspirations as reaching beyond any possible earthly situation and even beyond death. The point to be made is that where conditions seem unchanging and unchangeable by human hands, man's fulfillment tends to be portrayed either in terms of an intervention from without by a force greater than man or in terms of the removal of man from his earthly realm.

When the situation is drastically altered by the advent of science and technology, however, the above conceptualization becomes implausible and unreal. When, as we have seen, man's future on Earth appears undetermined and within his own hands to create or destroy, the notion of a pre-arranged future in some nonearthly sphere established by divine agency strikes a bizarre chord. The idea of an afterlife, usually imagined in these terms, thus strikes modern technical man as highly improbable, even prior to any serious consideration. Within the new time-orientation, no future existence which lies, imaginatively speaking, spatially outside or temporally beyond the present earthly scene and its astronomic environment can speak to man's experience. Any future can only be located as emerging from and ahead of that scene. Any transcendent reality can, if at all, be visualized only as a force or presence (perhaps even personal in some sense) situated ahead of the creative process, reaching towards man from the "far side" (rather than the "outside") or future of that process, drawing man to continually reach beyond himself and his present situation. A divinity becomes the basis of hope for the future of man. One variation of this theme is found in the writings of Teilhard de Chardin. While retaining a Christian expectation of the Second Coming of Christ, he asserts that such a divine intervention to fulfill human longings will occur only when man, in whom the evolutionary impulse is now conscious and free, has carried that process to a sufficiently high degree.[17] Man no longer asks whether God will rescue him from this vale of tears. It is rather a question of whether man's creative efforts, successful in part yet marred by failures, will lead him to reach for a "power of the future," a God on the far side of man's transformation of history.

We have glanced from beginning to end, so to speak, in relating the concept of creation to man's orientation towards the future. In so doing, the themes of science-fiction stories and novels as well as theological studies have influenced our approach. The same cultural factors discussed have, of course, helped to shape the thoughts and words of science-fiction authors. It is time now to examine explicitly how these writers do express, in some fashion or another, aspects of the concept of creation within the futurist perspective.

The most obvious creation of scientific man is the machine. In the guise of gadgets, weaponry, computers, robots, and spaceships, it enjoys a prominent place in speculative fiction. Nonetheless, the machine is the object of highly conflicting attitudes. On the one hand, mechanical products are viewed as outstanding assets, freeing man from drudgery and previous limitations, promoting human health and welfare, and indispensably assisting human progress and accomplishments. As vehicles carrying man to the stars, for example, in some novels of Arthur C. Clarke, they become vehicles and expressions of man's longing and ability to reach out, literally and figuratively, beyond himself. In Heinlein's *The Moon Is a Harsh Mistress* (1966) a winsome computer, the main character, makes possible a victorious outcome in the struggle of the ruggedly individualistic moon colonists against the decadent Earth civilization. The robot stories of Isaac Asimov present clear and logically thinking mechanical men, rationally dedicated to the good of men without the confusing clutter of human emotions. Charles Beaumont's beautiful story, "Last Rites" (1955, 1957), also tells of a "dying" robot who undergoes a painful inner conflict, resolved by reception of the last rites from a priest before its mechanism finally fails.

In such tales, the machine is looked upon positively as an instrument and expression of man's scientific progress, itself considered an index of human progress. It is a creation of man, essentially under his control and in the service of his goals. If in some ways the machine, as in the case of the computer and the robot, appears superior to man, at least to ordinary man, it remains an extension of man's new-found power and not a threat. Such confidence in the machine and its maker reflects a feeling of exhilaration at man's liberation from the ignorance and helplessness which had so long subjected him to the domination of his natural environment. Now at last he exults in the power presently within his grasp and envisions its increase in the future. Beneath this view lies the conviction that man is in control of his own destiny and able to direct the future to positive purposes, chiefly through science and the rationality it embodies.[18]

A more hesitant and somber approach to the machine is also found in science fiction. *Player Piano* (1952) by Kurt Vonnegut, for example, is set in the near future where automation has left unemployed and idle all but a very small elite. Following years of the dulling of minds and emotions by assembly-line monotony, this electronic revolution leads to a society of masses without jobs or purpose and singularly unprepared for any creative use of leisure. Such moral and spiritual consequences of a machine civilization are taken a step further by the classic story of E. M. Forster, "The Machine Stops" (1909). Except for a small remnant, man has become so dependent upon the machine for all his needs and wants that he becomes an infant in its mechanical womb, paralyzed by fear and unable to function when the machine finally breaks down. A closely allied theme deals with the use of the machine to achieve control of the human brain, manipulation of the emotions, and the fostering of an aquiescing dependency, as in *Synthajoy* (1968) by D. G. Compton. The strongest reaction is perhaps that of works continuing the tradition of Mary Shelley's *Frankenstein.* These convey the fear that man's inventions may turn against man and master or destroy him, as in Karel Čapek's *R. U. R.* (1921) or Robert Silverberg's *Tower of Glass* (1970).

The theme of a crippling overdependency upon the machine implies that newer and better outward changes do not of themselves grapple with or resolve all human problems. It indicates that man is more than the sum of physical needs to be gratified with or without his effort and consent, and his is more than sheer rationality. Man has deeper inner capacities of freedom and responsibility, of creativity and feeling, which must be challenged and actualized if he is to positively create himself and his future. The more skeptical outlook also evokes the spectre of darker human emotions and their influence upon the machines and their uses. Doubt is raised about the actual extent of man's control over his own handiwork, and the matter of the need for such control similarly arises. The question of control comes very strikingly to the fore in both the confident and the fearful attitudes. The former does express a conviction that reason needs to control emotion, which is either neglected or suppressed as messy and nasty.[19] The latter contain an uneasy premonition that man's machines, as a reflection of himself, may be either consciously put to corrupt and enslaving ends or may unconsciously enclose seeds of man's own destructiveness and hostility which will return to devour him.

At the deepest level of interpretation, the concern for control connotes at least a dim awareness of man's contingency, of the unnecessary character of his existence, and hence of the escape from his full control of his own destiny. This fear of not being in full control can become all the more alarming in an age when science has seemed to confer such great power. It is experienced as acute anxiety, as a threat to one's very self, as a sense of helplessness and loss of identity, only where there is a dread that the basic underlying character of reality is negative, frightful, or meaningless. The "man-eating" or man-destroying machine is the symbolic representation of such anxiety,[20] just as the spaceship reaching to the stars may symbolize man's trust in himself to confer meaning on all that falls within his purview. Whatever else it may be and whatever it may symbolize positively or negatively, the machine is a human product, and as such its treatment in science fiction illustrates our prior observation. Man today views creation in terms of his own self-creation in the future, or in the present looking towards the future. At the same time, within this context, he still inevitably confronts the question of the meaningfulness or meaninglessness of his own existence, a question formerly articulated in more direct fashion in terms of a God. Science fiction, in its ambivalent treatment of the machine, reflects some awareness that man's creation, while being a self-creation, includes elements which are beyond man's control and which leave room for a sense of awe, of mystery, or of fear.

Similar topics arise in the treatment of nature. On the one hand, there is the utilitarian and manipulative approach in which nature is chiefly raw material to be subjected to the power of man's technology. The beauty and cruelty, the profusion and chaos of nature are to be tamed by concrete, steel girders, and fences. Symmetrical parks are preferred to wilderness, neatly trimmed lawns to high flowering grasses. This viewpoint is captured in Clarke's *The City and The Stars* (1956). In the ultrarefined city civilization, all that is above, below, and outside the confines of the automated and artificial paradise is shunned through a lack of interest that masks a subtle fear. One is reminded of the observation of Marshall McLuhan that with the advent of television pictures from space capsules, the whole Earth becomes a stage contained within the artificial frame of the television cabinet. Here again the themes both of man's power to create himself through science and of his uneasiness over what escapes his control are prominent. One reaction to the solely manipulative view has been expressed in the romanticization of the rustic mode of life, as in Simak's *City* (1952). More recently in novels like Harry Harrison's *Make Room! Make Room!* (1966), emphasis has been placed upon the ecological crisis with the problems of pollution and overpopulation receiving considerable attention. Such works explore the idea of nature as resisting man's aggression, and of man as part of nature and reliant upon it for psychological as well as biological survival. They often launch bitter attacks upon human brutality, greed, exploitation, and rapacity.[21] Whether understood as beauty to contemplate or resource material to exploit, as hospitable environment or as threatening chaos, nature as well as the machine is the recipient of the science-fiction author's projected ideas and attitudes about himself and his society. To this subject we now turn.

What kind of society will man and his machines build on this Earth? An early yet typical instance of the utopian vision is *A Modern Utopia* (1905) by H. G. Wells. This novel gives form to the hope that, under the leadership and intelligent planning of an elite group of persons, applying the most advanced scientific and technological knowledge, man can build a progressively more ideal society. Asimov's *Foundation* series continues in this tradition, speaking of the development of "psychohistory," a truly scientific understanding of the human emotions, which thereby leads to their educated control and to the creation of a smoothly ordered society, unruffled by the shattering upheavals which had rent human history in the past. G. K. Chesterton's famous criticism, aimed at Wells, comes to mind: such utopias disregard the gravest problem, man's proneness to evil, his "original sin," while solving all the lesser difficulties. Indeed, the stubbornness of the human spirit, the unmanageability of man's emotions, and the stark brutality of his biological needs have led some to seek a kind of salvation for man involving passage from his bodily makeup to the level of pure energy or spirit, as in such works as Stapledon's *Last and First Men* (1930) and Clarke's *Childhood's End* (1953).

Not only the possibility but the very desirability of any utopian society has been questioned, even in Clarke's *Childhood's End*. From Huxley's *Brave New World* (1932) to Bradbury's *Fahrenheit 451* (1953) and James Gunn's *The Joymakers* (1961), a man's spirit stagnates and he loses personal identity when all challenge is removed, when hedonism prevails, when all disturbing thoughts are carefully shielded, and when anonymous conformity reigns. Pleasure, comfort, security, ease, all destroy—or at least put to sleep—the most deeply creative forces in man, who must either grow in the face of these challenges or wither. Such works give flesh to two very deep and polar human drives: toward familiarity, security, and certainty on the one hand; toward exploration, new growth, and risk on the other. The tension between them is set forth with particular clarity in Asimov's *The End of Eternity* (1955). A society, engineered to ensure "safety and security, moderation, nothing in excess, no risks without overwhelming certainty of adequate return," produces as its end result only "a loss of purpose, a sense of futility, a feeling of hopelessness." The reason given is that triumph and disaster are of a pair. "It is in the meeting of great tests that mankind can most successfully rise to great heights. Out of danger and restless insecurity comes the force that pushes mankind to newer and loftier conquests."[22] Man's profound need to be "saved" or rescued from all that threatens him confronts his equally profound need to wholly commit himself to goals which lie beyond his present situation, to continue his quest for the mysterious something which ever eludes his grasp, which is ever in the future. (One theologian, Steeman, observes that we have too long expressed concepts of a God in terms of the former rather than the latter need, and must now correct this approach.)

It is not just a matter of simple choice between security and courage. Many science-fiction works, such as the above, stress that the price of anything but a faceless conformity is extremely high. Sterile sameness and stable mediocrity are overcome only by unleashing, along with human freedom and creative genius, the forces of anxiety, chaos, and destruction. This theme is especially well exemplified in Anthony Burgess's *A Clockwork Orange* (1962). Through the protagonist, Alex, the horror of depraved violence is starkly contrasted with the hollowness of automatic, brainwashed "good" behavior. "My idea," Burgess is quoted as saying, "was that it is better for us to commit evil through free will than to have the good imposed upon us." He adds that he seeks to convey both the cost of maintaining freedom and moral choice, and its necessity, if there is to be hope for mankind.[23] In a related manner, *A Canticle for Leibowitz* (1959) by Walter Miller, portrays the quest to maximize security and minimize suffering at any price, and to build an earthly Eden upon this premise. Such a quest only increases man's sense of frustrated dissatisfaction as it nears apparent success, and inevitably issues into its opposites, violence and ruin, which permit hope to rise once more from the ashes of destruction.

Along with the recognition of the inseparability of creative and destructive forces within man, we find as well in science fiction vigorous satire and criticism of some attendant social ills. By projecting them into a future seen as evolving from present trends, authors like Cyril Kornbluth and Fred Pohl in *The Space Merchants* (1953) and *Gladiator-at-Law* (1955) communicate forcefully the consequences of greed and consumerism, of senseless and sadistic violence, of the relentless lust for domination. Some writers go as far as to warn that such destructive tendencies may inevitably prevail, that man is on a path of self-destruction, that his "fall" is imminent, if he does not find a creative outlet for his inner turmoil. *Level 7* (1959) by Mordecai Roshwald presents the diary of a man, written in the deepest underground nuclear shelter, the last human to die after an utterly pointless, push-button atomic war. The so-called "New Wave" trend in science fiction of the 1960s echoes at times a quite bleak pessimism about man's future. Such novels as J. G. Ballard's *The Drowned World* (1962) picture a post-catastrophe Earth in which the few survivors live in a kind of dreamworld where nothing ever happens. They exist without purpose, initiative, or sense of time, and simply give up to await the death they fear.

The progressive qualification, even rejection in some cases, of naively optimistic or utopian views of man reflects certainly the disillusionment of a war-torn century. It exhibits the increased awareness of powerful unconscious forces within man unveiled by Freud and his successors, the erosion of the myth of inevitable progress by the inroads of cynicism and despair, and the recognition that change and advance are not necessarily synonymous.

At the same time, there is expressed in many instances a confidence that man is able to cope with these anxious times and indeed to emerge the stronger from this challenge. On a deeper level, there is glimpsed in such works something of the essential ambiguity of the human condition and of man as he is presently constituted. There are unlit regions within man, as within nature, that resist the full light of human comprehension or control. They are thus broached both with a certain trepidation and with confidence, for they cloak negative and destructive as well as positive and creative forces. When this ambiguity is imaginatively extrapolated into the future of man, his society, and his history, there emerges a picture of the same continuing human struggle between light and darkness, good and evil, hope and despair. This puzzling creature, man, does experience himself today as one oriented to the future, and to a future within rather than outside history. Yet his furthest projections find increasing difficulty in visualizing any decisive resolution of this unending struggle within the historical process.

In projecting man as he is into the future, science fiction vividly uncovers the gap between man as he is and man as he would be, between human aspiration and human achievement. It intimates that man's deepest longings and severest conflicts are not fully capable of satisfaction and resolution here on Earth, present or future. It suggests further that what man most deeply craves is not just more of the same life but a different or new life; not merely a quantitatively longer life but a qualitatively higher life. This human desire for a higher life, expressed both in utopian wishes and dystopian dissatisfaction, is even more remarkably present in the treatment of the mutant and the alien.

The theme of the mutant is usually based upon the further evolution of man, either occurring in the natural course of things or else modified, deflected, or accelerated by other forces, such as a nuclear holocaust. The mutation may be biological or psychological, and it may be a step forward or a regression. It lies frequently in the direction of extrasensory perception or mental telepathy, chiefly regarded as a plus factor, but may contrariwise involve a reversion to idiocy or savagery. Set in a post-nuclear age, *The Chrysalids* (1955) by John Wyndham presents three groups of persons: those remaining much the same as contemporary man, those who have reverted to a more barbarous existence, and a new breed who have attained the mind-reading level and become an object of persecution. As in van Vogt's *Slan* (1940) and Stapledon's *Odd John* (1937), the most immediate intent is a firm indictment of bigotry; of man's tendency to fear, reject, and destroy that which is different. Beneath this criticism of intolerance, conformity, and racism, however, is implied the tacit conviction that the human race must evolve further if the future is not to be an endless treadmill of eternal recurrence. However positive or creative may be the continual struggle of man with contradictory forces within and outside of himself, it can finally lead nowhere if the human condition remains unaltered. The full actualization for which man yearns is beyond the scope of human life and history as we know it. Evolution therefore, must not stop at its present stage: *homo sapiens* must be superseded. Set within an evolutionary context, the mutation theme thus reflects, in contemporary dress, the inborn human drive to bridge the gap between limited human accomplishment and boundless yearnings, the desire for a new and higher form of existence than is presently accessible to man. The human drama can only be resolved at a higher level of life.

In addition, the contrasting juxtaposition of progressive and regressive evolutionary possibilities, as instanced in the poles of savagery and telepathy, are not only echoes of inner conflict or social strife. They also very curiously resemble, in space-age dress, the age-old themes of heaven and hell, salvation and damnation, at least insofar as they reach beyond man's present state and in two possible directions. Quite interestingly, in intimating a higher form of life to which man might aspire, certain themes recur. The evolutionary thrust itself suggests a dynamic and active idea of "salvation" rather than a passive, static condition. The use of telepathy repeatedly underlines the contention that greater understanding and communication rather than merely greater intellect alone are of critical importance. With the *homo gestalt* of *More Than Human* (1953), Theodore Sturgeon locates in this expanded or group consciousness a hope for man's future. A dynamic new personal wholeness channelled and realized in full communication would thus be integral to any higher life.

The truth of this interpretation is further accentuated by the generally negative attitude to stationary, dead-end utopias previously noted, but even more so in reactions to the prospect of endless living. The prototypical *Utopia* of Thomas More and its successors do, in fact, contain euthanasia chambers. As early as *Caesar's Column* (1890), Ignatius Donnelly speaks of boredom and the choosing of death out of a feeling of nothingness in the midst of technological wonders diverted to human gratification. In Vonnegut's story, "Tomorrow and Tomorrow and Tomorrow" (1954), for example, an indefinitely prolonged life-span, granting a practical immortality, is depicted as an intolerable burden. Man does not want to die, these tales observe, but his desire for life embraces much more than mere duration. As one author notes, "When we seriously think of living for eternity, even for millions of years, the project becomes tolerable only if we assume that not only our surroundings, but also ourselves will be so altered as to be almost unrecognizable."[24] Hence, the deepest desire of man is for life—for meaningful life, dynamic and relational. Yet such a life must involve a mutation to a higher form of existence rather than a mere continuation of more of the same; this same notion is stated quite distinctly, though in different language, by the Second Vatican Council.[25]

Throughout science fiction, modern man, a being shaped by science, reaches beyond security towards the future in order to attain a mysterious fullness of life which has hitherto eluded his grasp; yet at the same time he is tormented by fear, uncertainty, and destructiveness. As he stands before the immeasurably enlarged expanse of space and time, a small centre of consciousness in a vast and lonely universe, he wonders whether other intelligent beings, possibly more advanced than he, might not exist.

In the early decades of science fiction, the alien was predominantly depicted as a hostile agent, powerful and cruel, bent upon destroying or subjugating the earth. This approach, still found on occasion in stories and still common in late-night television movies, is perhaps explained as an outward projection of the inward fear, guilt, and hostility of colonizing nations who, for example, have slaughtered the indigenous population of the American continents and usurped their lands. "A Martian Odyssey" (1934) by Stanley Weinbaum is one of the first tales to sketch the alien as simply different, without that difference conveying the implication of inevitable animosity or conflict. There has been a general shift towards portraying aliens as keenly intelligent, genuinely benevolent beings of high moral calibre, to whom homage, humility, and even a kind of religious reverence is due. In some instances, there has been a complete reversal, with the superior alien becoming victimized by the viciousness, greed, and imperialism of man.

Reflecting upon such references to alien intelligences in science fiction and, in a broader context including the flying saucer phenomenon, Robert Plank observes that such imagined beings are expected generally to come either to save or to destroy us. He concludes that, from a psychological vantage point, such a relationship bears an uncanny resemblance to the love-hate Oedipal attitude of the small child to his father as perceived by that child. It reflects the childish wish for a "daddy" who will either punish us and get it over with or take care of us and make everything better.[26] This view, which contains a great deal of validity, is essentially an adaptation of Freud's interpretation of belief in God as the illusion that our parents run the universe for our benefit, thus exemplifying a refusal to face the harshness of reality.[27] A crucial element here is the association of the alien with a deity-figure. While the projection of a father-figure may be involved in many instances, the suggestion of deeper human wishes, already alluded to, need not be excluded.

We have noted the immense broadening of the frontiers of space and time. In this regard, the crux of the upheaval over Copernicus's heliocentric theory was not a dispute on the validity of astronomy. It gave rise to the problem of dissociating the fundamental Christian conviction of the dignity of man from the idea of Earth's physical centrality. To assert that the Earth was not central but peripheral to the universe was startlingly felt as a negation of human worth. Moreover, the gigantic distances of space conveyed to persons a feeling of their smallness and insignificance, as well as a sense of the silence, darkness, coldness, and emptiness of the universe. In addition, man, who must think within categories of space and time, had, as we have seen, imaginatively visualized a God—symbol and basis of human value and meaning—as located just beyond the spheres, hovering concernedly—or even retributively—near to man. But as the distance, spatial and temporal, is indefinitely extended, the same image of God results in pushing that God farther and farther away until he virtually disappears from the galactic universe. The same image which once expressed a close presence now communicates an absence. We have repeatedly stressed the importance of the category of the future rather than the past. In a similar vein, we may call to mind the insistence of Bishop Robinson's popular book, *Honest to God* (1963), on the greater appropriateness for today of metaphors of depth and interiority rather than of height and distance, in speaking of a divine reality.[28] In any event, the anxiety of man before this silent vastness, as well as his scientific confidence, has perhaps been instrumental in filling this void with airplanes, rockets, space probes, and in populating it in literature with alien intelligences.

Thus, the most immediate interpretation is that the alien is a substitute God-figure and father-figure, representing the projected wishful thinking and fright of an insecure child in a cruel universe. Though matters may often rest at this level, as with the popular belief in flying saucers, these imaginings about aliens may also reflect the more profound aspirations and fears which pertain to the human condition of the mature adult. Man, as science fiction recognizes, is a being who relentlessly searches for meaning and purpose in his life, yet is also threatened by anxiety, death, and meaninglessness. He craves a higher life transcending his present ambiguity. He has at least an inkling that this lies somehow beyond his grasp. The theme of the alien reflects, at its deepest level, man's profound craving that the universe be more than just man and nature. Man is forever in quest of "something more," a presence and depth of hope, of meaning, of value, which transcends him. Man is not enough for man. This is what is echoed in a variety of ways in modern science fiction, both in tones of hope and in tones of despair.

Science fiction thus poses to theology the challenge of discovering and articulating ways to affirm that the quest of man is not in vain, that the human enterprise is of worth and value. How may we enter fully into the ambiguity, negativity, and tragedy of the human condition and still pass through and beyond to a sense of beauty which envelops the whole, to a joy and even humor which does not allow tragedy the final word? How may we affirm a "something more" that is a source of meaning for the present and of hope for the future? There is possibly nothing startlingly new in works of science fiction, which is not also found, even perhaps more lucidly, in writings of a more strictly philosophical or psychological character. It is, however, important as a popular, more generally available form of literature, whose future orientation allows wide scope for the free play of speculative imagination. It thereby both expresses and reaches to the undercurrents of mood and attitude in our time. Science fiction is, indeed, one of the "signs of the times" to which theology must attend.

NOTES

1. See E. Schillebeeckx, *God the Future of Man* (New York: Sheed and Ward, 1968), pp. 51-90, 167-207; L. Gilkey, *Maker of Heaven and Earth* (New York: Doubleday Anchor Books, 1965), pp. 287-318.

2. See E. Kubler-Ross, *On Death and Dying* (New York: Macmillan, 1969); Ignace Lepp, *Death and Its Mysteries* (New York: Macmillan, 1968). Albert Camus brings this point home most forcefully in presenting man's wakening to his mortality. An individual in the springtime of his youth, he notes, looks forward to the future and the positive benefits it holds, only to be caught up short by the staggering realization that this relentless passage of time is also hurrying towards death. *The Myth of Sisyphus* (New York: Vintage Books, 1955), pp. 8-12.
3. See, for example, L. Dewart, *The Future of Belief* (New York: Herder and Herder, 1968); L. Gilkey, *Naming the Whirlwind* (Indianapolis: Bobbs-Merrill, 1969); and J. Ratzinger, *Introduction to Christianity,* trans. J. R. Foster (New York: Herder and Herder, 1969).
4. See, for example, M. Marty and D. Peerman, eds. *New Theology No. 5* and *New Theology No. 6* (Toronto: Macmillan, 1968-1969); C. Braaten, *The Future of God* (New York: Harper & Row, 1969); C. Braaten and R. Jenson, *The Futurist Option* (New York: Newman Press, 1970); and Vatican II, *Pastoral Constitution of the Church in the Modern World* (New York: Paulist Press, 1967).
5. On the theology of creation and, more specifically, its temporal dimension, see L. Gilkey, *Maker of Heaven and Earth,* esp. pp. 287-318; A. Hulsbosch, *God in Creation and Evolution* (New York: Sheed and Ward, 1965); and E. Benz, *Evolution and Christian Hope* (New York: Anchor Doubleday Books, 1968).
6. E. Schillebeeckx, *Marriage: Human Reality and Saving Mystery* (New York: Sheed and Ward, 1965), Vol. 1.
7. Ian Barbour, ed., *Science and Religion* (New York: Harper Forum Books, 1968); L. Newbiggin, *Honest Religion for Secular Man* (London: SCM Press, 1966), pp. 11-76.
8. Dewart, *The Future of Belief,* pp. 77-121. The vision of Teilhard de Chardin is, of course, also pertinent here. See *The Phenomenon of Man* (New York: Harper Torchbooks, 1961).
9. Note, for example, Sartre's observation that no definition of man is possible until after his death when self-choice is ended and man's nature becomes fixed. *Being and Nothingness,* trans. H. Barnes (New York: Washington Square Press, 1966). On 'futurology' see Alvin Toffler, *Future Shock* (New York: Bantam Books, 1971) and W. H. G. Armytage, *Yesterday's Tomorrows: A Historical Survey of Future Societies* (Toronto: University of Toronto Press, 1968).
10. Schillebeeckx, *God the Future of Man,* pp. 51-90, 167-207; C. Baum, *New Horizon* (New York: Paulist Press, 1972), pp. 51-70; T. Steeman, "What is Wrong with God?" in M. J. Taylor, ed., *The Sacred and the Secular* (Englewood Cliffs: Prentice Hall, 1968), pp. 154-74.
11. See, for example, A. Auer, "The Changing Character of the Christian Understanding of the World," in Karl Rahner et al., *The Christian in the World* (New York: P. J. Kennedy and Sons, 1965), pp. 3-44.
12. Auer, pp. 3-44; see also J. Y. Calvez, *La Pensée de Karl Marx* (Editions de seuil, 1969).
13. Gilkey, *Maker of Heaven and Earth,* pp. 209-46; A. Galloway, *The Cosmic Christ* (London: Nisbett and Co., 1959).
14. Chad Walsh, *From Utopia to Nightmare* (New York: Harper & Row, 1962).
15. L. Sprague de Camp, "Imaginative Fiction and Creative Imagination," in Reginald Bretnor, *Modern Science Fiction, Its Meaning and Its Future* (New York: Coward-McCann, 1953), pp. 119-54; Galloway, *The Cosmic Christ.*
16. S. Lyonnet, "The Redemption of the Universe," in Rahner et al., *The Church: Readings in Theology* (New York: P. J. Kennedy and Sons, 1963), pp. 126-56; L. Scheffczyk, "The Meaning of Christ's Parousia for the Salvation of Man and the Cosmos," in Rahner, *The Christian in the World,* pp. 130-57.

17. Teilhard de Chardin, *The Future of Man,* trans. N. Denny (London: Fontana Books, 1969), esp. pp. 321-23.
18. Articulations of this point of view may be found in the articles of G. Heard and R. Bretnor in Bretnor, *Modern Science Fiction.* A particularly striking fictional example is Fred Hoyle's *The Black Cloud* (New York: Harper & Brothers, 1957).
19. Kingsley Amis, *New Maps of Hell* (New York: Harcourt, Brace, 1960), pp. 64ff.
20. Bruno Bettelheim, *The Informed Heart* (New York: Avon Books, 1971). This book also cites a relevant article: E. Bernabeu, "Science Fiction," *The Psychoanalytic Quarterly,* 26 (October 1957), 527-35.
21. Two relevant anthologies are J. Stadler, ed., *Ecofiction* (New York: Washington Square Press, 1971) and R. Sauer, ed., *Voyages: Scenarios for a Spaceship Earth* (New York: Ballantine Books, 1971).
22. Isaac Asimov, *The End of Eternity* (Greenwich: Fawcett Crest Books, 1971) pp. 185-87.
23. The comments of Burgess are taken from an interview published in the *Toronto Globe and Mail,* 6 June 1972.
24. Basil Davenport, *Inquiry into Science Fiction* (Toronto: Longmans, Green, 1955), p. 70.
25. Vatican II, pp. 103ff.
26. Robert Plank, *The Emotional Significance of Imaginary Beings* (Springfield, Ill.: Charles C. Thomas, 1968). See also Philip Wylie, "Science Fiction and Sanity in an Age of Crisis," in Bretnor, pp. 221-41; Amis, pp. 80-86.
27. Sigmund Freud, *The Future of an Illusion* (New York: Doubleday Anchor Books, 1964).
28. John A. T. Robinson, *Honest to God* (London: SCM Press, 1963). See also his subsequent book, *Exploration Unto God* (London: SCM Press, 1967).

The Philosophical Limitations of Science Fiction

Patrick G. Hogan, Jr.

No one could be more aware of the presumptiveness of such a topic as the philosophical limitations of science fiction than a person who would be fool enough to think of such a topic in the first place. And in view of the possible implications of what may develop in treating the subject, this foolish writer may as well go on record early with a confession that his love affair with science fiction, like that of many others, goes well back into the time of the pulps, predating several of the flurries of faddishness of more recent decades and certainly the recent permissiveness which apparently encourages the writing of theses and dissertations about science fiction by eager university students. So to go on record elicits a mingled sadness and fierce protectiveness. Indeed, some of the more recent discoverers of the genre seem to give the offhand impression that they also invented it, or that they at least deserve extraordinary credit for bringing it to the attention of

---

This essay was presented as the keynote address of the 1973 SFRA meeting held at Pennsylvania State University September 14-17. A form of it has been published in *The Journal of General Education* 28 (Spring 1976), 1-15. That entire issue was devoted to papers given at the conference.

others, to whom they will be very happy to explain it. Perhaps there is also a trifle of sadness in the fact that if the degree of current interest could have been anticipated, more care would have been exercised in preserving copies of *Unknown, Amazing Stories,* or *Astounding Stories* as investments towards retirement—perhaps more valuable than the recent demands for genuine Confederate money. So much, then, for reassurance that current retrospectiveness has a sympathetic historical basis.

One other initial premise remains to be stated. As in many other areas, advocates of science fiction seem to be quite determined to create a special language in which to write and talk about their enthusiasm. A long list of examples would contribute little here; in fact, the matter is mentioned only in order to insist that insofar as possible what follows will be stated in the simplest language possible. Beginning with intentionally broad and sweeping generalizations, the discussion will turn to focus briefly upon utopian science fiction, not only because philosophical problems abound in that area, but as a subdued herald of "things to come," an ambiguous phrase at best.

The greatest danger in developing a thesis touching the philosophical limitations of science fiction is in one sense that which is on occasion generated by the contrary claims of the literary critic and those of the writer, whatever the nature of the latter's creation. However, the danger is doubled if the reader—perhaps the term critic is at once both too vague and too specific—addresses himself to matters philosophical rather than matters literary, assuming that even that distinction has validity. Naturally much of the imposing body of literary history or criticism is telling evidence that the reader-scholar has accepted one challenge or another and has written, if not lived, dangerously. Even so, the question of the philosophical intentions of the writer and the philsophical analysis of the reader creates an equation more often generated than solved.

Nothing to be said here is intended to suggest that there have not been many valuable contributions to the study of literature, whatever its vintage, of the sort which may be classified as philosophical, whether the subject of investigation be a single poem, play, story, or novel—or the totality of an author's works. Yet no reader who is obligated to divide his attention between primary material and the subsequent secondary material can honestly deny the existence of article upon article and volume upon volume of dubious contributions to both categories. Although the terminology may range from the excessively erudite to a pseudo-sophisticated parade of the latest jargon, carefully documented studies as well as casual reviews are too often prone to discover the presence of ideas or concepts quite likely foreign to authorial intent or to bemoan the absence of what the critic would have included if he had been creative enough to have been doing the writing.

Less a danger than a fairly simple problem is the postulation of a question somehow asking how much—to what degree and to what extent—literature can be expected to be philosophic. Obviously, one problem engenders another, for the problem of definition implicit in the topic presently under consideration cannot, unfortunately, be definitively solved here. Comments by way of indirection will have to suffice.

Philosophy, whether in its singular or plural form and with whatever ending, is too easy a term to use. Whether the subject matter to be examined be fiction or expository prose, too often lost somewhere in the shuffle is the glaring fact that by a philosophy is meant a system, and those philosophies which are systematic are few. Philosophies which tend towards completeness, attempting to encompass *both* man and the universe, are fewer still. In this respect it matters little whether the philosophy be ancient or modern. There can probably be no agreement here, for if no distinction is made between the past and the present on this point it would seem that no provision is made for science, which, to put it bluntly, would mean that the point has been missed.

Plato, it could easily be argued, would be less attractive to the modern writer than would be what the boob-tube would designate, if it were mentioned at all, as a "recent philosopher of one's choice." Here again, the point is slippery enough as it is, without trying to develop detailed comparisons and contrasts. But should it not be remembered that the usual passing reference to Plato is not to Platonism proper but to some stage of Neo-Platonism? And the curious reason for this is that Neo-Platonism, whatever its exact ilk, is more systematic than Platonism. In fact, most of the concentrated flurries of Neo-Platonic revival, but certainly not all, whatever the genesis of the renewed interest, at least attempted to improve the system. Plato has been mentioned instead of Aristotle because Aristotle, or Aristotelianism, was more systematic from the beginning; that would be another story. A philosophy as a system is the intended point. A mere collection of philosophical ideas, profound though they may be, does not constitute a systematic philosophy. The statement is not intended to be a negative one, nor does the lack of system seem to influence the acceptance or rejection of "philosophical ideas" by human beings. Even so, a surprising bulk of modern scholarship ignores such distinctions.

If that body of literature called science fiction is to be discussed with reference to its philosophical limitations or achievements, it is essential—and it is only fair—that such a discussion clearly establish the premises upon which it will proceed. Such a requirement should be demanded, *whatever* the nature of the fiction—for another reductive process is that fiction, ranging from story to trilogy, may as well be a focus, for this would include the bulk of science fiction, if movies and television productions are to be held in abeyance as being drama.

"Whatever the nature of the fiction" serves as a reminder that only a small proportion of that fiction which is other than science fiction has concerned itself with the development of or the fictional repetition or framing of systematic philosophies. There is no need to attempt a hand-list of significant exceptions. If any of this contains a grain of truth, all that needs to be said is that no more can be expected of science fiction than of any other kind of fiction. But to have said it may have been to be too hasty. There is reason to think that reader reaction, at least in some circles, *expects* science fiction to achieve what very, very little other current fiction seems to be attempting. If fiction is to be philosophic, with or without limitations, the writers of science fiction may have to meet the challenge.

So far, it has been hinted that in some mysterious fashion science fiction reveals evidence of philosophical limitations. To discuss these limitations presents yet another problem; in this case it may be a paradox. Should such a discussion be descriptive or prescriptive? *Can* it be either? No reminder is needed that writers are not especially receptive of advice about what they write and how they write about it. On occasion, even praise is grudgingly acknowledged. That laud and honor—richly deserved—which *is* taken kindly, such as that prefixed to the increasing variety of collections and reprints, is seldom based upon the philosophic content of the work. It will be remembered that about the same time—only a few decades ago, in fact—that American literature became an accepted part of the curriculum in colleges and universities, there was a renewed echo of the nineteenth-century pleas for the formulation of a distinctively American literature—with the one difference that the emphasis was upon the writing of the "great American novel." To the extent that this situation smacked of the prescriptive, there can be no doubt that a legion of major writers marched to one drummer or another, to which the more recent parade of college courses devoted to a single writer serves as testimony. But the specific prescription is seldom mentioned any more, either as a challenge or as reference to an acknowledged victory.

Yet, is it being prescriptive to speculate that if in the remainder of a waning century there is to be a significant body of fiction dealing seriously with those manifestations of human thought and experience called philosophy, then it is up to the writers of science fiction to produce it? If so, it may be the function of that kind of reader who is willing to be cursed as critic to attempt to describe it. Such a description cannot be a substitute for the creative act, but it does seem quite clear that Western culture has reached a curious stage which demands some kind of closer coordination. Circumstances no longer permit the time lag that may be observed and described between the Neo-Platonism of, say, Plotinus and that of Ficino and the Florentine School. (Whatever time may be, a time lag is *not* fictional.)

If then, to date, science fiction has evidenced philosophical dimensions, and if the prescriptive approach must be avoided, what purposes may be served by descriptive observations?

Perhaps this convoluted question has a partial answer, one which may be at least suggested by briefly touching a very few of the topics and themes which make up the almost unlimited subject matter available to the writer of science fiction.

One intriguing clue emerges from the recurrence in science fiction of concern with utopias. Much has been said and will be said in this respect, but a few comments are imperative here. First, it is not difficult to remember that the accurate term may be, not "utopia," but "antiutopia" or "dystopia" or whatever. Secondly, it must be remembered that it is precisely here that the writer must succeed in doing something that whole literary movements, such as Realism and Naturalism, have failed to do, and that is to take fully into account the relationships between science and technology and the human beings who generated them and who must live or die by them. (A culture, too, can sicken and die!)

Are there not partially helpful hints from the past here? Grossly ignoring the biographical facts, is it not worth a moment's speculation to consider that one reason Sir Francis Bacon did not complete his *The New Atlantis* was his growing realization that the perfect society could not be founded upon scientific principles alone, even science as he conceived or misconceived it? To argue that if Bacon could have imagined or intuited robots or servomechanisms he could have completed his system is, of course, nonsense. But there is another deceptively simple point tucked in here somewhere. The modern writer of a utopia, or its counterpart, must give science its proper due, which undoubtedly means he must know more about it than is often apparently the case. Only partial knowledge means that the writer has little choice other than a negative account of a possible utopia. That may be the horrible truth, but, contrariwise, it may be that the available evidence, and the speculation—the fiction—based thereupon demands re-examination. Or, to take another isolated example, the relationship of man to the machines he has invented and developed, although a topic treated in an almost infinite variety of ways, still leaves much territory to be explored. Whether the device is a starship, with or without space-warping capabilities, or a sketchily described vehicle for time travel, does not much matter. The challenging philosophical implications implicit here, if the here may be specified as the concept of interstellar travel by any sort of manned vehicle or device, have perhaps been best described by a writer whose own fiction does not fit comfortably either the classification of science fiction or fantasy. In one of his less well known essays ("Will We Lose God in Outer Space?"), the late C. S. Lewis, although remarking that we are still a long way from journeying to other worlds inhabitated by intelligent beings, poses several questions about the possible conduct of Man in his relationships with other beings if and when and wheresoever he may encounter them. By way of superficial treatment, his questions can be summarized as asking, "What is man to do *if* he finds thinking creatures on a distant planet?" There is no value in trying to dismiss Lewis's queries as smacking of the theological; they are philosophical enough to demand speculation on the part of writers of science fiction. Indeed, with or without an awareness of Lewis's questions, some of the best recent science fiction has addressed itself to these questions. Once again, manifestly *without* trying to spread credit where it is rightly due, it may still be observed that more needs to be done than has yet been accomplished. Many stories and novels have approached these matters, suggesting a current need for synthesis, but only science fiction provides at once both a laboratory and a forum for the development and airing of the theories which would provide some faint hope that Man can meet his potential challenges. Only philosophy, not science alone, can generate and sustain such hope.

Almost any topic with which science fiction has concerned itself, with the possible exception of gimmick stories intended only to be funny or clever and the intrusive preoccupation in a few instances with sex, deserves scrutiny in point of its possible philosophical implications—if any. But in an attempt to be a trifle more specific in the present discussion, a reversion to utopias will have to serve. Since he is praised or blamed for popularizing, if not coining, the term "utopia," Thomas More is a logical writer with whom to begin.[1]

Curiously, it is a science-fiction novel, rather than the wealth of scholarship devoted to Thomas More, which provides one of the keenest insights into what his *Utopia* was all about. In R. A. Lafferty's *Past Master* (1968), the More who is "transported" from his own time in the Old World of Old Earth[2] to the dubious utopia of Golden Astrobe, and who because of his complete honesty is to be elevated to the high, albeit temporary, capacity of "past master," comments on his own *Utopia:*

> 'I once wrote an account of as sick a world as I could imagine. You see, my second claim to fame is that I coined the word and the idea Utopia. I wrote in bitter and laughing irony of that sickest of all possible worlds, that into which my own world seems to be turning.'
>
> —p. 31.

More even professes to know what the future reaction to his own work is to be:

> 'I am told by time travelers that my angry humor piece has always been misunderstood. It came to be believed that I wrote of an ideal world. It even came to be believed that I wrote with a straight face. My mind boggles at the very idea, but I'm told that it is so. . . . There is something very slack about a future that will take a biting satire for a vapid dream.'
>
> —p. 31.

There is little point in arguing the validity, or the lack thereof, of the comments Lafferty puts into More's mouth. If these and others be true, and it is very probable that they are, the whole tradition of utopian writing, whether science fiction or not, may demand additional intensive meditation—and re-evaluation.

It must also be remembered that Thomas More cannot be accused of being a systematic philosopher, certainly not as the history of philosophy suggests that the term be defined. This is not a negative charge, even though it can lead to speculation that More's *Utopia* is perhaps more properly to be classified with Machiavelli's *The Prince* than either is to be compared with, say, Plato's *Republic.* There is little question that social criticism, "sociology" not having been invented, and political philosophy are legitimate areas of concern in both More and Machiavelli, as well as rather early perceptions of matters psychological—if epistemology is too dated a discipline. The somewhat quaint juxtaposition of More and Machiavelli is intended only to suggest the serious difficulties which can arise in considering More's *Utopia* as a philosophical treatise. Notwithstanding the number of scholarly investigations appertaining thereto,[3] a strong case can be made that the philosophical content of More's *Utopia* is limited. Yet it is often used as a touchstone in discussions of utopian science fiction.

Actually, since he has a better claim to classification as a philosopher, the previously mentioned Sir Francis Bacon, with his interest in science (as he knew it and foresaw it), in his unfinished *The New Atlantis,* should be more influential in science-fiction circles than Thomas More. But he obviously is not, whether because *The New Atlantis* was never completed or because his science was so technologically primitive.

It has probably never been conjectured that the utopian work which is yet to be written would need to be a masterpiece by a systematic philosopher. Nor, for that matter, has it been suggested that the anti-utopia or the dystopia which would preclude any attempt to develop some future positive utopia would require such authorship. Usually, however, it appears that the judgment of one or another so-called utopia, no matter how influential in the history of ideas, is one of failure because of impracticability, not of failure because of lack of philosophical soundness.

Somewhat slowly, a self-developing key question begins to formulate itself which either justifies the present line of reflection or renders it invalid: Is it possible for a work classified as utopian to be the result of systematic philosophical speculation? Cannot the same question be asked about these works which are called dystopian? Moreover, if the fairly common complaint about partly philosophical utopias is that they are impractical, why do utopian concerns drawn from a spectrum ranging from human engineering to a robot-centered culture or from behavioristic psychology to agrarian reform on a virgin planet so often end up in fiction as dystopias? How many dystopias were first formulated in an author's mind as a possible utopia? Is it less demanding of a writer's intellect to compose a dystopia than to write the modern utopia, or, to be more precise, an account of the possible future utopia? Rather than a single key question, one question seems to beget another.

It is not the purpose here to attempt the impossible task of a chronological account of even typical utopias, early or late; for dystopias the prospect would be even more forbidding. Even a book-length study would be hard pressed to make other than a selective survey, presupposing that some attempt at thoroughness would be desired. Those interested in book-length studies which have attempted to deal with the general subject, and with varying degrees of interest and effectiveness, will find wealth aplenty in Thomas D. Clareson's bibliographies in *Extrapolation.*[4] There is no intent to imply that among these volumes there are not numbers of serious evaluations of the utopia-dystopia enigma. Nor is a familiarity with all of these works boasted. But, as yet, answers to some of the questions posed above, along with a host of similar questions, seem to be elusive.

Suggestions which might lead to some sort of answers abound. As a random example, Chad Walsh in *From Utopia to Nightmare* (1962) writes: "Theoretically, the loss of utopian hopes could mean that man is abandoning his humanistic delusions and returning to Christian realism. But it can equally well mean that a mood of total pessimism, as unreasoned as the earlier utopian hopes, is engulfing our minds and our spirits."[5] Keeping in mind that Walsh tends to treat traditional utopias and dystopias rather than quite recent examples, and that his own angle of vision is slightly religious, if not theological, he does provide a framework which makes it possible to say of Thomas More as a fictional character in Lafferty's previously mentioned *Past Master* that More emphatically denies having "humanistic delusions," whatever they may be, and that his meeting essentially the same fate in the novel that he did in life does not come clear as a return to "Christian realism." And if the character More is more pessimistic than optimistic, it is a strangely cheerful pessimism. After More loses his fictional head, the statements are made that:

> All life and heat and pulse went out of the world. It died in every bird and rock and plant and person of it, in every mountain and sea and cloud. It died in its gravity and light and heat, in its germ-life and in its life-code. Everything ceased. And all the stars went out.
>
> —p. 190

Yet only a few short paragraphs later the question is posed, "Does a new world follow the old . . . ?" Lafferty's final paragraphs are interspersed by "*Be quiet. We watch. . . . Be quiet. We wait.*" And the novel concludes with "*Be quiet. We hope.*" (p. 191).

In a related vein it may be remarked that early in the massive reading and rereading program which was considered essential as additional preparation for the present comments, the rather arbitrary decision was made to exclude science-fiction writers other than of American vintage. Unfortunately, this determination—as extended—does not permit brief reference to C. S. Lewis, whose trilogy—*Out of the Silent Planet* (1938), *Perelandra* (1943), and *That Hideous Strength* (1945)—would certainly be appropriate for analysis according to the framework attributed above to Walsh. Moreover, if not excluded, it might be possible to say a little more about whether Lewis was writing fantasy or science fiction or both, for, to quote out of context, "Compounding the irony," Clareson says, "the modern form of fantasy that we call science fiction is best understood as 'the other side of realism'. . . ."[6]

To take another tack, it is rather odd that in the dim light of relative preoccupation with dystopias one weighty contribution to the twentieth-century utopian tradition is often overlooked. Perhaps the year of appearance of Wright's *Islandia* (1942)[7] had something to do with its subsequent neglect. More likely is the book's detailed concern with an agrarian rather than a technical society, its setting on a mythical continent on Earth rather than the Earth-like planet of a distant star, and its stress upon leisure and meditation rather than scientific advancement or the complexities of coping with an imaginary alien culture. The book does contain discussions of improving the economy of the "utopia," a project involving political overtones, but it may well lack the excitement of other appeals to man's reason, if not to his imagination. If nothing else, it could be argued that this kind of account is more nearly the stuff dreams are made of than nightmares.

In this respect, the typical dystopia may be described as the product of a writer's logical mind as distinguished from those mental processes classified as his imagination. A typical by-product may well be a misplaced seriousness leading to a preoccupation with satirical intent, not infrequently with a questionable grasp of effective techniques of satire. Something of this problem is revealed in a review of a quite recent book by Fred and Geoffrey Hoyle:

> . . . The Hoyle stories are the playthings of genius. Because they carry around no portentous sociological baggage, the Hoyles are all the more effective at the classical task of science fiction, which is to satirize grotesque social reality in the mirror of scientific possibility. More than that, the tales have that rarest of qualities in fiction, science or otherwise: gaiety.[8]

Whether the high praise is justified or not is beside the point. It is the questioning of certain characteristics as effective means of achieving a given effect and the suggestion that some kind of humor is a better means that may provide a clue to both limitations and potentialities even in utopian science fiction. In short, unrelieved satire, so frequently a quality of the dystopia, and deadly seriousness, often associated with utopian writing, are not likely to produce significant results. It should be noted however, that even the brief passage cited disparages, or at least questions, the sociological approach partly in order to praise the combination of satire and gaiety. The more closely the passage is examined, its provocative questioning quality having been admitted, the more ambiguous it becomes. When, or by whom, was it established that the "classical task" of science fiction is to "satirize grotesque social reality," and why only "grotesque social reality"? To linger no longer, it may be observed that the quoted comments are an excellent example of the kind of sequential argument that after tempting a reader to agreement on one point causes him to overlook a medial disagreement on the way to a terminal positive observation, in this case the ingredient of gaiety, or humor. Nor is this a matter of picking at nits, if it is recalled that a multiplicity of nits could lead to varying degrees of discomfort. Who has not felt somewhat uncomfortable after reading one of the increasing number of paperback collections of stories called "new science fiction," sometimes the product of special writing workshops, only to find that few of the selections are science fiction, whatever else they may be. Fortunately, the strictures of biology forbid nits from having kittens.

Naturally, it may be expected that the seemingly unlimited potential of science fiction would have attracted—as it has—writers with widely diverse backgrounds, be they scientific, humanistic, or otherwise. Even the fairly recent fad of teaching science fiction has attracted as teachers persons from a number of disciplines other than literature. One refreshing direction in the writing of science fiction has been what is called the anthropological approach, or fictional exercises by trained anthropologists. To mention but a single example, the implications of which may relate to utopian science fiction, the six stories by Chad Oliver published as *The Edge of Forever* (1971) may suffice. In a section entitled "Afterthoughts" at the end of the book, the author states:

> One repetitive theme is the idea that if you are going to manipulate culture you have to do it on the sly. . . . It is not a popular concept. I

don't advocate it, except in fiction. (The joker, of course, is who decides to manipulate what, and on what basis?)[9]

The concept suggested here that is of prime importance to utopian projections is the necessity of manipulating culture. In other words, the only way for utopian planning to be effective is for it to provide a blueprint of changes which must be made in order to achieve the better society or culture which has been envisioned. *Change* is the essential element in the formula. Utopian writing, of necessity often largely fictional, is normally concerned with what might be, not what is. The only way to transform what might be into reality is for change to take place; change requires the passage of time; therefore, the sequence of changes which equals change is almost always concerned with future time. The relative preoccupation of science fiction with the future, certainly with what might be, is one of the reasons most modern utopian writing falls into the genre of science fiction. As the last quotation suggests, planned changes in culture can present serious problems, even though the intent is utopian.

Among the problems which cultural change may contribute is that a culture, or society, consists of human beings, who are notoriously unpredictable when confronted with change. Men seem to be more responsive in some instances than others. Without multiplying examples, men appear to be quick to make a change which promises material gain, or to accept a technological development which contributes to creature comfort, or to participate in a new activity which they think will result in pleasure or excitement. But human beings are slow to accept changes which require serious readjustment of their thought processes; it matters very little whether or not their understanding of what they think is systematic or sound. Education does not seem to have helped very much in these matters. Students prefer to study psychology and sociology rather than philosophy, and those who do study philosophy too seldom let it influence their own thinking, with the possible exception of fads such as existentialism and the like. In short, if that be possible among such complexities, one philosophical limitation of utopian science fiction may be that its practicality, considering its necessary focus upon human beings, exists in direct proportion to the decrease in its philosophical content. Men more easily change to accept automation, and therefore robots, than they do to consider the possibility that they must in some way change their essential nature.

Additional problems are added in another passage from Oliver and in deceptively simple terms:

> A great deal of culture is way down deep, automatic, taken for granted. I cannot even imagine a culture that was entirely rational (using anyone's definition), entirely conscious, all on the surface. I don't think it would *work*. Certainly the most sweeping changes in our lifeways have been largely accidental—the un-anticipated consequences of fooling around with that hunk of flint, domesticating that cow, planting that seed.[10]

These observations can be taken to clarify some of the reasons dystopias tend to outnumber utopias. For a culture to be "entirely rational," it may be presumed that ideal circumstances would be required, not the least of which would be rational men to create such a culture, live in it, and maintain its rationality. Since men are not always rational in unusual circumstances, which outnumber the ideal variety, the raw material for dystopias is more abundant than for utopias. Moreover, if Oliver is correct in his diagnosis of "sweeping changes," utopian science fiction may be immune to philosophical limitations, addressing itself to the hardware necessary to comfortable survival on a distant planet.

Or is it? A piece of flint can be shaped into a tool, a weapon, or an ornament. Sooner or later, one consequence of the development is the determination of its significance, which requires thought, however unsophisticated. Thought sometimes becomes philosophical, sometimes utopian. Interestingly, the fictional Thomas More is represented as being "boggle-eyed" at the importance of material developments in the presumed utopia he is observing:

> 'Of course I'm impressed by the thousands of years of technological advance since my time. . . . And in my day I had the name of being a

> forerunner in these things. I didn't know what questions to ask about the future when—well, when I talked to certain traveling men on this subject a long time ago, or at least a long time from here. I asked them questions of philosophy and theology and the political formation of commonwealths, and of the arts and tongues and of the mind understanding itself. It never struck me that the changes would be in material things. We had already made great advances in these, far beyond the Greeks and Romans, and I thought the cycle would swing back and the thousand years after myself would be devoted to advances in the intangibles.'
>
> —p. 52

But for More the tangibles are no substitute for the intangibles; he may have no solution that would transform the utopian dream into a tangible reality, but he knows that technological advances are not enough: "The fact that there are no sick of mind among you would entice me also, had I not discovered for myself that so many of you are dead of mind" (p. 52).

Therefore, to try to knot together such devious threads, it must be admitted that in all fairness to the writers of utopian science fiction it may be grossly unfair to expect, much less to demand, of them a resolution of the philosophical limitations with which they are confronted. It is absolutely no reflection upon their often high competence as writers to point out that those with sound scientific backgrounds frequently produce fine science fiction, but they cannot be expected to have an equally firm grasp of the philosophical, and perhaps other, principles which would enable them to create the utopian science-fiction novel that would at once weld together the utopian dream and a cold, hard world of technological reality. Nor would a philosopher, however defined, fare better; both philosophers and theologians are currently experiencing an unhappy confusion, especially if they are trying to adapt previous philosophy to fit a technological society or to formulate a new system in the face of changes that continue to change. There is little point in any process of elimination, but there is the bare possibility that the anthropologist or the historian of science, by stretching the boundaries of knowledge and understanding, may be better candidates for such authorship than representatives of diverse other disciplines.

The possibility, if not the probability, is very strong that a hoped-for solution will be found neither in utopian attempts nor in the apparently more abundant anti- or dystopias but in some new dimension, if not undreamed of at least unthought of to a degree that an adequate system may be developed in fiction. There *is* the inevitable paradox in the vacillation between man's beastly limitations and his as yet unrealized potential. Too few attempts have been made to take man where he is—whatever that may mean and wheresoever he may be considered to be—and to provide him with a blueprint which he can follow, rather than attempts to escape into or from such a projection.

Perhaps it is both wishful and wistful thinking that whatever philosophical system may be predicated to insure the continuity of the total being called Man will emerge from the typewriters of writers of science fiction. It may be a hope begot of desperation, but there are those who think that it *will* emerge. For through the medium of science fiction, whatever the genesis of the concepts, it is possible for writers to present to a growing audience an account, not of what was, or of what is, but of what may, perhaps even *can,* be. It would be a pity were the challenge of philosophical limitations not met, for never has mankind had greater need of such an achievement.

NOTES

1. A condensed version of the comments in the present study touching utopian science fiction appeared in *Journal of the American Studies Association of Texas,* 6 (October 1975), 55-62; permission for the use thereof has been granted by the editor.
2. R. A. Lafferty, *Past Master* (New York: Ace Books, Inc., 1968), p. 8. Subsequent references to this work are indicated in the text.
Studies Association of Texas, 6 (October 1975), 55-62; permission for the use thereof has been granted by the editor.
3. A brief sampling could include: R. P. Adams, "Designs by More and Erasmus for a New Social Order," *Studies in Philology,* XLII (1945), 131-45; W. E. Campbell, *More's Utopia and His Social Teaching* (London, 1930); J. H. Hexter, *More's Utopia: The Biography of an Idea* (Princeton, 1952); M. Smelser, "Political Philosophy of Sir

Thomas More," in *Studies in Honor of St. Thomas Aquinas* (St. Louis, 1943), pp. 12-32.

4. Thomas D. Clareson, "An Annotated Bibliography of Critical Writings Dealing with Science Fiction (Books and Pamphlets)," *Extrapolation,* 11 (May 1970), 58-66; 12 (May 1971), 110-18. The recent and copious compilations of Lyman Tower Sargent, currently being circulated in mimeographed form, should also be consulted.
5. Walsh, as quoted by Clareson in *Extrapolation,* 11 (May 1970), 66.
6. Thomas D. Clareson, as quoted by Gerald Jonas, "Onward and Upward with the Arts: S. F.," *The New Yorker,* 29 July 1972, p. 48; see also Clareson's "The Other Side of Realism," in *SF: The Other Side of Realism,* pp. 1-25.
7. Austin Tappan Wright, *Islandia* (New York and Toronto, 1942); reprinted recently by Arno Press in a series of forty-one books called "utopian literature."
8. Horace Judson, review of *The Molecule Men,* by Fred Hoyle and Geoffrey Hoyle (New York: Harper & Row, 1972), in *Time,* 24 July 1972, p. 82.
9. Chad Oliver, *The Edge of Forever* (Los Angeles: Sherbourn Press, Inc., 1971), p. 296. It is not intended naively to imply that this direction is a new one; "refreshing" is the emphatic word.
10. Oliver, p. 297.

Critical Methods: Speculative Fiction

Samuel R. Delany

The historical discussion of the development of some area of art, while often illuminating, does not necessarily exhaust that area. The development of a particular literary technique or theme over several decades through several writers, often in several countries, is not completely solved by a chronological listing of who did what first.

The historical literary critic tends to see literary progress as a process rather like this: some seminal genius invents a form; another refines it; still a third brings it to heretofore unimagined perfection; while a later fourth now takes the form into decadence; finally a new genius appears who, reacting against this decadence, invents a new form, and the cycle begins again.

But this view only traces a single thread through what is essentially a tapestry of aesthetic productions. The line, by definition, tries to connect the high points. Frequently enough, these high points are, in reality, connected. But just as frequently

---

This article was originally published in *quark/#1*, edited by Samuel R. Delany and Marilyn Hacker (New York: Paperback Library, 1970), pp. 182-95. It is reprinted with the permission of the author.

they are connected more strongly to other works and situations totally off this line. Historical artistic progress only exists by virtue of the perspective lent by hindsight.

Of the many ways in which an artist can be influenced by other art, the historical art-critic overconcentrates on two: the desire to imitate excellence, which, in genius, sometimes results in former excellence surpassed; and the distaste for the mediocre, the stultified, the inflexible, which, again in genius, can result in new forms.

But there are other ways to be influenced. One artist may find a work that seems to him to have an interesting kernel, but strikes him as so badly executed that he feels he can treat the same substance far more rewardingly. More frequently, I suspect, he finds an interesting technique employed to decorate a vapid hollow center, and uses it to ornament his own central concerns. It is still a little odd to look at whom some major authors felt to be their greatest influences. Thus Coleridge says that the sonnets of the country Reverend William Lisle Bowles, insipid and artificial by today's standards, were the literary epiphany of his youth. And Keats was practically fixated on the eighteenth-century boy-poet Thomas Chatterton, who, after perpetrating a series of forgeries of Middle English poems, allegedly the work of a nonexistent monk, Thomas Rowley, came to London and within the year committed suicide by taking rat poison, aged seventeen years and nine months.

Let us look at the development of one of the narrative techniques that practically alone supports science fiction: expertise—that method by which an author, deploying a handful of esoteric facts, creates the impression that he, or more often a character in his story, is an expert in some given field. It was formulated as an outgrowth of French Naturalism by a writer who began as a younger disciple of Zola, Joris Karl Huysmans. He brought the technique to pitch in his extremely influential novel *A Rebours,* published in 1884, a year after *Treasure Island,* a year before *She*. But where the Naturalists employed exhaustive research to give density to their endless chronicles of common people at common professions, Huysmans used comparatively superficial research to give an impression of thorough familiarity with a whole series of bizarre and exotic subjects, including late Latin literature, horticulture, and perfumery, to list only a few.

Till its recent reissue, I doubt if many currently working SF writers had read Huysman's plotless, characterless, yet totally enthralling novel. But you can find the technique employed in exactly the same manner in something as recent as Thomas Disch's *Camp Concentration.* Still, though I cannot prove it, I am sure there is a line (more likely a web) of writers who read writers who read Huysmans, and who took from one another this obviously effective technique, as directly as Wilde took the cadences and repetitions in the dialogue for *Salome* from Poe's *Politian.*

Indeed, we know Huysmans was familiar with Poe. Poe and Baudelaire are the most frequently mentioned authors in *A Rebours.* Huysmans undoubtedly knew Poe through the superb Baudelaire translations, which, from their impact on French literature, quite possibly have more merit than the originals. In *A Rebours, The Narrative of A. Gordon Pym* is mentioned by name, a work which Poe dots with much nautical expertise to make his sailor narrator convincing, on a thoroughly unreal voyage to the South Pole, that ends with the appearance of the White Goddess herself. This, and the similar use of expertise in the tales of ratiocination, could easily have prompted Huysmans to make the jump between using expertise to validate the commonplace to evoking the exotic and bizarre. (For those of you interested who are unable to acquire the book, you can get some idea of the flavor of *A Rebours* from Chapter Eight of Oscar Wilde's *Picture of Dorian Grey,* which is a pastiche of Huysmans; the mysterious yellow-backed French novel after which Dorian patterns his life was immediately identified by the Victorian public as *A Rebours,* which was confirmed by Wilde during the Queensbury trial; the book had achieved a reputation for decadence and corruption, as sexual oddities were another subject that Huysmans explored with his newly perfected technique.)

One place where the connection is clearly drawn is in Alfred Bester's early horror novella, *Astarte Was a Lady*. The opening of the novella is practically a rewrite of the opening movements of *A Rebours*. The relation is so close that I am fairly sure that Bester, an erudite author who studs his work with overt and covert literary references, was undoubtedly familiar with it when *Astarte* was published in the late thirties in *Unknown*. And Bester is easily the SF writer who brought expertise to its full fruition in his work.

Thus an SF literary technique has its burgeonings in an American fantasist, passes over the ocean to be translated by a great poet, is furthered by a French *fin de siècle* decadent, and returns a hundred years later to American magazine fiction. In the early sixties, it moved away to support the pseudo-SF James-Bond-style thriller, which would thoroughly collapse without it. But this is the way the web of influence works, passing in and out of the genre, crossing national and language boundaries, and returning, completely frustrating the historical critic who would keep everything in its proper path.

In the same way, the didactic methods of Robert Heinlein owe a great deal to Shaw's comedies of ideas, far more than to Wells and Verne. Indeed, part of the mystical optimism that pervades so much of SF is a product of a process that we can see in the ending of Shaw's *Man and Superman,* Twain's *Mysterious Stranger,* Kipling's "Children of the Zodiac," and Poe's *Eureka,* a process shared by such SF classics as Heinlein's *Stranger in a Strange Land,* Clarke's *Childhood's End,* Sturgeon's *More Than Human,* and Disch's *Camp Concentration*: any attempt to be totally rational about such a basically mystical subject as man's ultimate place in the universe tends to squeeze all the mysticism into one bright chunk that blurs all resolutions at the end.

Contrary to what might be expected, it is much harder to trace the development of a strictly limited subject than of a general one. To take an absurd example: it would be fairly intriguing to discuss the growth of interest in late medieval, Gallic song-forms among poets of the past hundred years. From Joyce's villanelle in *Portrait of the Artist* to Pound's and Auden's experiments with the sestina and canzone, or in the turn-of-the century profusion of rondels and rondolets, there is great give and take among the general run of poets, with a few enduring examples that give significance to the whole discussion. It would be quite another matter to discuss the use of only one medieval song form, let us say the triolet, over the same period. One could cite, in a historical list, Rimbaud's "Le Coeur vole," go on to mention Ernest Dowson's and Lionel Johnson's attempts (contemporaries of Yeats) and perhaps Sara Teasdale's "Why Do You Walk Through the Fields in Gloves" from the twenties. For what little it's worth, I would hazard a guess that Dowson had read Rimbaud and that Teasdale had read Dowson. But this gives us only a list, not a development. The fact is, the impulse to write one's first triolet is simply to see if one can do it. But once the form is learned, the impulse for the second or third might just as easily come from reading Gray's *Anatomy* as reading Milton, from the ubiquitous unhappy love affair, or the poached egg you had for breakfast.

To explore the development of SF poses a similar problem. Though its audience is growing, it is still a limited form, a specialized genre. The historical approach has been tried many times. But the fact is, if SF had been influenced only by itself, it would have strangled long since. If it did not continually influence areas outside itself, we would not have the present increase of interest. Simply because it is limited, a simple listing of which writer wrote what first will not do, whether one starts with Wells or Lucian.

The usual historical approach, at present, is the common intellectual property of practically anyone who knows that SF stands for science fiction. It begins with Wells and Verne and more or less ends with Heinlein and Bradbury. Anyone whose interest extends to actually reading it knows that an editor named Campbell caused some major changes, and before that an editor named Hugo Gernsback was important.

My own feeling is that, in an attempt to give respectability to American SF, much too much has been made of the relation between English Victorian, or Wellsian SF, and post-Gernsback, or Modern. Risking the other extreme, I propose that the relation actually is no stronger (or weaker) than the passage of the idea that it was possible to write stories and novels set in the future. Let me make some sweeping statements about areas that have been covered much more thoroughly by a host of other writers. Wells's "Romances of the Future" come from much the same impulse that produced his monumental multivolume *An Outline of History*. The future stories were an outgrowth of the perfectly viable fancy that history might well continue beyond the present. Both the historical work and the SF, however, fell out of the same twin Victorian views: that man's knowledge, in general, and his technology, in particular, develop in a more or less orderly way; and also that, in a given situation, human behavior will always be more or less the same, no matter when, or where.

Both of these views, however, are Victorian prejudices.

Technology has always run in both constructive and destructive directions at once. While Rome's engineers built amazing stone aqueducts with engineering techniques that astound us today, her aristocracy was unintentionally committing mass suicide with lead-based cosmetics and lead-lined wine jars. Pasteur invented vaccination, which prevented smallpox, and which, when the technique was finally extended to typhoid, typhus, diphtheria, and yellow fever, made possible the Second World War—till then, it would have been unthinkable to mass so many soldiers in such unsanitary conditions without having them completely wiped out by communicable diseases. Yet, from modern military medicine come the new discoveries in bioelectronics, and the science which Pasteur invented to preserve life is ultimately rushed on a step. Man's technical achievements, like his aesthetic ones, do not form a single line, but a web, in which numerous lines can be traced. Indeed, they sit in the same web. Any new discovery, from Oveonic devices to the revelation of a new ecological relationship, may spark changes in all directions, with good and bad results, that will cycle and echo, perhaps for centuries, in science, economics, and art.

Nor is human behavior any more stable from age to age, place to place. In seventeenth-century India, a Buddhist priest went to sit at the gate of a Sultan who had treated his people too harshly.

At the gate, the priest refused to eat or drink, and inside the house, the Sultan died from guilt and shame; while, in eighteenth-century France, the Queen, upon being told that the people had no bread, responds with the line that has become an emblem of political irresponsibility, "Then let them eat cake." In Greece in the ninth century B.C., the accidental revelation of incest between mother and son resulted in suicide and self-mutilation; five hundred years later in Persia, parents and children who could prove that they had indulged in carnal relations were elevated to the rank of holy men and women with great honor and reverence. A Mediterranean, upon discovering his wife in the arms of another man, commits a brutal double murder, while an Eskimo, receiving a stranger into his igloo, graciously offers his wife for sexual pleasure during the length of the visitor's stay. (And the unbiased student of anthropology could further cite societies or times in which incest was neither holy nor anathematic, but commonplace, or in which the disposal of her own, and possibly her spouse's, sexual favors was the woman's prerogative.) In nineteenth-century Russia, certain aristocrats organized weekend hunts for their guests, with dogs, horses, and rifles. The quarry, slaughtered and hung up for show in the barn, was thirteen- and fourteen-year-old peasant boys. Today, in Vietnam, seventeen- and eighteen-year-old American boys amuse themselves shooting at war prisoners through the stockade fence, while, in the states from which these boys hail, the death penalty is finally declared illegal as a primitive and barbaric custom.

There is nothing universal about the laws of human nature, at least as the Victorians pictured them. My readers sensitive to cultural resonances will probably sense them from all these examples of behavior as they look around our own culture. But that is because the human mind resonates. To try and construct historical chains of causation between these types of behavior and our own society is to miss the point. The human animal is potentially capable of any behavior. The feeling of resonance is a personal response to that potential.

Not only can the human animal behave in any way, the human psyche can approve or disapprove of any behavior. Thus, in one cultural enclave, the supreme moral act is the eating of bread and the drinking of wine; in another it is the act of sexual congress itself; while in another it is the disemboweling of babies. One group feels that avarice and selfishness are the roots of all evil. Another feels that uneducated altruism is the source of all the world's mismanagement, and that altruistic acts are the basic sins that rot the society. One group feels that ignorance is the cause of all the world's trouble. Another feels that all knowledge leads to pain.

No, the Victorian supposition of the linear moral logic of human progress and the inflexible catholicity of human nature have been left rather far behind. But these ideas are as inchoate in Wells's SF as they are in his history.

To look at Gernsback—or rather, Gernsback and his progeny—in relation to Wells, questions of literary merit set momentarily aside, immense differences appear immediately.

Gernsback was interested solely in the wonderful things progress might bring. As a popular entertainer, he was just as interested in the possible as he was in the probable. In his own novel, *Ralph 124C41+,* there is the chaste ghost of a love interest, but it vanishes amidst a host of marvelous gadgets. His use of behavior went only so far as it showed what things could do. Most of the objects were socially beneficial. When they were not, they were in the hands of the criminals that Ralph triumphed over. But there was none of the socially functional logic in which Wells indulged: *Since this is scientifically infeasible, it would not be socially beneficial to discuss what might come out of it.* The logic behind Gernsback's view of SF, which persists today, is rather: *Even though current technology claims this is impossible, if we were to achieve it, look at what marvels might result.*

It is just this basic concern with thingness that makes me insist that the initial impulse behind SF, despite the primitive and vulgar verbal trappings, was closer to the impulse behind poetry than it was to the impulse behind ordinary narrative fiction.

As another critic has said, in another context, "Poetry is concerned with the thingness of things." The new American SF took on the practically incantatory task of naming nonexistent objects, then investing them with reality by a host of methods, technological and pseudo-technological explanations, imbedding them in dramatic situations, or just inculcating them by pure repetition:

Television
Rocketship
Waldo
Spacesuit

But this is SF at its most primitive. The incantatory function—a better word than "predictive"—is no more the chief concern of modern SF than it is the concern of modern poetry; though remnants of it still linger in everything from Cordwainer Smith's "ornithopters" to Greg Benford's "brain tapping." Here is the place to note, I think, that when the British SF magazine *New Worlds* was awarded a London Arts Council subsidy, one of the testimonials, from a member of the editorial board of the *Oxford Unabridged Dictionary of the English Language,* explained that science fiction was the most fertile area of writing in the production of new words which endured in the language—a position held up till the mid-thirties by poetry.

Because it was unconcerned with behavior at its beginnings, SF was eventually able to reflect the breakdown of Victorian behavioral concepts which, for all his advanced thinking, had strictured Wells. It has been remarked, everywhere that man has noted in detail what goes on around him (you will find the idea in Confucius and in Plato) that the objects around him do influence his behavior, as well as how he judges the behavior of himself and others. The philosophers of aesthetics never tire of reminding us that the man who grows up in a beautiful and aesthetically interesting environment behaves very differently from the man raised among ugly, squalid surroundings. The Victorian progressives added to this that a person raised in an efficient, healthy, leisurely environment behaves quite differently from one raised amidst harrying inefficiency and disease. The aesthete quickly points out that the behavior of the person brought up with efficiency is still not the same as that of the person brought up with beauty.

McLuhan formulates this more precisely when he explains that any man-made object, and a good many natural ones, as they express or reflect aspects of man's inner consciousness, become factors in the equations governing communication as soon as they come into our perception.

But well before McLuhan had put this so succinctly—indeed, SF was to prompt McLuhan to this statement, another example of influence across boundaries—American SF writers, freed from the strictures of the probable, left to soar in the byways of the possible, not bound by the concept of universal human nature, in a country that was itself a potpourri of different cultural behavior patterns, sat contemplating marvelous objects in the theater of the mind. Slowly, intuitions of the way in which these objects might affect behavior began to appear in their stories. Editor Campbell was astute enough to see that this was perhaps the most powerful tool in the realization of these marvelous inventions. He encouraged his writers to use this tool, to make the focus of the stories the juncture between the object and the behavior it causes. As the writers followed Campbell, SF began to grow up.

By much the same process that poetry expanded beyond its beginnings in ritualistic chant and incantation, to become a way to paint all that is human, and etch much that is divine, so SF became able to reflect, focus, and diffract the relations between man and his universe, as it included other men, as it included all that man could create, all he could conceive.

Already, how much more potentially complex a template we have than the one left us by Victorian utopian fiction. The utopian fictions of Butler, Bellamy, Wells, as well as the later Huxley and Orwell, exhaust themselves by taking sides in the terribly limiting argument: "Regard this new society. You say it's good, but I say it's bad." Or, "You say it's bad, but I say it's good."

Auden has pointed out in his collection of essays, *The Dyer's Hand,* and then gone on to examine in his cycle of poems, *Horae*

Canonicae, that this argument is essentially a split in temperaments, not a logical division at all.

There are, and always will be, those people who see hope in progress. Auden calls their perfect world New Jerusalem. In New Jerusalem, hunger and disease have been abolished through science, man is free of drudgery and pain, and from it he can explore any aspect of the physical world in any way he wishes, assured that he has the power to best it should nature demand a contest. There are, and always will be, people who wish, in Auden's words, to return to Eden. He calls their perfect world Arcadia. In Arcadia, food is grown by individual farmers, and technology never progresses beyond what one man can make with his own hands. Man is at one with nature, who strengthens him for his explorations of the inner life; thus all that he creates will be in natural good taste; and good will and camaraderie govern his relation with his fellows.

To the man who yearns after Arcadia, any movement to establish New Jerusalem will always look like a step toward Brave New World, that mechanized, dehumanized, and standardized environment, where the gaudy and meretricious alternates with the insufferably dull; where, if physical hardship is reduced, it is at the price of the most humiliating spiritual brutalization.

In the same way, the man who dreams of New Jerusalem sees any serious attempt to establish an Arcadia as a retreat to the Land of the Flies; that place of provincial ignorance, fear, disease, and dirt, where man is prey to the untrammeled demons of his own superstition, as well as any caprice of nature: fire, flood, storm, or earthquake.

The final argument for either of these views must ultimately be expressed: in the environment I prefer, I would find it easier to treat the variety of my fellows with affection, tolerance, and respect. And this, as Auden says, is a statement of personal preference, not a logical social dictum. With the variety of fellow beings what it is, the argument will probably always be here.

Modern SF has gone beyond this irreconcilable utopian/dystopian conflict to produce a more fruitful model against which to compare human development.

The SF writers working under Campbell, and even more so with Horace Gold, began to cluster their new and wonderful objects into the same story, or novel. And whole new systems and syndromes of behavior began to emerge. Damon Knight, in *In Search of Wonder,* notes Charles Harness's *The Paradox Man* as the first really successful "reduplicated" novel where an ordered sarabande of wonders reflect and complement each other till they have produced a completely new world, in which the technological relation to ours is minimal. Now the writers began to explore these infinitely multiplicated worlds, filled with wondrous things, where the roads and the paintings moved, where religion took the place of government, and advertising took the place of religion, where travel could be instantaneous between anywhere and anywhere else, where the sky was metal, and women wore live goldfish in the transparent heels of their shoes. Within these worlds, the impossible relieves the probable, and the possible illuminates the improbable. And the author's aim is neither to condemn nor to condone, but to explore both the worlds and their behaviors for the sake of the exploration, again an aim far closer to poetry than to any sociological brand of fiction.

As soon as the Wellsian parameters are put aside, far more protean ones emerge from modern SF almost at once.

In the most truly utopian of New Jerusalems, sometime you will find yourself in front of an innocuous-looking door; go through it, and you will find yourself, aghast, before some remnant of the Land of the Flies; in the most dehumanized Brave New World, one evening as you wander through the dreary public park, sunset bronzing fallen leaves will momentarily usher you into the most marvelous autumn evening in Arcadia. Similarly, in either Arcadia or the Land of the Flies, plans can be begun for either Brave New World or New Jerusalem.

SF has been called a romantic and affirmative literature. J. G. Ballard has gone so far as to point out, quite justly, that the bulk of it is rendered trivial by its naively boundless optimism. But we do not judge the novel by the plethora of sloppy romances or boneheaded adventures that make up the statistically vast majority of examples; if we did, it might lead us to say the same of all areas of literature, novel, poetry, or drama; with no selection by merit, I'm afraid on a statistical listing, expressions of the vapidly happy would far outnumber expressions of the tragic on whatever level. As any other area of art is judged by its finest examples, and not by the oceans of mediocrity that these high points rise above, this is the way SF must be judged. There are threads of tragedy running through the works of Sturgeon and Bester (they can even be unraveled from Heinlein), not to mention Disch, Zelazny, and Russ, as well as Ballard's own tales of ruined worlds, decadent resortists, and the more recent fragmented visions of stasis and violence. And one would be hard-pressed to call the comic vision of Vonnegut, Sladek, and Lafferty "naively optimistic."

If SF is affirmative, it is not through any obligatory happy ending, but rather through the breadth of vision it affords through the complexed interweave of these multiple visions of man's origins and his destinations. Certainly such breadth of vision does not abolish tragedy. But it does make a little rarer the particular needless tragedy that comes from a certain type of narrow-mindedness.

Academic SF criticism, fixed in the historical approach, wastes a great deal of time trying to approach modern SF works in utopian/dystopian terms—works whose value is precisely in that they are a reaction to such one-sided thinking. It is much more fruitful if modern works are examined in terms of what they contain of all these mythic views of the world. (Carl Becker has suggested that New Jerusalem and Brave New World are the only two new myths that the twentieth century has produced.)

It is absurd to argue whether Asimov's *Foundation* trilogy represents a utopian or a dystopian view of society; its theme is the way in which a series of interrelated societies, over a historical period, force each other at different times back and forth from utopian to dystopian phases.

In *The Stars My Destination,* the Jaunt Re-education program is clearly a product of New Jerusalem. Equally clearly, the Presteign Clan, with its four hundred ninety-seven surgically identical Mr. Prestos, is from Brave New World. And they exist side by side in the same work. Gully, though he has been uniformed by Brave New World, begins as an unformed lump of elemental violence, ignorance, and endurance from the Land of the Flies. Robin Wednesbury's home in the re-established forest of Greenbay, insulated from its neighbors, with her collection of books and records, exists in Arcadia. Gully/Caliban implodes into it with violence and rape; and Robin and Arcadia survive to both help and hinder him as the novel goes on. This sort of optimism, emblematically as it is handled, is far more true to life than the Victorian convention that equates "dishonor" with death—though in black Robin's eventual marriage to the only other non-Caucasian in the book, the Oriental Yang-Y'eovil, there is a hint of acceptance of an equally nasty American convention.

Because all four visions are offered in the best modern SF, no single one is allowed to paralyze us with terror or lull us into muddle-headed euphoria.

What I would like to see in serious SF criticism, among other things, is an examination of how all four of these mythic visions sit in concert in given works. And I would like to see an end to the lauding (or dismissal) of works because they do (or do not) reflect only one.

Index

Index

Index

Index

Contributors

Robert H. Canary is a member of the English Department at the University of Wisconsin—Parkside, and co-editor of the interdisciplinary journal CLIO.

Thomas D. Clareson, Professor of English at the College of Wooster, has been editor of *Extrapolation: A Journal of Science Fiction and Fantasy* since 1959, and has served as the Chairman of the Science Fiction Research Association since its founding in 1970. He has been elected to a five-year term on the Executive Committee of the MLA Section on Popular Culture. His previous book with Kent State University Press is *SF Criticism: An Annotated Checklist* (1972). He is now on leave-of-absence working on a history of American science fiction and fantasy during the period 1870-1926 and is completing a biography of the popular nineteenth-century British novelist, Charles Reade.

Samuel R. Delany is one of the outstanding young writers of science fiction to come to the fore in the 1960s. His most recent titles include the experimental *Dhalgren* (1975) and *Triton* (1976).

S. C. Fredericks, Department of Classical Studies, Indiana University, is a member of SFRA. He is at work on an extended study of the patterns of myth in modern science fiction.

Beverly Friend is editor of the *SFRA Newsletter.* A resident of Chicago, she has led numerous seminars for teachers of science fiction and has written *Science Fiction: The Classroom in Orbit* (1974).

Patrick G. Hogan, Jr., Department of English, University of Houston, is one of the founders of the MLA Seminar on Science Fiction. He has long been editor of *South Central Bulletin,* the newsletter of The South Central Modern Language Association.

Steven Kagle, Department of English, Illinois State University, is editor of the journal, *Exploration.*

J. Norman King, Department of Theology, University of Windsor, uses science fiction as a basis of a course in Religious Studies which focuses "upon images of man and issues of meaning and value."

Carolyn Rhodes, Department of English, Old Dominion University, has undertaken several studies of science fiction for HEW and has contributed to various journals. A member of SFRA, she is also active in the MLA Women's Studies Program.

Stanley Schmidt, Department of Physics, Heidelberg College, combines his role as teacher with that of professional science-fiction writer. His most recent story is "A Thrust of Greatness" in the June 1976 issue of *Analog.*

Patricia Warrick, Department of English, University of Wisconsin—Fox Center, is currently one of the editors of a joint SFRA-SFWA anthology, *Science Fiction: Contemporary Myth Makers.* She is also working on a study of Mack Reynolds.

Gary K. Wolfe, College of Continuing Education, Roosevelt University, has an interest in popular literature as well as science fiction and fantasy. He is now working on a book-length critical study of science fiction.

Thomas L. Wymer, Department of English, Bowling Green University, has been responsible for the Science Fiction Programs at recent Popular Culture Association Meetings. He has written major critical essays on Kurt Vonnegut, Jr. and Philip José Farmer.